NO KING,
NO POPERY

Recent Titles in
Contributions in American History

NO KING, NO POPERY

Anti-Catholicism in Revolutionary New England

Francis D. Cogliano

Contributions in American History, Number 164
Jon L. Wakelyn, Series Editor

GREENWOOD PRESS
Westport, Connecticut • London

Library of Congress Cataloging-in-Publication Data

Cogliano, Francis D.
    No king, no popery : anti-Catholicism in Revolutionary New England /
Francis D. Cogliano.
        p.   cm.—(Contributions in American history, ISSN 0084–9219 ;
no. 164)
    Includes bibliographical references and index.
    ISBN 0–313–29729–0 (alk. paper)
    1. Anti-Catholicism—New England—History—18th century.   2. New
England—Church history—18th century.   3. New England—History—
Revolution, 1775–1783.   I. Title.   II. Series.
BR520.C64   1995
305.6′2074′09033—dc20   95–19322

British Library Cataloguing in Publication Data is available.

Library of Congress Catalog Card Number: 95–19322
ISBN: 0–313–29729–0
ISSN: 0084–9219

First published in 1995

Greenwood Press, 88 Post Road West, Westport, CT 06881
An imprint of Greenwood Publishing Group, Inc.

Printed in the United States of America

The paper used in this book complies with the
Permanent Paper Standard issued by the National
Information Standards Organization (Z39.48–1984).

10 9 8 7 6 5 4 3 2 1

For Mimi and Edward

Contents

Acknowledgements

Research and writing are not solitary tasks. In the course of producing this book I have relied on the help and advice of many friends and colleagues who deserve my sincerest thanks.

My parents, Ann and Frank Cogliano, nurtured and supported my early interest in history. As an undergraduate, John Brooke and George Marcopoulos encouraged me to pursue the study of history at an advanced level. This particular project had its genesis in David Hall's seminar on popular culture at Boston University. Along the way various scholars offered their advice, support, and criticism. Alfred F. Young contributed to this project in ways only he can appreciate properly. My contact with him has taught me much about the historical profession. I am especially grateful to Richard D. Brown who read and commented on an earlier version of my manuscript. My greatest intellectual debt is to Alan Taylor, who nurtured this project from its inception, admonishing and encouraging me as circumstances required.

Many other friends and colleagues provided encouragement and support for this project. At Boston University, Jim Dutton and Mitch Allen have been good friends who have always been eager to help with all problems great and small. Jussi Hanhimäki read early versions of my manuscript and routinely beat me at squash in an effort to keep both my mind and body fit. During the course of researching and writing this book I have come to value the wit, wisdom, and friendship of Charles Hanson. Over the past several years, Charles has shared his ideas with me in the true spirit of scholarly cooperation. I am certain this book is better for the experience. Additionally, I am grateful to my colleagues at La Sainte Union College in Southampton, England, who have provided the convivial atmosphere in which this book was completed. I am particularly grateful to Derek Edgell for his comments on my manuscript and his friendship. Margit and P.O. Källman deserve thanks for providing me with computer facilities and a congenial place to write. Alan Swartz also merits special mention. Although his interest in early American history is minimal, Alan's friendship and computer skills have left their mark on the present work.

The research for this book could not have been completed without generous financial assistance from Boston University, La Sainte Union College, and the Higher Education Funding Council of England. I am grateful to the staffs of the Archives of the Archdiocese of Boston, the Boston Public Library, the Huntington Library, the Massachusetts Archives, Massachusetts Historical Society, Mugar Memorial Library, and the Peabody Essex Museum for their aid with my research. Bill Milhomme of the Massachusetts Archives deserves special mention. His enthusiasm for this topic was an inspiration and his willingness to track the vaguest references was invaluable. I wish to thank the Archives of the Archdiocese of Boston, the Huntington Library, and the Massachusetts Historical Society for permission to quote from their manuscript collections.

Finally, and most important, this book is dedicated to my wife and son. Without them this project would not only be incomplete, but so would my life. To them I offer this book as a small measure of my esteem.

Abbreviations

AABo:	Archives of the Archdiocese of Boston
CP:	Samuel Cooper Papers, Huntington Library
MA:	Massachusetts Archives
MHS:	Massachusetts Historical Society
MHSC:	Massachusetts Historical Society, *Collections*
MHSP:	Massachusetts Historical Society, *Proceedings*
NEHGR:	*New England Historical and Genealogical Register*
NEQ:	*New England Quarterly*
WAL:	*Warren-Adams Letters* (Boston, 1917-25)
WMQ:	*William and Mary Quarterly*, 3rd series

NO KING,
NO POPERY

Introduction

On June 17, 1745, a combined force of New England militiamen and British naval vessels captured the supposedly impregnable French fortress at Louisbourg, Nova Scotia. Under the terms of the capitulation, the French residents of Louisbourg were allowed to practice Catholicism until arrangements could be made to transport them to France. This temporary circumstance allowed the Yankee soldiers to witness Catholic worship, a rare opportunity since Catholicism was illegal in colonial New England. One soldier from Springfield, Massachusetts, observed: "This day I went into the Hospital to See the French People Say Mass. I Could'ent help wondering to See Gentlemen who were men of Learning . . . so Led Aside as to worship Images, to Bow down to A Cross of wood, and to see so many of all Ranks Seemingly Devout, when we've Reason to think They never had any Communion with God through the Course of their Lives."[1] The anonymous soldier expressed a view of Catholicism common to most colonial New Englanders. They found Catholicism antithetical to their way of life as Protestants. Indeed, anti-Catholic sentiment was one of the primary factors that drove the soldier and four thousand of his neighbors to Cape Breton for the siege of Louisbourg. As a New Englander, the soldier could not comprehend how intelligent people could practice what he perceived as idolatry.[2]

The soldier from Springfield was not alone. The overwhelming majority of his friends and neighbors shared his outlook with respect to Catholicism. Anti-Catholicism, or anti-popery to use the contemporary term, was one of the most prevalent characteristics of New England culture before the American Revolution.[3] Expressions of anti-popery could be found in the churches, schools, taverns, streets, and newspapers of colonial New England. It was an important part of the rhythm of life in New England before the American Revolution.

Eighteenth-century New Englanders were Protestants in the most fundamental sense. They were opposed to the Roman Catholic Church. Whatever their other theological, intellectual, political, or social differences, almost all New Englanders agreed on this point. For New Englanders, anti-popery provided a vocabulary of good and evil which they used to define their enemies and themselves and to order their world. This vocabulary found expression in learned treatises, sermons, the law, and in the streets during popular demonstrations and celebrations. The vocabulary of anti-popery helped New Englanders define the parameters of what was acceptable and unacceptable in their society. It promoted unity among an otherwise disparate people. One may call the collective ideas expressed by New Englanders about popery "the anti-papal persuasion."[4] This "persuasion" was a concise expression about the world as New Englanders viewed it.

Despite its prominence, anti-popery has been one of the most neglected cultural traditions by historians of colonial America.[5] The purpose of the present study is to chronicle the changing role of anti-popery in New England from the siege of Louisbourg in 1745 until 1791 when John Carroll, archbishop of Baltimore, head of the Catholic church in America, visited Boston. First, I will demonstrate the importance of anti-popery to colonial New Englanders. Second, I will show that assumptions about Catholicism colored the way New Englanders reacted to the imperial crisis between 1765 and 1775. When they opposed the king, New Englanders saw themselves behaving as true Protestants, as well as Englishmen, defending their nation against incipient popery just as their seventeenth-century forbears had. Anti-popery was an important intellectual source for the American Revolution. Third, I will examine the impact the Revolution had on anti-popery in New England. With the participation of the Catholic French as allies to the Americans, New Englanders were compelled to reevaluate their attitudes toward Catholicism during the Revolution. The result was a prolonged debate over the place of the anti-papal persuasion in the cultural life of revolutionary New England. As a consequence of this debate, limited toleration supplanted anti-popery in the wake of the Revolution.

I argue that cultural change, the decline of anti-popery during the Revolution, was elite-directed in eighteenth-century New England. I agree with David Hackett Fischer that "small groups dominate every cultural system. They tend to do so by controlling institutions and processes so that they become 'governors' of a culture in both a political and mechanical sense."[6] This is especially true in the early modern period. Elite-driven reform was not unusual in the eighteenth century.[7] In revolutionary New England, members of the Whig elite—political and military leaders, ministers, and newspaper publishers, the "cultural governors"—actively campaigned against anti-popery once they became convinced that expressions of anti-Catholic sentiment endangered the success of the Revolution. Their campaign against anti-popery was a gradual process which began with the first tentative approaches to Quebec and the Catholic Eastern Indians of Maine, and culminated in granting religious freedom under the new state constitutions. The campaign was successful because the cultural elite forced the change, both by suppressing anti-popery and by promoting toleration.

Although cultural change was elite-directed, I do not assume that the non-elite was a benighted mass molded at the whims of its leaders. As Fischer notes, "the relation between elites and other cultural groups is highly variable. Every culture might be seen as a system of bargaining" between elites and non-elites.[8] In revolutionary New England, there was strong, sustained popular and regional opposition to the elite campaign against anti-popery. Despite elite attempts to eradicate anti-popery, anti-Catholic feeling was never entirely eliminated there. The cultural debate over anti-popery in revolutionary New England reveals the limits of the powers of the region's cultural governors.

NOTES

1. As quoted in Louis Effingham De Forest, ed., *Louisbourg Journals* (New York, 1932), 11.

2. Francis D. Cogliano, "Nil Desperandum Christo Duce: The New England Crusade against Louisbourg, 1745," *Essex Institute Historical Collections*, 128 (1992), 180-207.

3. According to Thomas M. Brown, "in the colonial period of American history no intellectual tradition was more prominent, or more omnipresent than anti-Catholicism." Thomas More Brown, "The Image of the Beast: Anti-Papal Rhetoric in Colonial America," in Richard O. Curry and Thomas M. Brown, eds., *Conspiracy: The Fear of Subversion in American History* (New York, 1972), 1-20, quotation, p.1. Brown uses the term "anti-Catholicism." I prefer "anti-popery," which I believe is

more accurate: "popery" was the term generally used by colonial Americans when referring to Catholicism. It is an intellectual shorthand for everything that Americans believed and feared about eighteenth-century Catholicism.

4. My use of the word "persuasion" is derived from the work of Marvin Meyers. He defined a "persuasion" as "a matched set of attitudes, beliefs, projected actions: a half-formulated moral perspective involving emotional commitment. The community shares many values; at a given social moment some of these acquire a compelling importance. The political expression given to such values forms a persuasion." Meyers developed the term to describe the ideas and beliefs that bound Jacksonian Democrats together in the 1830s, but I believe it can fruitfully be applied to colonial New Englanders with respect to popery. Anti-popery was a shared set of assumptions, that compelled emotional commitment. Colonial New Englanders were as fervent foes of popery as Jacksonian Democrats were of the "Monster Bank." Marvin Meyers, *The Jacksonian Persuasion* (Stanford, 1960); see chap. 1 for the term "persuasion" quotation, p. 10.

5. The literature on anti-popery in colonial America is brief. See Timothy W. Bosworth, "Anti-Catholicism as a Political Tool in Mid-Eighteenth-Century Maryland," *Catholic Historical Review*, 61 (1975), 539-563; and Joseph J. Casino, "Anti-popery in Colonial Pennsylvania," *Pennsylvania Magazine of History and Biography*, 105 (1981), 279-309. Only one monograph has been devoted to the subject, Mary Augustina Ray's *American Opinion of Roman Catholicism in the Eighteenth Century* (New York, 1936). Although helpful, Ray's work is also outdated. Gayle Kathleen Pluta Brown, "A Controversy Not Merely Religious: The Anti-Catholic Tradition in Colonial New England" (Ph.D. dissertation, University of Iowa, 1990), updates Ray's work but does not consider the impact of the American Revolution in detail. Apart from the present work, the most complete work on the Revolution is Charles Hanson, "From the Quebec Act to the French Alliance: The Catholic Question in Revolutionary New England" (Ph.D. dissertation, University of California at Berkeley, 1993).

6. I would not go so far as Fischer does to characterize this situation as an "iron law of cultural elites," but his model of cultural relations accurately describes revolutionary New England with respect to the question of anti-popery. David Hackett Fischer, *Albion's Seed: Four British Folkways in America* (New York, 1989), 896.

7. E. P. Thompson recently demonstrated that eighteenth-century English plebeian culture was traditional and resisted change, whereas the culture of the patrician elite was more innovative (often at the expense of the plebeians). E. P. Thompson, *Customs in Common* (London, 1993), 7-9. The debate over anti-popery in revolutionary New England reveals a similar pattern of cultural interaction.

8. Fischer, *Albion's Seed*, 896.

1

Exposing the Idolatry of the Romish Church: Anti-popery and Colonial New England

By the mid-eighteenth century it was impossible for Englishmen in Britain or America to divorce anti-popery from their notion of what it was to be English. The anti-Catholic tradition that the colonists brought with them to the New World can be traced at least as far back as 1563 when the Protestant martyrologist John Foxe published the first English edition of his *Actes and Monuments*. Commonly called *The Book of Martyrs*, Foxe's book chronicled in brutal, graphic detail the suffering and torture allegedly inflicted upon Protestants by Catholics. Although the architect of Catholic oppression was ultimately the pope, Foxe paid careful attention to the actions of his supposed minions, the kings of France and Spain. Foxe also paid particular attention to the fate of Protestants persecuted during the reign of Mary Tudor. It is to Foxe that Queen Mary owes her reputation as "Bloody Mary." Foxe did more than simply chronicle Catholic atrocities. He also laid the groundwork for the marriage of Protestantism to the concept of what it was to be English. Queen Mary was nefarious not only for her persecutions, but because she had wed the Catholic king of Spain, thereby endangering the Protestant succession in England. *The Book of Martyrs* demonstrated that tyranny came from abroad: Versailles, Madrid, and ultimately the Vatican, from which the pope attempted to control the world. Conversely, freedom resided wherever true Englishmen and women lived. By definition a true Englishman was a Protestant.[1]

Foxe depicted England as a uniquely Protestant nation and the English people as the chosen people of God.[2] From the *Actes and Monuments* readers learned that true Englishmen were Protestants and that Catholics were bloodthirsty zealots who served foreign despots and would stop at nothing to extirpate Protestantism. *The Book of Martyrs* is one of the earliest expressions of a cultural formula that became a commonplace in the Anglo-American world during the seventeenth and eighteenth centuries: to be English was to be Protestant, to be Protestant was to be free, therefore Englishmen were by nature free men. The association between Protestantism and the vaunted "liberties of Englishmen" was a close one for Englishmen in England and in the colonies.

The influence of Foxe's *Book of Martyrs* should not be underestimated. It went through many editions and held a prominent place in English Protestant churches well into the nineteenth century. In many Anglican churches the *Book of Martyrs* had a place next to the Bible on the altar. Readings from the *Actes and Monuments* were also made part of the liturgy in some parishes. By the seventeenth century the message of the *Book of Martyrs* had filtered throughout English society. In England, Protestantism became wed to the notion of being a good Englishman. Catholicism, or popery, was antithetical to the survival of England and had to be countered.[3]

Foxe's book was popular because it resonated so strongly among the people of sixteenth- and seventeenth-century England. The Englishman or woman born in 1550 could easily recall the Marian persecutions, the rising of the Catholic northern earls against Queen Elizabeth in 1570, the attempt by the Spanish to conquer England in 1588, as well as the 1605 Gunpowder Plot of Guy Fawkes and a small band of Catholic conspirators who attempted to assassinate King James I and destroy Parliament. The struggle between Spain and England in the early modern period gave rise to a potent variant of English anti-popery which was oriented against the Iberian power. According to this "Black Legend," the Spanish were the most powerful and ruthless of papists. They were especially bent upon conquering England and subjecting the English to their infamous Inquisition. The image of captured English sailors enslaved on Spanish galleys was particularly powerful and common in the sixteenth century. The frequent conflicts between Spain and England made the fear and hatred of Spain and things Spanish a common element of English nationalism.[4] Each of these incidents reinforced the theme of Foxe's *Book of Martyrs*: Catholics were forever scheming to return England to Rome, and they would stop at nothing to achieve their goal, including regicide.

Ironically, the only British regicides of the seventeenth century were

Protestants who killed a king they suspected of harboring popish sympathies. Only when the English fear of things Catholic and the belief that popery and tyranny were synonymous are taken into account, can the political upheavals of seventeenth-century England be properly understood. For example, Charles I was widely suspect, in part, because his wife was a French Catholic and because his archbishop had introduced "popish" innovations into the Anglican church. Questions about Charles' alleged Catholicism helped make his overthrow and execution justifiable in the minds of many Protestants. After the Stuart Restoration, the fear of resurgent Catholicism became more pronounced. Protestants even suspected that the great London fire of 1666 was the work of Catholic saboteurs. In 1679 a wave of anti-Catholic paranoia swept the country in the wake of the so-called "Popish Plot" of Catholics to take over the country. Charles II, like his father, was widely suspected of being a crypto-Catholic. His brother and successor, James II, was a practicing Catholic. The prospect of a Catholic succession after the birth of his son in 1685 was the primary cause of the Glorious Revolution. Forevermore the Stuarts were linked in the popular mind with popery and tyranny. They reinforced their place as a treacherous Catholic dynasty during the two eighteenth-century attempts by the Stuart Pretenders to seize the throne and overturn the Catholic succession.

Anti-Catholicism permeated English culture by the end of the seventeenth century. It found expression not only in Foxe's *Actes and Monuments* but in the streets of England as well. David Cressy has demonstrated that a "Protestant calendar" existed in Elizabethan and Stuart England that gave the people ample opportunity to commemorate important days in the English Protestant year. For example, the English regularly celebrated Guy Fawkes Day (Gunpowder Treason Day) with the ringing of bells and the burning of bonfires. Each year Englishmen honored the anniversary of Queen Elizabeth's accession (November 17) in a similar manner. By the end of the seventeenth century, public demonstrations in England frequently included the burning of the pope and the devil in effigy.[5]

Popular anti-popery remained a feature of English life during the eighteenth century. In 1715 and 1745 angry Protestant crowds attacked Catholics during the attempts of the Stuart Pretenders to seize the throne. Crowds burned the pope in effigy on Gunpowder Treason Day as well as in more spontaneous demonstrations such as the street fights between Whigs and Tories in 1715. Popular celebrations with an anti-papal theme occurred whenever Britain defeated one of her Catholic foes. Crowds gathered to salute Vice-Admiral Edward Vernon and to celebrate his triumph over the Spanish at Porto Bello in 1739. Similar celebrations greeted the news of the fall of Louisbourg in 1745 and the capture of Quebec in 1759. The potency and persistence of popular anti-Catholicism became apparent in 1780 when thousands of Londoners participated in the Gordon Riots which were sparked by a parliamentary act to repeal anti-Catholic legislation.[6]

English settlers brought the English anti-papal tradition to New England during the seventeenth century. Foxe's *Book of Martyrs* was a commonly owned book in seventeenth-century Massachusetts. The town of Concord owned a copy which it made available to interested townsmen. Adaptations of Foxe's stories appeared in children's books. New Englanders embraced the Protestant calendar of early modern England.[7] During the seventeenth century, New Englanders occasionally celebrated Guy Fawkes Day.[8] The people of colonial New England also embraced the political and patriotic aspects of anti-popery. For them the opposition to Catholicism and their loyalty as Englishmen and women were one and the same.

During the eighteenth century, New England anti-popery, while similar to its English cousin, developed along its own lines according to local circumstances. While popery threatened the liberties of New Englanders, they feared the Catholic Indians of Canada and their French sponsors more than Spanish galleys. Until the end of the Seven Years' War, anti-popery remained a potent force in New England life. The New England variant of anti-popery would play an important role in the coming of the American Revolution.

II

In 1750 Judge Paul Dudley of the Massachusetts Supreme Court of Judicature, a prominent colonist, died at age seventy five. Dudley willed to his alma mater, Harvard College (Dudley received his A.B. from Harvard in 1690 and his A.M. in 1693), £133.6.8 to endow a series of four lectures to be given annually at the college.[9] According to Dudley's will, the third lecture should be devoted toward "exposing the Idolatry of the Romish church, their tyranny, usurpations and other crying wickedness, in their high places; and finally that the church of Rome is that mystical Babylon, that man of sin, that Apostate church spoken of in the New Testament."[10] Dudley's will reflected three of the most important criticisms of the Catholic Church among eighteenth-century New Englanders: the beliefs that the Catholic Church was idolatrous, tyrannical, and represented the Antichrist of the Book of Revelation.

One of the most consistent criticisms of the Catholic Church among eighteenth-century New Englanders was its idolatry. Pierre Berault, a former Jesuit who had become a Protestant and wrote an exposé of his former faith, declared: "That it is flat Idolatry to worship God in any Image is expressed and manifested by the Children of Israel when they made the Golden Calf to be a representation of God." Berault concluded, "The Idolatry of Rome is as gross and wicked as theirs was."[11] The author of an anonymous catechism published in 1746 explained in no uncertain terms the view that New England Protestants took toward Catholic idolatry: "it is not lawful to make Images of God; nor to direct our Worship to an Image or to give religious Worship to any Creature." To do so would be an expression of superstition, not faith. The author continued, "It were innumerable to account the many vain Fopperies in their Devotions, which they place Religion in; As the tooth of St. Christopher; the Hair of St. Peter's Beard."[12] The Catholic attachment to religious relics was unacceptable idolatry and superstition in the eyes of New England's Protestants.

The idolatrous nature of Catholicism was more than the alleged hair and teeth of long-dead saints. In Protestant eyes, idolatry lay at the very heart of the Catholic liturgy. The outspoken pastor of Boston's West Church, Jonathan Mayhew, devoted the 1765 Dudleian Lecture to the subject on May 8, 1765. In a sermon titled *Popish Idolatry*, Mayhew attacked the doctrine of transubstantiation and the eucharist as the chief forms of idolatry in the Catholic Church: "The host is often carried in procession with great solemnity: and those who are but casually present when it passes are obliged to kneel down in an act of worship to God; unless perhaps, they will run the risque of the inquisition, or of being knocked on the head by the devout rabble that attend it." Mayhew went on to allege that the very absurdity of transubstantiation was proof that it was an idolatrous belief. In so doing, Mayhew attacked the very heart of the Catholic liturgy, and the most important tenets of the Catholic faith.[13]

New Englanders believed that the Catholic clergy promoted idolatry in order to keep the laity in a state of scriptural and spiritual ignorance. A former priest explained popish bigotry as the product of "blind faith in what the preachers and Priests tell them; and next to this, that it is not allowed to them to read scriptures, nor books of controversy about religion."[14] In the 1777 Dudleian Lecture, Edward Wigglesworth criticized the Catholic Church for "setting up oral traditions as of equal authority with sacred Scriptures, [which] has opened the door for the admission of doctrines and precepts into that church, subversive to those delivered by Christ and his Apostles."[15] To eighteenth-century New Englanders, ignorance of the scripture was a certain invitation to eternal damnation in the eyes of God. Scriptural illiteracy led to anti-Christian idolatry, which in turn made it impossible for individuals to enjoy God's saving grace. In their attitudes toward scripture, Catholics were the antithesis of New Englanders.

David Hall has persuasively argued for the importance of scriptural literacy in colonial New England. According to Hall, New Englanders defined literacy as the ability to read and understand the Bible. In this New Englanders believed they differed from most Catholics.[16] Judge Dudley concluded, "nothing Contributed more to the blessed Reformation from Popery, than the Translating and Printing of the Bible in the several Languages of the Nations, and restoring the free use of Scriptures to the people."[17] This democratic notion of scriptural access—the belief that individuals can come to know God through the scripture without the interference of clerical mediators—was at the heart of New England Protestantism.

New Englanders believed that the Catholic clergy promoted idolatry in order to keep the laity ignorant of the spiritual truths of scripture. In this manner Catholics were denied salvation and were easily controlled by priests. Anti-Catholic writers devoted extensive space to decrying the power and influence of the Catholic clergy. Antonio Gavin, a former Jesuit, described the Catholic clergy as "wolves in sheep's clothing, that devour [the laity], and put them in the way of damnation."[18] Three attributes dominate the descriptions of the clergy in eighteenth-century literature: carnality, greed, and cruelty.

Perhaps the most popular literary portrayal of Catholic priests in colonial New England was that of the priest as lecher. It was a common belief that all Catholic priests took advantage of their positions to gratify their sexual desires. New Englanders believed that the origins of popish carnality lay in church doctrine. They held that priestly celibacy was unnatural and impossible. According to *A Protestant's Resolution*: "The Popish doctrine forbidding [priests] to marry, is a devilish and wicked Doctrine . . . it leads to much Leudness and Villainy, as Fornication, Adultery, Incest, Sodomy, Murder &c."[19] New Englanders had an apparently insatiable appetite for tales of popish carnality. While such accounts probably more accurately reflect the prurient interests of colonial New Englanders than the indiscretions of the eighteenth-century Catholic clergy, the belief that the clergy consisted of adulterous, immoral lechers whose first priority was to gratify their own depraved desires was widespread in colonial New England.

According to New Englanders, priests took advantage of the confessional to induce unsuspecting young women to succumb to their advances.[20] A small book entitled *The French Convert*, published anonymously in Boston in 1725, offers a typical example of the way New Englanders portrayed the Catholic clergy. In *The French Convert*, a drunken priest offered absolution to a French woman whose husband was away in the army in exchange for sex. Antonio the priest, a "Gray-bearded Satan," attempted to seduce the young wife while administering the sacraments. The woman, named Deidamia, refused the priest's advances. In the meantime she converted to Protestantism. When Father Antonio discovered her conversion, he tried to blackmail her for sex. When Deidamia still failed to succumb, Antonio hired two Russian mercenaries to kill her. They were unsuccessful, and Deidamia was saved by her husband who had also converted.[21]

The story presents several archetypal figures in colonial New England culture. Antonio, the priest, was depraved and ruthless. He took advantage of his position and Deidamia's loneliness to gratify his own wolfish desires. Moreover, Antonio was a Jesuit. Of all the clerical orders, the Jesuits, New Englanders believed, were the most lascivious, greedy, and cruel. They were also the most dangerous because they were the best trained and wielded the most power of all the clerical orders.[22] Deidamia, by contrast, was a virtuous woman loyal to God and husband who would rather die than lose her virtue. Before her conversion, Deidamia lived in ignorance. She was exposed to holy writ by her industrious Huguenot gardener, Bernard, who devoted his life to hard work and God. The contrast between the simple, industrious Bernard, who embodied the virtues of Protestantism—piety and hard work—and the lazy, lecherous Antonio, who lived off the wealthy Deidamia's family, is striking testimony to the different perceptions that New Englanders had of themselves and their Catholic adversaries.[23]

Colonial New Englanders believed that Catholic priests like Antonio were avaricious as well as lecherous. The greed of the clergy is the second major theme in New England descriptions of them. In *The French Convert*, Bernard explained to Deidamia that the purpose of Catholic miracles, relics, and indulgences was "to get Money; [for] the Whoredoms, Murthers and Incests of the many Popes, Cardinals and Prelates of the Roman Church."[24] New Englanders believed that the primary reason the Catholic hierarchy had instituted all the unscriptural, idolatrous innovations in church practices, such as auricular confession, the sale of indulgences, and prayer to the saints, was to extort money from the ignorant laity. They believed this on the good authority of former priests. Pierre Berault told them, "the Pope to fatten his Cheeks and fill his Trunks with Money, will have us to have recourse unto saints, and take them for our Advocates." According to Antonio Gavin, "the confession is the mint of Fryars and Priests, the sins of the penitents the metals, the absolution the coin of money, and the Confessors the keepers of it." According to Paul Dudley, the church's ill-gotten wealth was used to "maintain the Pope with his Cardinals, and other Ecclesiasticks in a Grandeur and Luxury, equal, if not superior, to the Richest Court in Europe."[25] Thrifty New Englanders saw in the clergy a grasping, hungry hierarchy eager to be fed the hard-earned money of the laity.

Clerical extortion undermined the desire of the laity to work hard and earn money at all. Colonial New Englanders routinely characterized Catholic countries as havens not only of tyranny but its byproducts, sloth and corruption. Reverend Samuel Cooper, of the prestigious Brattle Church in Boston, declared with reference to Catholic Italy, "we cannot wonder to see the Idleness prevail in those Countries where Tyranny riots upon the Fruits of honest diligence."[26] When the clergy robbed the benighted laity of their money, they also took their economic initiative and industriousness. To colonial New Englanders, who prided themselves on their hard work, Catholic indolence was as odious as Catholic idolatry.

The Catholic clergy was more than greedy and lascivious in New England eyes; they were also inhumanely cruel, especially to Protestants. According to Antonio Gavin, "The Roman Catholics with the Pope say . . . that no man can be saved out of their communion, and so they reckon enemies of their faith all those that are of a different opinion. And we may be sure that the Protestants . . . are their irreconcilable enemies."[27] Priests taught Catholics that they were not required nor expected to show mercy to heretics. The subtitle to a pamphlet entitled *Popish Cruelty Displayed* is testimony to the connection between the clergy and persecution in the minds of New Englanders:

Being a full and true Account of the Bloody and Hellish Massacre in Ireland, Perpetrated by the Instigation of the Jesuits, Priests, and Fryars, who were the chief Promoters of those Horrible Murthers, unheard of Cruelties, barbarous Villainies and inhuman Practices, executed by the Irish Papists upon the English Protestants in the Year 1641.[28]

According to this pamphlet, the Catholic clergy instigated the alleged massacres of 1641 by providing eucharist to the Irish "upon the condition they should neither spare, Man, Woman, nor Child of the Protestants. . . . They openly professed, that they held it as lawful to kill a Protestant as to kill a Dog."[29] Colonial New Englanders had little problem believing that Catholic priests were the authors of such massacres when they looked to the north and saw the results of Jesuit influence among the Native Americans of Canada who occasionally raided the New England frontier.

The ultimate engine of popish cruelty was the infamous Court of Inquisition employed to root out heresy in Catholic countries. According to Samuel Cooper, "the inhumanity of her court of inquisition is not to be equalled among the most barbarous nations, nor by any court erected by the gravest tyrant."[30] The Inquisition was especially galling to New Englanders because it existed to forbid free expression, especially in matters of religion. In 1750 Jonathan Mayhew declared, "God be thanked, one may in any part of the British

Dominions, speak freely . . . without being in danger either of the bastille or the inquisition."[31] According to former Inquisitor Antonio Gavin, "the Inquisitors have a despotic power to command every living soul; and no excuse is to be given, nor contradiction to made to their orders, nay the people have not liberty to speak nor complain."[32] The methods of the Inquisition were enough to make the blood of the staunchest Protestants curdle. Gavin described an oven with a large pan in it, a wheel "covered on both sides with thick boards . . . all the circumference of the wheel set with sharp rasors," and a pit full of serpents and toads. According to Gavin:

The dry pan and gradual fire are for the use of Hereticks, and those that oppose the Holy Father's will and pleasure, for they are put all naked and alive into the pan, and the cover of it being locked up, the executioner begins to put in the oven a small fire, and by degrees he augmenteth it till the body is burnt into ashes. The second is designed for those that speak against the Pope and the Holy Fathers; and they are put within the wheel, and the door being locked, the executioner turns the wheel till the person is dead. And the third is for those who contemn the images, and refuse to give the due respect and veneration to ecclesiastical persons, for they are thrown into the pit, & there they become food of the serpents and toads.[33]

For a people well versed in Foxe's *Book of Martyrs*, such behavior from Catholic clergymen, while frightening, was certainly not surprising.

New Englanders so feared and hated the Catholic clergy that they took legal action to insure that they would not have to suffer the presence of Catholic clerics in their midst. With the exception of James II's brief reign, Catholics were denied religious freedom in all the New England colonies.[34] Massachusetts adopted the strongest measures to prevent the presence of Catholicism within its borders. In 1647 the Great and General Court, "taking into consideration the great wars, combustions and divisions which are this day in Europe, and at the same are observed to be raised chiefly by the secret underminings and solicitations of those of the Jesuitical order," adopted a law banishing all Catholic clergymen from Massachusetts. Any priests found in Massachusetts who had once been banished, were to be executed.[35] Massachusetts lawmakers reenacted the law on June 17, 1700, against "divers Jesuits, priests, and popish missionaries" not for instigating trouble in Europe but "who by their subtile insinuations industriously labor to debauch, seduce and withdraw the Indians from their due obedience to his majesty."[36] The 1700 law reflects the specific New England context for the fear of Catholicism as the eighteenth century began. Rather than focus on the threat popery posed to the Protestant succession in Britain, New Englanders were more concerned about the activities of the popish missionaries who threatened them from Canada. The anti-priest law of 1700 remained in force until the American Revolution.

New Englanders primarily feared the Catholic clergy as the agents of popish oppression. Exposing "the tyranny, usurpations and other crying wickedness in their high places" was the second heading in Judge Dudley's bequest against popery. In New England eyes, the Catholic clergy were part of a vast hierarchy that oppressed lay people, stifled free discourse, and hampered free trade. At the head of this hierarchy was the pope, an omnipotent, bloodthirsty bigot who would stop at nothing to extirpate Protestantism.

For eighteenth-century New Englanders, well versed as they were in English history, popery and tyranny were synonymous. Jonathan Mayhew declared: "we ought in reason and prudence to detest the church of Rome, in the same degree that we prize freedom. Her laws, more arbitrary than those of Draco, are, in effect, like his, all written in blood. Popery and liberty are incompatible; at irreconcilable enmity with each other."[37] Tyranny was the corollary of popery. Conversely, liberty was the corollary of Protestantism. Just as there could be no reconciliation between Protestantism and tyranny, there could be no compromise between popery and liberty.

New Englanders believed that Catholics were part of a vast international conspiracy to seek world domination. They believed that Catholics owed their loyalty first and foremost to that conspiracy and its head, the pope. They held that the pope used his religious influence to maintain his tyrannical grip. Because they owed their allegiance to the pope, Catholics could not be trusted with any civil power in Protestant countries. Englishmen cited this belief as a justification for their anti-Catholic laws. New Englanders readily concurred. In 1772 the freeholders of Boston voted that Catholics should be excluded from voting because "those they call hereticks may be destroyed without mercy; beside their recognizing the Pope in so absolute a manner, in subversion of the Government leading directly to the worst anarchy and confusion, civil discord, war, and bloodshed."[38] A subject could not have two masters, and, since the pope required blind and absolute obedience, Catholics could not be trusted with civil power.

The papal threat concerned more than religion. The freedom of humanity was at stake in the battle between Catholicism and Protestantism. Jonathan Mayhew explained:

Our controversy with her [the Catholic Church] is not merely a religious one . . . but a defense of our laws, liberties and civil rights as men, in opposition to the proud claims and encroachments of ecclesiastical persons, who under the pretext of religion, and saving men's souls, would engross all power and property to themselves and reduce us to the most abject slavery.[39]

Such a view fostered a manichean outlook toward Catholicism and Catholics among New Englanders. They believed there could be no compromise between popish tyranny and Protestant liberty.

III

At no time was anti-papal feeling higher than during the last great conflict between the French and the English in North America, the French and Indian War (1754-63). New Englanders participated in the conflict in extraordinary numbers.[40] For them the conflict was an anti-papal crusade. As Sylvanus Conant, the pastor at Middleborough, Massachusetts, told the militia of the town on April 6, 1759, "our Enemies in the present bloody Controversy are no less Enemies to God, to Religion, Liberty, and the pure Worship of the Gospel than to us."[41] Samuel Bird assured a group of soldiers, "you are to fight for King George, the best of Kings, against proud Lewis; . . . you are to draw the Sword in the Cause of King JESUS, the King of Kings, in the Defence of his Subjects: against the Emissaries and Incendiaries of Hell and Rome."[42] Such conclusions were a natural consequence of an anti-papal perspective which recognized no room for compromise between popery and Protestantism.

The anxiety of New Englanders was very great in the early years of the conflict when the French enjoyed repeated successes on the battlefield. The prospect of French victory terrified New Englanders. Jonathan Mayhew described the dreadful consequences of French victory in the Massachusetts election sermon he delivered on May 29, 1754. The annual election sermon was probably the single most important sermon delivered throughout the year, for the minister had the collective ear of the political and clerical leaders of the colony. Mayhew made the most of his opportunity.

According to Mayhew, if the French defeated the English, tyranny would triumph over liberty and evil over good. The minister described a chilling vision of New England after a French victory.

Do I behold them spreading desolation thro' the land! Do I see the slaves of Louis with their Indian allies dispossessing the freeborn subjects of King George of the inheritance received from their forefathers? . . . Do I see this godly patrimony ravished from them by those who never knew what property was, except by seizing that of others for an insatiable Lord![43]

Mayhew struck a nerve in all New Englanders with such a vision. The prospect of Catholic slaves and Indians ravishing the property of free-born English

Protestants was the worst nightmare of colonial New Englanders. The minister skillfully described a conquered New England where the French had conquered not only the people but their history. How, after all, could New Englanders stand by and see their patrimony stolen from them by popish slaves? To do so would be to lose all that the settlers of New England had achieved.

True Christianity was at stake in the conflict. Mayhew described the religious life of post-conquest New England:

Do I see Christianity banished for popery! The Bible for the mass-book! The oracles of truth, for fabulous legends! Do I see the sacred edifices erected here to the honour of the true God and his Son . . . laid in ruins themselves! Instead of a train of Christ's faithful, laborious ministers, do I behold an herd of lazy monks, and Jesuits, and exorcists and inquisitors!

If the French were not defeated, Mayhew warned, "liberty, property, religion, happiness" would be "changed, or rather transubstantiated into slavery, poverty, superstition, wretchedness."[44] Mayhew's election sermon is a masterpiece of anti-papal propaganda. The minister cleverly and effectively drew a contrast between a Protestant and a Catholic New England to demonstrate to his fellow Yankees what was at stake in the conflict with France. Mayhew's sermon is the most famous of hundreds of similar sermons delivered throughout New England in the early years of the war.[45]

New England anxiety turned to cautious optimism in 1758, when, for the second time in thirteen years, an Anglo-American expedition captured Louisbourg. Revitalized by the ministry of William Pitt, the English captured Quebec in September 1759. In 1760 they captured Montreal. When the Treaty of Paris was signed in 1763, the British had won the war and driven the French from North America. Nathaniel Appleton explained the victory in true New England fashion, "as Canada was the only Province of Roman Catholicks in these Northern Parts of America, so God has now made himself known by [the] awful Judgements which he has executed upon Them."[46] Though it might enjoy some early success, popery could not triumph because God would not permit it.

The conquest of Canada became one of the highlights in the triumphal story of Protestantism in New England. In a style reminiscent of Mayhew, Eli Forbes described his post-war vision of Canada as a Protestant utopia.

Canada is subdued-how pleasing the sound . . . Methinks I see Towns enlarged, Settlements increased and this howling wilderness become a fruitful Field, which the Lord hath blessed; and to complete the scene, I see Churches rise out of the Superstitions of Roman Bigotry and flourish in Every Christian Grace, and divine

Ornament, where has been the seat of Satan, and Indian Idolatry.[47]

Freed from the shackles of popery, Canada would flourish under Protestantism just as New England had. Where popery hindered industry, Protestantism encouraged it. Protestant enlightenment would supplant popish ignorance. Above all, exclaimed Nathaniel Appleton, "Romish corrupt Principles [would] be extirpated so as never to have Root again in this new World!"[48] In the twelve years between the Peace of Paris and the fighting at Lexington, concern over Catholicism in Canada would be a major preoccupation in New England.

IV

The various elements of colonial New England anti-popery combined to form what I have called the anti-papal persuasion. This was a coherent intellectual system with an internal logic which helped define colonial New England culture. The system was greater than the sum of its parts. As an intellectual system, anti-popery was cyclical: Protestants were free because they had the intellectual freedom to read scripture; in turn, their intellectual freedom permitted their religious and political freedom; religious and political freedom produced economic initiative and drive which produced economic prosperity—the emblem of a free society; prosperity allowed the freedom and education to study scripture. Popery promoted a contrary cycle: Catholics were denied access to scripture, therefore they were ignorant; ignorance, in turn, made them easy dupes for tyrants, secular and religious, thus the church hierarchy was able to steal the wealth of its laity; therefore Catholics were mired in poverty and ignorance which cost them their freedom and their souls.

The image of Catholicism that prevailed in colonial New England was a nightmarish inversion of all that New Englanders held dear. Catholics embodied all the vices and weaknesses that New Englanders abhorred and were determined to avoid. They were licentious, ignorant, lazy, and illiterate. They had no self-control. They did not control their property. They did not exercise their own judgment in matters of politics or religion. Rather, Catholics were controlled by a domineering, scheming, grasping hierarchy headed by the pope who was in league with Satan. The papal world was a caricature of all that colonial New Englanders detested and feared.

In defining their foes, anti-popery also helped New Englanders define themselves. In decrying the characteristics of Catholicism, New Englanders defined themselves as sober, industrious, literate, and, above all, free. The comparison with Catholicism is significant for it gave New Englanders an important yardstick by which they could measure their own society. They were able to reach the conclusion that they were "God's New English Israel" when they compared their society to the decadent corruption and oppression they saw in France, Spain, and Italy.

Anti-popery provided the people of eighteenth-century New England with a sense of control and order in an uncertain and dangerous world. Since the majority of colonial New Englanders were nominally Calvinists of various stripes, most would not presume to claim control over the destiny of their souls. However, by comparison with Catholics, they exercised remarkable autonomy over their lives and property in this world. In politics they enjoyed local control of their governments, unlike Catholics who were ruled by tyrants at the beck and call of the pope in Rome. In religious matters, their ministers were answerable to their congregations in stark contrast to the Roman hierarchy. New Englanders did not pay tithes to support an indolent, lascivious, unprincipled, clergy. There were no priests in New England to ravish its virtuous Protestant maidens or to rob its freemen of their hard-earned patrimony.

Anti-papal values bound colonial New Englanders together despite their pronounced economic, political, religious, and intellectual divisions. The anti-papal persuasion muted social divisions by appealing to common cultural values. The pervasiveness of the anti-papal persuasion and the vital social role it played in eighteenth-century New England are most apparent in Boston's commemoration of Guy Fawkes Day.

NOTES

1. British anti-popery has received much more complete coverage than its American variant. William Haller's *The Elect Nation: The Meaning and Relevance of Foxe's Book of Martyrs* (New York, 1963) is an excellent place to begin for Elizabethan anti-popery. Also see Peter Lake, "The Significance of the Elizabethan Identification of the Pope as Antichrist," *Journal of Ecclesiastical History*, 31 (1980), 161-178. Anti-popery during the Stuart period has been the subject of some excellent scholarship. Caroline M. Hibbard, *Charles II and the Popish Plot* (Chapel Hill, 1983) and David Cressy, *Bonfires and Bells: National Memory and the Protestant Calendar in Elizabethan and Stuart England* (Berkeley, 1989) are recent works that adress the subject. See also Carol Z. Wiener, "The Beleaguered Isle: A Study of Elizabethan and Early Jacobean Anti-Catholicism," *Past and Present*, 51 (1971), 27-62; Robin Clifton, "Popular Fear of Catholics during the English Revolution," *Past and Present*, 52 (1972), 23-55; John Miller, *Popery and Politics in England, 1660-1688* (Cambridge,

1973); John Kenyon, *The Popish Plot* (London, 1972); K. H. D. Haigh, "'No Popery' in the Reign of Charles II," in J. S. Bromley and E. H. Kassman, eds., *Britain and the Netherlands* (The Hague, 1975), 102-119; Ian Y. Thackray, "Zion Undermined: The Protestant Belief in a Popish Plot during the English Interregnum," *History Workshop Journal*, 18 (1984), 28-52; and Jeremy Black, "The Catholic Threat and the British Press in the 1720s and 1730s," *Journal of Religious History*, 12 (1983), 364-381. Also useful are D. G. Paz, "Popular Anti-Catholicism in England, 1850-1851," *Albion*, 11 (1979), 331-359; D. G. Paz, "Anti-Catholicism, Anti-Irish Stereotyping and Anti-Celtic Racism in Mid-Victorian Working-Class Periodicals," *Albion*, 18 (1986), 610-617; E. R. Norman, *Anti-Catholicism in Victorian England* (New York, 1968); and Steve Bruce, *No Pope of Rome: Anti-Catholicism in Modern Scotland* (Edinburgh, 1985).

2. This theme is developed extensively in Haller, *The Elect Nation*, especially 224-250.

3. See Haller, *The Elect Nation*, 13-18.

4. See William S. Maltby, *The Black Legend in England* (Durham, NC., 1971).

5. David Cressy, "The Protestant Calendar and the Vocabulary of Celebration in Early Modern England," *Journal of British Studies*, 29 (1990), 31-52; O. W. Furley, "Pope-burning Processions of the Late Seventeenth Century," *History*, 44 (1959), 16-23; Timothy Harris, *London Crowds in the Reign of Charles II* (New York, 1987).

6. See Nicholas Rogers, "Popular Protest in Early Hanoverian London," *Past and Present*, 77 (1978), 70-100; Robert B. Shoemaker, "The London 'Mob' in the Early Eighteenth Century," *Journal of British Studies*, 26 (1987), 273-304; Kathleen Wilson, "Empire, Trade and Popular Politics in Mid-Hanoverian London: The Case of Admiral Vernon," *Past and Present*, 121 (1988), 74-109; and George Rudé, *Paris and London in the Eighteenth Century* (New York, 1973), 268-292.

7. David D. Hall, *Worlds of Wonder, Days of Judgement: Popular Religious Belief in Early New England* (New York, 1989), 45, 51, 75. *The New England Primer* always retold the story of John Rogers who was "Minister of the Gospel in London, was the first Martyr in Q. Mary's Reign and was burnt at Smithfield, February the fourteenth 1554 . . . [who] died courageously for the Gospel of Jesus Christ." *The New England Primer* (Boston, 1727 and many other editions).

8. See Cressy, *Bonfires and Bells*, 202-206.

9. Pauline Maier, "The Pope at Harvard: The Dudleian Lectures, Anti-Catholicism, and the Politics of Protestantism," *MHSP*, 97 (1985), 16-41. Also see Douglas C. Stange, "The Third Lecture: One Hundred and Fifty Years of Anti-Popery at Harvard," *Harvard University Library Bulletin*, 16 (October 1968), 354-369.

10. "The Will of Judge Paul Dudley," *Colonial Society of Massachusetts Publications*, 16 (1925), 854-857.

11. Pierre Berault, *The Church of Rome Evidently Proved Heretick* (Boston, 1685), 4-5.

12. *A Protestant's Resolution* (Boston, 1746), 16, 29.

13. Jonathan Mayhew, *Popish Idolatry* (Boston, 1765), 9-10.

14. Antonio Gavin, *A Master-Key to Popery* (Newport, 1773), 146.

15. Edward Wigglesworth, *The Authority of Tradition* (Boston, 1778), 7.

16. Hall, *Worlds of Wonder, Days of Judgement*, 22-31.

17. Paul Dudley, *An Essay on the Merchandize of Slaves and the Souls of Men* (Boston, 1731), 43.

18. Gavin, *A Master-Key to Popery*, 49.

19. *A Protestant's Resolution*, 18-19.

20. See Gavin, *A Master-Key to Popery*, 31, 33, 46, for a few of many examples.

21. [A. D. Auborn], *The French Convert* (Boston, 1725).

22. See Gavin, *A Master-Key to Popery*, 80-83.

23. *The French Convert*, 18-19.

24. *The French Convert*, 40.

25. Berault, *The Church of Rome Evidently Proved Heretick*, 7; Gavin, *A Master-Key to Popery*, 98; Dudley, *An Essay on the Merchandize of Slaves*, 32-33.

26. Samuel Cooper, *A Sermon Preached . . . Before the Society for the Encouragement of Industry* (Boston, 1753), 28.

27. Gavin, *A Master-Key to Popery*, 117-118.

28. *Popish Cruelty Displayed* (Boston, 1753), title page.

29. *Popish Cruelty Displayed*, 5.

30. Cooper, *A Discourse on the Man of Sin*, 44.

31. Jonathan Mayhew, *A Discourse on Unlimited Submission* (Boston, 1750), preface.

32. Gavin, *A Master-key to Popery*, 212-213.

33. Gavin, *A Master-Key to Popery*, 234-235.

34. Catholics did not obtain religious freedom in Massachusetts until 1780, Rhode Island in 1783, New Hampshire in 1784, and Connecticut until 1791. See Arthur J. Riley, *Catholicism in New England to 1788* (Baltimore, 1936), 92-136. This theme will be treated in chapter 7.

35. N. B. Shurtleff, ed., *Records of the Governor and Company of the Massachusetts Bay in New England*, 5 vols. (Boston, 1853-54), II, 193.

36. *Acts and Resolves of the Province of Massachusetts Bay*, 21 vols. (Boston, 1869-1922), I, 423-424.

37. Mayhew, *Popish Idolatry*, 49.

38. *Votes and Proceedings of the Freeholders and Inhabitants of the Town of Boston* (Boston, 1772), 4.

39. Mayhew, *Popish Idolatry*, 48-49.

40. See Fred Anderson, "A People's Army: Provincial Military Service in Massachusetts during the Seven Years' War," *WMQ*, 40 (1983), 499-527.

41. Sylvanus Conant, *The Art of War* (Boston, 1759), 12.

42. Bird, *The Importance of the Divine Presence*, 17.

43. Jonathan Mayhew, *Election Sermon* (Boston, 1754), reprinted in A. W. Plumpstead, *Wall in the Garden: Selected Massachusetts Election Sermons, 1670-1775* (Minneapolis, 1968), 283-319.

44. Mayhew, *Election Sermon*, 311.

45. For example, in 1755 New London's Solomon Williams described a vanquished New England where the meeting houses were destroyed and Protestants "forced into gallies, or nunneries, the Ministers shot." See Solomon Williams, *The Duty of Christian Soldiers* (New Haven, 1755), 24. For a discussion of New England preaching during the French and Indian War, see Nathan O. Hatch, "The Origins of Civil Millennialism in America: New England Clergymen, War with France and the Revolution," *WMQ*, 31 (1974), 407-430. For an extensive bibliography of sermons published during the war, see Hatch's *The Sacred Cause of Liberty: Republican Thought and the Millennium in Revolutionary New England* (New Haven, 1977). Also see Kerry Trask, *In the Pursuit of Shadows: Massachusetts Millennialism and the Seven Years War* (New York, 1989), and Harry Stout, *The New England Soul: Preaching and Religious Culture in Colonial New England* (New York, 1986), especially chap. 12.

46. Appleton, *A Sermon Preached October 9*, 26.

47. Forbes, *God the Strength of His People*, 33.

48. Appleton, *A Sermon Delivered October 9*, 26.

2

Deliverance from Luxury: Pope's Day, Social Conflict, and the Anti-papal Persuasion

I

Anti-popery was not confined to the quadrennial Dudleian Lecture at Harvard College. The pope was not a bogeyman who resided solely in the minister's study. Anti-Catholic sentiment was richly manifested in the popular culture of colonial New England. New England almanacs routinely noted the various important days in the Protestant calendar. For example, *Freebetter's Almanac* reminded Connecticut readers in 1774 of the anniversaries of the beheading of Charles I, the 1745 conquest of Louisbourg, and the discovery of Guy Fawkes' Gunpowder Plot in 1605.[1] The last date, November 5, was an important anniversary in the popular culture of colonial New England. According to Peter Oliver, New Englanders "Uniformly practiced the exhibiting of a pageant on every 5th of November representing the Pope and Devil upon a stage."[2] At the end of the evening the participants burned the stages. This celebration was known in New England as Pope's Day. Pope's Day was the unofficial, though widely celebrated, anti-Catholic holiday in colonial New England.

Both elite and plebeian New Englanders valued the celebration of Pope's Day. The elite appreciated the stabilizing impact of anti-papal rhetoric, which unified and bound a socially disparate people together. Wealthy New Englanders, who sympathized with the day's anti-papal theme, hoped that if the crowd expressed its anger at popery, it would not direct it at them. The celebration of Pope's Day gave New England's common people a voice with which to assert their agreement with the very foundation of New England culture, Protestantism. However, it also gave them an opportunity to vent their anxieties and frustrations. In the pre-revolutionary period, therefore, Pope's Day had two functions: to validate the anti-papal persuasion of the common people of colonial New England, and to allow the them to define their own group identity and express their own interests.

II

In England, the fifth of November was traditionally met with bonfires to celebrate the deliverance of the people from tyranny. During the seventeenth century the celebration of Guy Fawkes Day was frequently merged with that of Queen Elizabeth's Accession Day (November 17). Both were greeted by bonfires, pealing bells, and mock coronation processions and executions of the pope and the devil. In combining the holidays, Britons stressed their Protestantism in the face of the crypto-Catholicism of the Stuarts. Because of their anti-Catholic, patriotic premise, the Protestant churches in New England accepted these celebrations.[3] The earliest recorded celebration of Pope's Day in New England occurred on November 5, 1623, when a group of sailors built a bonfire at Plymouth Plantation that burned out of control and consumed several homes. By the second half of the seventeenth century, the commemoration of Guy Fawkes Day became a regular occurrence. As it evolved in the seventeenth century, Pope's Day was a celebration for the lower orders in Anglo-American society. The rowdy sailors at Plymouth in 1623 were but the earliest in a long line of mariners, artisans, and apprentices who celebrated the fifth of November with increased vigor throughout the seventeenth and eighteenth centuries.

The prominence of sailors in the celebration is not coincidental. Pope's Day was most popular in the seaports of New England. Prominent celebrations were held in Marblehead, Newburyport, Newport, Salem, and Portsmouth. In 1702 Marbleheaders met the fifth of November with a bull-baiting, with the meat distributed to the poor. This rather unusual celebration reflects the plebeian focus of the festival and its participants.[4] Bostonians celebrated Pope's Day most consistently and vigorously. This chapter will focus on the commemoration in Boston in order to examine the role anti-popery played in the amelioration of social conflict in colonial New England.

During the first decades of the eighteenth century, the celebration of Pope's

Day became increasingly more elaborate and violent. Simple bonfires gave way to the burning of the pope and the devil in effigy. In the 1720s Bostonians began to parade the pope's effigy through the streets on a platform prior to its being committed to the flames. Benjamin Walker recorded in his diary in 1729 that "some men brought through the North End . . . the Pope in a chair . . . others before him."[5] Frequently, Bostonians carried more than one pope through the streets, and fighting often resulted when parades crossed paths. November 5th was a night of heavy drinking for the celebrants. The dangerous nature of the evening was certainly made clear in 1735 when four apprentices drowned while canoeing from Boston Neck, where the pope had been burned.[6]

By the 1730s the ritualized celebration of Pope's Day had three elements: a procession in which the celebrants paraded the effigy of the pope through the streets and exacted tribute from the populace, a violent confrontation between the rival processions, and finally the burning of the popes. The celebration began in the afternoon or early evening with a procession of floats prepared in the weeks before November 5th. The large floats were preceded by young boys who carried their own small effigies of the pope. According to a broadside published by the "Printshop Boys" and distributed during the procession in the 1760s:

The little Popes they go out first
With little teney Boys:
In frolics they are full gale
And make a laughing noise.[7]

Printer's apprentice Isaiah Thomas, who participated in the celebration of Pope's Day in the 1750s and 1760s, remembered, "Little boys had them [popes] placed on shingles, bigger boys on a piece of board, some no bigger than one boy could carry in his hands, others would require two or more boys and so on."[8]

The procession of the boys signaled the beginning of the larger parades through the streets. Geography, rather than age or occupational group, was the prime factor in determining which pope gang a man belonged to. In Boston, two rival neighborhoods—the North End and South End—traditionally exhibited rival popes.[9] The neighborhoods spent days and even weeks preparing their popes for the celebration. Isaiah Thomas provides the best description of one of the larger popes:

On the front of these stages, was placed in proportion to the dimensions of the Stage, a large lantern framed circular at the top and covered with paper. Behind this lantern was placed an effigy of the pope sitting in an armed Chair. Immediately behind him was the imaginary representation of the Devil, standing Erect with extended arms. . . . The larger Effigies had heads placed on poles which went thro' the bodies & thro' the upper part of the stages which were formed like large boxes, some of them not less than 16 or 18 feet long, 3 or 4 feet wide and 3 or 4 feet in depth. Inside of the Stages and out of sight sat a boy under each effigy whose business it was to move the heads of the Effigies by means of the poles before mentioned, from one side to the other as fancy directed.[10]

Youths played a central role in the Pope's Day ritual. An unidentified seventy-year-old man wrote to the *Columbian Centinel* in 1821 to describe the Pope's Days of his youth. He recalled, "On the stage was music and something to drink—also boys, clad in frocks and trousers well covered with tar and feathers who danced about the pope, . . . and frequently climbed up and kissed the devil."[11]

The symbolism of the Pope's Day parades reflected the concerns of colonial New Englanders. In contrast to their British counterparts who placed the effigy of the would-be regicide, Guy Fawkes, at the center of their ritual, New Englanders reserved their attention for the pope. The substitution of the pope for Guy Fawkes indicates that New Englanders were more concerned with expressing their distaste for Rome than their allegiance to London.[12] In their symbolic rendering of the pope, there was no doubt as to where he figured in the outlook of most New Englanders. The creators of the floats placed the effigies on the stages in such a way as to demonstrate symbolically what they believed was the relationship between the pope and the devil. David Robinson, a Philadelphian visiting Boston in 1761, wrote: "His Holiness was in a very antique dress and had a really Roman nose. The Devil, out of complisance wore one about two inches longer and had a key in one hand and a pitch fork in the other." Isaiah Thomas remembered that "the Effigy of the devil was always well tarred in order to hold a thick coat of feathers." Peter Oliver concurred: "sometimes both of them [the pope and the devil] are tarred and feathered, but it was generally the Devil's luck to be singular."[13] On the floats, New Englanders deliberately rendered the pope as the servant of Satan.

Although viewed by patrician observers as an unruly mob, the Pope's Day crowd was an organized affair. There was a definite hierarchy among the celebrants. Each year the participants elected officers to oversee the construction of the pope and to lead the procession.[14] Perhaps the best-known Pope's Day celebrant was Ebenezer Mackintosh. Born to an impoverished family, he was a shoemaker of marginal success. Despite his humble circumstances, "General" Mackintosh could be found at the head of the South End pope attired in a blue and gold uniform and a lace hat bearing a rattan cane and a speaking trumpet throughout the 1760s.[15] The presence of elected officers like Mackintosh indicates the development of a lower-class leadership outside the traditional sociopolitical channels of power.

Under the leadership of officers like Mackintosh, the Pope's Day celebrants dragged the various popes through the streets. Crowds of bystanders verbally abused the effigies as they passed. According to the Printshop Boys:

The great ones next go out, and meet
With many a smart rebuff,
They're hall'd along the street
And called bad names enough.[16]

Eventually the processions visited the homes of the wealthier members of the Boston community where a "purser" stepped forward and exacted tribute from the homeowners to defray the expenses of the evening's revelry. The demand for tribute followed certain ritual forms as well. This element of the Pope's Day celebration is probably an American version of the English mummers' play with the pope supplanting the traditional mummers' hero, Father Christmas.[17] It was quite common for the celebrants to rap upon the sides of the houses with staves or clubs. There was an implied threat of violent destruction in this rapping that surely did not go unnoticed by the homeowners. According to Isaiah Thomas, the purser rang a hand bell and recited a poem at the homes of "every person who had the appearance of having money in his pocket." After the crowd repeated the verses, the purser took up his collection.[18] James Freeman, a Bostonian who cast a disapproving eye on the celebration, noted that a throng accompanied the popes which was "very abusive to inhabitants, insulting persons and breaking windows of such who did not give them money and even of those who had given liberally."[19]

After the popes had been paraded through the streets, the next phase of the celebration was a violent contest between the rival groups. There was a rich tradition of competitive violence between the North and South Ends, as the two crowds struggled to capture the pope of the opposition. Isaiah Thomas remembered: "A competition it seems early arose between each part of town which made the best Popes and Devils. Hostilities soon commenced . . . In those battles stones, brickbats, besides clubs were freely used and altho' persons were seldom killed, yet broken heads were not infrequent."[20] Thomas was nearly killed when he was struck in the head with a brickbat one year. James Freeman noted in 1745 that when the two popes met, "their followers fell on one another with the utmost rage and fury. Several men [were] wounded and bruised and some left for dead and rendered incapable for a long time."[21]

Throughout the 1750s and 1760s, the violence associated with Pope's Day apparently intensified. In 1752 a sailor named John Crabb died from a scuffle with "a lad named Chubb and a Negro Fellow."[22] Thomas Chubb, a sailor, and

Abraham, a slave of William Pitman, clubbed Crabb to death. The court records do not indicate what happened to Abraham, but Chubb received a brand on the hand and twelve months in prison for his part in the episode.[23] Indeed, by the mid-1760s the melee between the two gangs became the central focus of the evening. In 1764 Freeman observed:

It was formerly the custom on this anniversary for the lower classes to celebrate the evening in a manner peculiar to themselves. . . . But of late . . . instead of spending the evening agreeably, the champions of both ends of town engage each other in battle under the denominations North and South End. . . . At about eight o'clock the two parties met near the Mill Bridge where they fought with clubs, brickbats for about a half an hour, when those of the South End gained victory, carrying off not only their own, but their antagonists' stages which they burned on Boston Neck. In the fray, many were much bruised and wounded in their heads and arms, some dangerously.[24]

The Pope's Day celebration culminated with the burning of the popes on Boston Neck where the public gallows were located. Sometimes the crowd subjected the pope to mock trial and execution. The victors in the conflict between the rival gangs won the honor of burning their float as well as that of their opponents, "to which were added all the wash tubs, tar barrels, and stray lumber which they could lay their hands on," usually stolen along the routes of the processions.[25] With the burning of the platforms and the symbolic killing of the pope, and a good deal of hearty drinking, the evening drew to a close.

III

In his characterization of popular festival, Peter Burke writes, "Carnival was an enactment of 'the world turned upside down', a favorite theme of the culture of early modern Europe."[26] In Burke's model, Carnival allowed for ritualized disorder and aggression on the part of the lower orders of society. It is a wonderful irony that the premier expression of anti-Catholicism in colonial British America, Pope's Day, was similar in both form and function to the carnivals of Catholic Europe. According to Burke, the elite both appreciated and feared Carnival. They valued it as a social release for the lower orders. They preferred that the world be turned upside down ritually for one day rather than in permanent reality. But the upper classes also feared Carnival as a subversive threat to their way of life. The ritualized disorder and violence could easily spill over into the anarchic violence of riot and social rebellion such as Emanuel Le Roy Ladurie described in sixteenth-century Romans.[27] But, according to Burke's model, popular rituals such as Carnival or Pope's Day were, in the main, social safety valves which allowed society's discontented to expend their energies in a fashion that was relatively unthreatening to the social hierarchy. Viewed in this way, Pope's Day did not challenge the established social order but reinforced it.

However, to view Pope's Day as merely a "safety valve" is limiting. As Natalie Davis has written in her exploration of the "Abbeys of Misrule" in early modern France: "rather than being a mere 'safety valve' deflecting attention from social reality, festive life can on the one hand perpetuate certain values of the community (and guarantee its survival) and on the other hand criticize political order. Misrule can have its own rigor and can also decipher king and state."[28] Pope's Day served a similar function in colonial New England. Because the major theme of the celebration was anti-popery, the common folk were able simultaneously to validate one of the core values of New England culture, Protestantism, and to express the interests of their particular social group. Because they did so under the umbrella of anti-popery, the common folk were allowed a relatively wide latitude in their expressions of social discontent on Pope's Day. In order to appreciate the social function of Pope's Day, we must consider exactly who participated in the ritual, and assess what the experience meant to the participants.

In 1753 the Great and General Court described the participants in the Pope's Day revelry as "tumultuous companies of men, children and negroes." James Freeman described them as a "vast number of negroes and white servants with clubs."[29] The participants in Pope's Day came primarily from that class of eighteenth-century society usually termed "the lower orders": day laborers, sailors, lesser artisans, apprentices, servants, slaves, and the unemployed. A survey of the relevant court records for the period from 1745 to 1765, when the celebration was at its height, reveals that thirty-three Pope's Day celebrants were arrested in 1749, 1752, and 1764. Among them were six shipwrights, five mariners, three bakers, two slaves, two chairmakers, two cordwainers, one leather dresser, one cooper, one sailmaker, one shipjoiner, one chocolatemaker, one distiller, one bricklayer, one caulker, one tailor, one ropemaker, and one housewright.[30] As the court records indicate, the tradition was especially popular among those engaged in the maritime trades. Sailors were at the bottom of the social hierarchy.[31] As a major port, Boston had a ready supply of landless, often rootless men who were happy to participate in a celebration that involved drinking, fighting, and the chance to insult some of their employers. Other participants were young apprentices, like the four who drowned in 1735, and the printer's imp, Isaiah Thomas. The majority of the participants were lesser artisans who were eager to join their nautical counterparts in a celebration at the expense of their social betters. This was especially true in the mid-eighteenth century when an economic decline exacerbated social tensions in Boston.[32]

The social pressures of the mid-eighteenth century manifested themselves in the celebration of Pope's Day. The celebration had a decided anti-authoritarian theme as well as an anti-papal one. The participation of boys in the parade combined with the mockery of the ritual to foster the anti-authoritarian atmosphere. The Pope's Day processions were styled after papal coronations.[33] By having children serve as the mocking "attendants" of the pope, Bostonians expressed their distate not only for popery in particular, but for authority in general. As James Freeman recorded in 1754, the whole reason for dragging the pageantry through the streets was so that "the vulgar might impress them [the wealthy] with a sense of deliverance from luxury."[34]

Occasionally, members of the crowd literally delivered their wealthy peers from luxury. For example, in 1746 the following advertisement appeared in the *Boston Gazette*: "Some of the Pope's attendences had some supper as well as Money given 'em at a House in Town, One of the Company happen'd to Swallow a silver Spoon with his Victuals, Marked IHS. Whoever it was is desired to return it when it comes at hand."[35] There must have been some bitterness when a crowd of poor artisans stood in the November cold outside the home of a wealthy merchant to exact tribute. The increased violence between 1745 and 1765, against both property and persons, reflects the discontent that gripped Boston during the period.

The celebration of Pope's Day reflected a plebeian criticism of the patrician class whose trappings were increasingly inaccessible. An observer noted that the effigy of the pope "was dressed in gorgeous attire with a large white wig on, over which he has an enormous gold-laced hat."[36] The association of aristocratic finery with popery in such effigies was clear. According to historian Peter Shaw, the Boston popes were usually attired in breeches, in contrast to the trousers of workingmen, for just such a purpose. The Boston crowd not only burned the symbols of political and spiritual tyranny, but also those of economic superiority.[37]

The anti-papal theme of the Pope's Day celebration made such demonstrations, while irritating, acceptable. The common folk deliberately exploited a socially acceptable popular demonstration to give expression to their own grievances. Because they sincerely enunciated the values of the anti-papal persuasion, Boston's lesser artisans, apprentices, and sailors were also able to give voice to their own values and aspirations. It was only because the celebration of Pope's Day fell within the acceptable parameters of the anti-papal persuasion that it was permitted. Bostonians were not unaware of the protest within the celebration. The Governor's Council decried the "pretence of commemorating the preservation of the king and Parliament" and criticized the celebration for, "instead of encouraging an abhorrence of Popery & forming a Spirit of Loyalty in the Youth of the Town, the aforesaid Practices have been attended with horrible Profaneness and the greatest immoralitys."[38] The popular protest expressed within the anti-papal persuasion posed a dilemma for those who opposed the celebration. How could the excesses of Pope's Day be limited and the anti-papal message maintained?

After 1745 the local and colonial authorities made occasional half-hearted efforts to limit the violence and scope of Pope's Day. For example, in 1748 the Justices of the Peace in Boston gave public notice that "whereas sundry persons have heretofore gone about the streets the evening following 5th of Novr. armed wh. clubs & demanding money of ye inhabitants and breaking ye windows of ye who refuse it, they are determined to send out constables the present 5th of Novr. to prevent such disorders."[39] Apparently the proclamations were of little consequence. On November 23, 1752, the Governor's Council reported that "many grievous disorders have been committed in the town of Boston on the evening of the fifth of November and the Pageants or Shows generally made use of on that occasion having of late years been greatly multiplied the disorders have proportionally increased."[40] The General Court created a committee to consider legislation to stem the disorders. As a consequence, in 1753 the legislature passed an "Act for further preventing all riotous, tumultuous and disorderly Assemblies or Companies of Persons" from "carrying pageants and other shews through the streets and lanes of the town of Boston and other towns of this province, abusing and insulting the inhabitants by menaces and abusive language." The assembly passed similar acts in 1756, 1758, and 1763.[41] Despite these legal restrictions, the celebration of Pope's Day continued unabated. More significantly, political leaders made no serious efforts to enforce the laws. As long as the celebrants confined their activities to one day, and limited their violence, prudence and custom dictated that little could or should be done to put a stop to it.

The mercantile elite in Boston looked upon Pope's Day with ambivalent feelings. Given their subscription to the anti-papal persuasion, they endorsed its overall theme. Moreover, they valued the festival as a social release. In decrying the violent nature of Pope's Day, James Freeman conceded that, "these parties do not much [act violently] at any other time." However, since they were frequently harassed by the Pope's Day crowd, members of the elite must have experienced trepidation and even fear every November 5th.[42] Indeed, Boston merchant John Rowe called Pope's Day "that foolish custom" and took care to note the behavior of the crowd each November 5th in his diary.[43] That Rowe took the time each year to note the behavior of the crowd indicates that it was a matter of concern for him. Most homeowners in Boston must have shared his concern each November.

What happened when the celebration of Pope's Day exceeded the acceptable standards of social expression? How did the elite respond to more serious threats to the social order? The answers to these questions emerge from consideration of the Pope's Day celebrations of 1764 and 1765. The 1764 event exceeded the bounds of acceptable popular expression. Premature rioting associated with the holiday occurred on October 31, November 2, and November 3. On the afternoon of the fifth, before the parade, a young boy fell under a wheel of the North End pope and was "killed on the spot."[44] In the wake of the tragedy, the sheriff and militia were called out to destroy the popes and prevent the processions. The officials destroyed the North End pope but were driven back by a South End crowd. In the meantime, the North Enders rebuilt their pope and processed through the streets.[45] No doubt the inability of government officials to take control of the streets in the wake of the fatality caused a good deal of consternation among the elite of the town. The celebration of 1764 left many Bostonians with a sense that the acceptable limits of authority and social order had been breached. Constables arrested Ebenezer Mackintosh, as captain of the South End pope. He was tried and acquitted on February 7, 1765.[46]

Pope's Day 1764 is an excellent example of the role that it played in colonial Boston. The rioting that year demonstrated that Pope's Day could serve as both a vehicle for social protest and a social safety valve. The 1764 celebration was a protest insofar as the crowd openly defied and stifled the authority of the government. Despite this challenge, the defiance of the crowd was limited. The members of the crowd directed their violence at one another. The crowd did not injure any members of the elite.

Nonetheless, in the wake of the 1764 Pope's Day, the Boston elite demonstrated concern over the behavior of the crowd. Elite trepidation was reinforced during the Stamp Act crisis of the following summer. News of the Stamp Act reached Boston in the spring of 1765. The following August two major riots rocked Boston, directly inspired by opposition to the Stamp Act. During the second riot, a crowd attacked and destroyed the home of Thomas Hutchinson. Both opponents and supporters of the Crown among the elite criticized the Hutchinson riot. The thorough destruction of Hutchinson's house proved that Pope's Day alone was not a sufficient outlet for the social anxieties of the Boston crowd. The ritual gathering of tribute and breaking of windows had, apparently, given away to more substantial social violence.[47]

In the autumn of 1765 the elite took steps to stem such social disruptions.

During the last week in October, according to James Freeman, "several gentlemen" tried to establish "a reconciliation between the two parties."[48] They accomplished this through shrewd manipulation and bribery. The Whig elite employed Ebenezer Mackintosh, with his followers, to keep order during the first week of November. In this way they brought him under their influence while allowing him to exercise a degree of authority.

Perhaps the most remarkable Pope's Day since the sailors set fire to Plymouth in 1623 occurred in 1765. The event contrasted sharply with the bloody encounter of the previous year. The two neighborhoods did not engage in their annual melee. James Freeman observed:

about noon the pageantry . . . were brought on stages and met at King Street where the Union was established in a very ceremonial manner, and having given huzzas they interchanged ground, the South marched to the North and the North to the South . . . until they again met . . . the whole proceeded to the Liberty Tree . . . they refreshed themselves for a while and retreated to the northward agreeable to plan. They reached Copp's Hill before six o'clock where they halted. Having kindled a fire, the whole pageantry was committed to the flames.[49]

No incidents of violence marred the celebration, for, as the *Boston Gazette* reported, "not a club was seen among the whole, nor was any Negro allowed to approach the Stage."[50]

As restrained by the Whigs, Pope's Day lost its plebeian, though not its anti-papal, nature. In exchange for this relatively mild celebration, "many gentlemen seeing the Affair well-conducted contributed to make a handsome purse to entertain those who carried it off."[51] The gentlemen sponsored a "Union Feast," at the Royal Exchange Tavern, the following week. The supper was attended by "several leading gentlemen" and about two hundred of the leading members of the Pope's Day crowd. The diners were seated according to their rank in society.[52] In this way the Whigs reinforced the social hierarchy which had been occasionally challenged during the previous year.

The celebration of 1765 reinforced the traditional anti-papal persuasion. The distinctly anti-papal aspects of the festival—the parading and burning of the pope—remained. In this way Pope's Day of 1765 was a traditional affirmation of the values that bound New Englanders together. At the same time, the celebration diminished those elements of the festival that were distinctly plebeian—the demand for tribute and the festive violence. The elements of social conflict were subsumed by the anti-papal persuasion of colonial New England.

IV

The celebration of Pope's Day provides insight into the complex interaction between the anti-papal persuasion and New England culture. While anti-popery promoted unity in that it appealed to the near universal abhorrence of Catholicism in colonial New England, it also provided poor Bostonians with a means to express their own interests, values, and aspirations. In short, while the anti-papal persuasion appealed to almost all New Englanders, it did not appeal to them in the same ways.

The occupations of the Pope's Day celebrants are vivid testimony that the aversion to popery was a sentiment that transcended social boundaries in colonial New England. For plebeian New Englanders, anti-popery meant that they were not illiterate dupes blindly and stupidly supporting a leisure class of clerics and nobles. The anti-papal persuasion told poorer New Englanders that they were freer than the peasantry of popish countries. Implicit in their freedom was a higher standard of living and greater political freedoms than their counterparts in Catholic countries enjoyed. Appropriately, when poor Bostonians felt their economic and political position declining, they resorted to the vocabulary of anti-popery to express their grievances. By burning the pope, Pope's Day celebrants declared that they were free and would not suffer to live like papists.

The anti-papal persuasion appealed to wealthier New Englanders as well. For them anti-popery also meant freedom. It meant that they were free to pursue their own material and spiritual interests without catering to clerical interference. It also meant that they lived in a stable, well-ordered society, not a society of caprice, but one of law. No inquisition threatened their independence. Importantly, anti-popery stifled the social discontent manifested in the celebration of Pope's Day by appealing to common values. Thus in 1765, rather than attempting to prohibit the celebration, members of the elite publicly embraced anti-popery in an effort to avoid a recurrence of the disturbances of 1764.

While the anti-papal persuasion meant different things to different groups of New Englanders, its strength, its very persuasiveness, derived from the unity it promoted. The people of eighteenth-century New England were divided by a number of factors. They differed according to wealth, geography, education, occupation, theology, and politics. The one thing they most agreed on was their aversion to popery. Pope's Day contributed to the stability of New England society by appealing to common values. As Pope's Day 1765 demonstrated, the Whig elite appreciated the value of appealing to anti-popery. Throughout the 1760s and 1770s, Whig leaders deliberately and successfully utilized the rhetoric of anti-popery to rally support for their cause.

The universal fear and hatred of Catholicism, expressed on Pope's Day, colored the way New Englanders of all social classes responded to British activities in the 1760s and early 1770s. The belief that Britain was becoming "popish" would contribute in a very real fashion to the coming of the American Revolution. Between 1763 and 1775 New England Whigs gradually came to believe that Britain was reverting to popery. They were encouraged in this belief by their cultural leaders, especially ministers and politicians. Their immediate reaction would be to claim that they were the true Englishmen and Britain had strayed from its historical anti-Catholic mission. When this proved an untenable intellectual position, the people of New England would embrace a complete break with Britain rather than a compromise with popery.

NOTES

1. [Nathaniel Daboll, ed.], *Freebetter's Connecticut Almanac for 1774* (New London, 1773). For the impact of the Protestant calendar on British North America, see David Cressy, *Bonfires and Bells: National Memory and the Protestant Calendar in Elizabethan and Stuart England* (Berkeley, 1989). I am grateful to Charles Hanson who alerted me to the prominence of anti-popery in colonial almanacs and generously allowed me to read the manuscript from his talk, "From the Quebec Act to the French Alliance," delivered at the American Antiquarian Society on February 27, 1992.

2. Douglas Adair and John R. Schutz, eds., *Peter Oliver's Origins and Progress of the American Rebellion* (Stanford, 1961), 84.

3. Cressy, *Bonfires and Bells*, 203-205; Peter Shaw, *American Patriots and the Rituals of Revolution* (Cambridge, Mass., 1981), 204-208; George L. Kittredge, "Burning the Pope in Effigies in London, 1678," Colonial Society of Massachusetts *Publications*, 18 (1915-16), 12-14; J. E. Etherington, "Lewes Bonfire Night Celebrations," *Sussex History*, 1 (1977), 8-21.

4. Josiah Cotton to Rowland Cotton, October 17, 1702, *MHSC*, 80 (1972), 271. Also see Joseph B. Felt, *Annals of Salem*, 2 vols. (Salem, 1849), II, 50-55; and Joshua Coffin, *History of Newbury* (Boston, 1845), 248-249.

5. Benjamin Walker, Diary, MHS, entry for November 5, 1729.

6. *Boston News-Letter*, November 20, 1735; *Boston Weekly Journal*, November 20, 1735; "The Diary of the Rev. Samuel Checkley, 1735," *Colonial Society of Massachusetts Transactions*, 12 (1908-9), 270-305, quotation, p. 305.

7. *North End, South End Forever* (Boston, 1768).

8. Isaiah Thomas, *Three Autobiographical Fragments* (Worcester, 1962), 22.

9. The North and South Ends were divided by the Mill Creek which bisected the Boston peninsula in the eighteenth century. The North End was more densely populated than the South, though the South End included the Common as well as Boston Neck where the popes were burned. Nathaniel B. Shurtleff, *A Topographical and Historical Description of Boston* (Boston, 1872), 124-125.

10. Thomas, *Three Autobiographical Fragments*, 22-23.

11. *Columbian Centinel*, November 10, 1821.

12. Shaw, *American Patriots and the Rituals of Revolution*, 18.

13. Letter from David Robinson to William Preston, November 5, 1761, *MHSP*, 32 (1918-19), 184; Thomas, *Three Autobiographical Fragments*, 23; Adair and Schutz, *Peter Oliver's Origins and Progress of the American Rebellion*, 84. According to Alfred F. Young, tarring and feathering combined the traditional English rituals of popular punishment—the skimmington and the public execution—in a "uniquely American way" that emphasized public humiliation and pain. See Alfred F. Young, "English Plebeian Culture and Eighteenth-Century American Radicalism," in Margaret and James Jacob, eds., *The Origins of Anglo-American Radicalism* (London, 1984), 185-212, quotation, p. 194.

14. Thomas, *Three Autobiographical Fragments*, 25.

15. George P. Anderson, "Ebenezer Mackintosh: Stamp Act Rioter and Patriot," *Colonial Society of Massachusetts Transactions*, 26 (1924-26), 15-64; see also Pauline Maier, *From Resistance to Revolution: Colonial Radicals and the Development of Opposition to Britain, 1765-1776* (New York, 1972), 69-70.

16. "North End, South End Forever."

17. Shaw, *American Patriots and the Rituals of Revolution*, 209.

18. Thomas, *Three Autobiographical Fragments*, 25; Thomas could remember only a fragment of the poem when he wrote his autobiography. Joshua Coffin (*History of Newbury*, 251) transcribed a more complete verse said to have been recited in Newbury in the eighteenth century, a portion of which follows:
You'll hear our bell go jink, jink.
Pray madam, sirs, if you'll something give,
We'll burn the dog [the pope] and never let him live.

19. James Freeman, The Notebook of James Freeman of Boston, Describing the Activities at Boston from 1745 to 1765, MHS; quotation from November 5, 1745.

20. Thomas, *Three Autobiographical Fragments*, 23-24.

21. Freeman, Notebook, November 5, 1745.

22. *The Boston Weekly News-Letter*, November 23, 1752; and Massachusetts Council Records, November 23, 1752, MA 47:357-359.

23. Suffolk County Court Files 70058 and 70433, MA.

24. Freeman, Notebook, November 5, 1764.

25. Coffin, *History of Newbury*, 251.

26. Peter Burke, *Popular Culture in Early Modern Europe* (New York, 1978), 188. For early American crowds, see Dirk Hoerder, *Crowd Action in Revolutionary Massachusetts, 1765-1780* (New York, 1977); and Paul Gilje, *The Road to Mobocracy: Popular Disorder in New York City, 1763-1834* (Chapel Hill, 1987).

27. Emanuel Le Roy Ladurie, *Carnival in Romans*, trans. Nancy Foeny (New York, 1979).

28. Natalie Z. Davis, "The Reasons for Misrule," in Natalie Z. Davis, *Society and Culture in Early Modern France: Eight Essays by Natalie Zemon Davis* (Stanford, 1975), 97-123, quotation, p. 97. For work on popular culture and religion, see Robert Darnton, *The Great Cat Massacre and Other Episodes in French Cultural History* (New York, 1984); Natalie Z. Davis, *Society and Culture in Early Modern France*; Natalie Z. Davis, "Some Tasks and Themes in the Study of Popular Religion," in Charles Trinkaus and Heiko A. Oberman, eds., *The Pursuit of Holiness in Late Medieval and Renaissance Religion* (Leiden, 1974), 307-336. For anthropological studies that consider the issues of social control and social protest in festive life, see Stanley Brandes, *Power and Persuasion: Fiestas and Social Control in Rural Mexico* (Philadelphia, 1988); Robert Da Matta, "Carnival in Multiple Planes," in John J. MacAloon, ed., *Rite. Drama. Festival. Spectacle: Rehearsals Toward a Theory of Cultural Performance* (Philadelphia, 1984), 208-240; and David Gilmore, "Carnival in Fuenmayor: Class Conflict and Social Cohesion in an Andulusian Town," *Journal of Anthropological Research*, 31 (1975), 331-349.

29. *Acts and Resolves of the Province of Massachusetts Bay*, 21 vols. (Boston, 1869-1922), III, 647; Freeman, Notebook, November 5, 1745. Although such descriptions are typical clichés employed by the elite to describe all colonial crowds, they should not be completely disregarded. Melvin Wade has demonstrated that there was a vibrant festive life among African Americans in colonial New England in which the social boundaries between African Americans and poor whites were crossed. It is probable that this also occurred on Pope's Day. See Melvin Wade, "Shining in a Borrowed Plumage: Affirmation of Community in the Black Coronation Festivals of New England, ca. 1750-1850," in Robert B. St. George, ed., *Material Life in America, 1600-1860* (Boston, 1988) 171-182.

30. See Suffolk County Court of General Sessions of the Peace, Docket Book, 1749-54, 22; and Suffolk County Court Files, 70058, 70433, 100493, 100494, MA. All those arrested were males. Males were active performers in the ritual; females played an important role in the ritual as onlookers. As the Printshop Boys noted with respect to Pope's Day, "The girls run out to see the sight"; see *North End, South End Forever*.

31. Jesse Lemisch, "Jack Tar in the Streets: Merchant Seamen in the Politics of Revolutionary America," *WMQ*, 14 (1968), 374-375.

32. In Boston, the middling orders—the master artisans, lesser merchants, and small property holders—all suffered from worsening economic conditions. In 1687 the middle 60 percent of the population controlled 52.3 percent of assessed wealth in the city; by 1771 this portion had shrunk to 38.6 percent. By 1771 nearly one in three Bostonians was a propertlyess laborer. The economic decline of the middling and lower classes had political as well as social ramifications. Many artisans lost the franchise when they could no longer meet property requirements. According to Dirk Hoerder, "even the most optimistic scholarly estimate is that only 56 percent of the adult white males (or about 1,500) were enfranchised" during the 1760s. Dirk

Hoerder, "Boston Leaders and Boston Crowds, 1765-1776," in Alfred F. Young, ed., *The American Revolution: Explorations in the History of American Radicalism* (DeKalb, 1976), 237-238. For the economic situation in Boston, see Alan Kullikoff, "Progress and Inequality in Revolutionary Boston," *WMQ*, 28 (1971), 375-412; James Henretta, "Economic Development and Social Structure in Colonial Boston," *WMQ*, 22 (1965), 75-92; Gary B. Nash, "Urban Wealth and Property in Pre-Revolutionary America," *The Journal of Interdisciplinary History*, 6 (1976), 545-584; Gary Nash, *The Urban Crucible* (Cambridge, 1979); and G. B. Warden, "Inequality and Instability in Eighteenth-Century Boston: A Reappraisal," *The Journal of Interdisciplinary History*, 6 (1976), 585-620.

33. Shaw, *American Patriots and the Rituals of Revolution*, 187-188.

34. Freeman, Notebook, November 5, 1754.

35. As quoted in Esther Forbes, *Paul Revere and the World He Lived In* (Boston, 1942, repr. 1969), 94.

36. *Columbian Centinel*, November 10, 1821.

37. Shaw, *American Patriots and the Rituals of Revolution*, 11-12. Paul Gilje has argued that the Pope's Day effigies in New York in 1747, in the aftermath of the rising of the Stuart Pretender, represented a similar form of social protest. The effigy of the Stuart Pretender, which was exhibited along with the pope and the devil, was made to represent a Scottish aristocrat. According to Gilje: "the effigy may have stood as a muted symbol of the aristocracy. Under the guise of patriotism, the common folk could denigrate and humiliate this effigy, which represented an individual normally untouchable." Gilje, *The Road to Mobocracy*, 29.

38. Massachusetts Council Records, November 23, 1752, MA 47:357-359.

39. Freeman, Notebook, October 1748.

40. Massachusetts Council Records, November 23, 1752, MA 47:357-359.

41. *Acts and Resolves*, III, 647-648; IV, 78, 617-618.

42. Burke, *Popular Culture*, 178-204; Freeman, Notebook, November 5, 1764.

43. For example, in 1768 Rowe recorded, "The People have behaved Well being Pope Night." Anne Rowe Cunningham, ed., *The Letters and Diary of John Rowe* (Boston, 1903), 194.

44. Suffolk County Court Files, 100493, 100494, MA. Quotation from the "Journal of John Boyle," *Colonial Society of Massachusetts Transactions*, 12 (1908-9), 290.

45. Rowe, *Letters and Diary*, 67.

46. Rowe (*Letters and Diary*, 67) mentions the trial of Mackintosh in passing; Anderson ("Ebenezer Mackintosh," 26) reports that Mackintosh was tried and acquitted.

47. See Maier, *Resistance to Revolution*, especially chaps. 1-2; and Bernard Bailyn, *The Ordeal of Thomas Hutchinson* (Cambridge, 1974), especially chap. 2; also Shaw, *American Patriots and the Rituals of Revolution*, chap. 1.

48. Freeman, Notebook, November 5, 1765.

49. Freeman, Notebook, November 5, 1765.

50. *Boston Gazette*, November 11, 1765.

51. *Boston Gazette*, November 11, 1765.

52. *Boston Evening Post*, November 18, 1765; Hoerder, "Boston Leaders and Boston Crowds," 245; Maier, *Resistance to Revolution*, 70.

3

The Pope of Canada and the Fool of England: Anti-popery and the Ideological Origins of the American Revolution

I

Between 1763 and 1775 New Englanders gradually came to believe that the greatest threat of popery came not from Rome or Paris but from London. It would have been impossible to accuse George III of popish sympathies in 1763. Indeed, under his direction and that of his grandfather, British arms had vanquished the preeminent Catholic powers, France and Spain. However, by 1775 New Englanders indicted the king and his ministers for their popish tendencies. This critical transition was often overshadowed by more immediate events such as the Stamp Act or the Townshend Duties. Nonetheless, throughout the period of crisis that preceded the Revolution, the fear of popery colored the lenses through which New Englanders viewed British actions.

The shift in the anti-papal persuasion, however, was a slow, subtle process. Circumstances favored the change. The French menace, while still potent, had retreated before the triumph of British arms in the French and Indian War. With the strongest external popish threat removed, New Englanders were able to concentrate on the threat of popery from within the British Empire. Most importantly, leading Whigs, especially ministers like Jonathan Mayhew and

Samuel Cooper, encouraged New Englanders to view British actions in the light of the anti-papal tradition.

Whig leaders appreciated the potency of anti-papal rhetoric, and between 1765 and 1775 they successfully applied it to describe British actions. The apprehension of popery in New England increased when discussions began in the 1760s over whether an Anglican bishopric should be established in British America. Parliament further exacerbated New England fears in 1774 with its passage of the Quebec Act which gave legal sanction to Catholicism in Canada. When coupled with other British actions such as the Stamp Act, Townshend Acts, and Coercive Acts, these actions made it easy for New Englanders to conclude that Britain and its leaders had been corrupted by popery. Once New Englanders reached this conclusion, history taught them that, as good Protestants, they must resist.

II

In 1815 John Adams wrote that "the apprehension of Episcopacy contributed . . . as much as any other cause, to arouse the attention not only of the inquiring mind, but of the common people, and urge them to close thinking on the constitutional authority of parliament over the colonies."[1] While scholars disagree as to how real the threat of an Anglican episcopal establishment in the American colonies was, the spirited debate over the prospect of such an establishment was genuine.[2] New Englanders feared that the establishment of an Anglican hierarchy in America would be the first step toward the establishment of popery in New England.

For New Englanders, the final debate over the Anglican episcopacy began in August 1760 when the new royal governor of Massachusetts, Francis Bernard, and an Anglican missionary, East Apthorp, arrived in Boston. Characterized by Carl Bridenbaugh as the "unwitting provocateurs of Church and State," these men represented the more vigorous attitude of London toward the colonies in the wake of the British triumph over France in the Seven Years' War.[3] Bernard, an Anglican, was a royal placeman, and Apthorp came to fill a mission established by the Anglican Society for the Propagation of the Gospel in Foreign Parts (SPG) not among the Catholic Indians of Maine but among the Congregationalist Yankees of Cambridge! Apthorp built a mansion within sight of Harvard Yard and rumors quickly spread that it would house the first American bishop. Both Apthorp and Bernard were potent symbols to the people of New England of the encroaching power of the Anglican Church and the

English state.

During the next fifteen years, a vigorous transatlantic debate took place over the wisdom of sending an Anglican bishop to America. The debate took many forms, from learned treatises published as pamphlets to vicious insults traded in newspapers. Innuendo and rumor served the adversaries as well as careful research and reason. New Englanders were well represented in the debate. Some, such as Connecticut's Samuel Johnson and Thomas Bradbury Chandler, defended the Anglican cause. Most, such as Noah Welles of New Haven and Boston's Jonathan Mayhew, were staunch opponents of episcopacy. Indeed, New England's cultural elite—its ministers, editors, and politicians—played a leading role in opposing an episcopal settlement in America. Anti-papal rhetoric was one of their chief weapons. Consistently and effectively, the opponents of an Anglican establishment linked their opponents to the Catholic Church.

The Anglicans, too, attempted to enlist anti-popery in their cause. Thomas Bradbury Chandler, a Connecticut native who presided over King's College in New York, declared that some "will oppose it [an Anglican bishopric] from an Enmity, either open or secret, to the Protestant Religion; of which the Church of England is confessedly the strongest Barrier against Popery." Even the archbishop of Canterbury condemned the persecution of his church which he saw in New England, declaring "now the plain Truth is, that all Protestants learnt this Practice from the Church of Rome." These prominent men argued that only popish sympathizers could oppose an Anglican establishment in America.[4] That both sides in the Episcopal Controversy employed the language of anti-popery is evidence of its prevalence and importance in pre-revolutionary New England.

The opponents of episcopacy were more successful than their adversaries in employing anti-papal rhetoric. After all, New England Congregationalists had been employing the language of anti-popery against various enemies, including Anglicans, for a century and a half. For them anti-papal rhetoric provided a highly refined set of symbols ideal for attacking an entrenched hierarchy such as that of the Church of England. The superficial similarities between the Anglican and the Roman churches—both hierarchical and liturgical—made the appeal to anti-popery quite appropriate to enemies of episcopacy. When Anglicans employed anti-papal rhetoric, they sounded shrill; when their opponents did, they struck a nerve.

The opponents of episcopacy were well aware of the utility of anti-papal rhetoric. As the English libertarian Thomas Hollis advised them in April 1764, "The Conduct of the Church of England in Respect to Papists and Popery . . . is the WEAK side of the Leaders of that Church and they may be constantly attacked on it with very great advantage."[5] New England's ministers and publishers needed little encouragement. They willingly and effectively picked up anti-papal rhetoric and used it as a metaphorical cudgel against their enemies. In so doing they came to appreciate that political benefits could be won by appealing to New England's anti-papal persuasion.

Among the foremost opponents of an episcopal settlement was Jonathan Mayhew. The pastor of the West Church in Boston, Mayhew had become an international sensation in 1750 with the publication of *A Discourse on Unlimited Submission*. In the *Discourse*, Mayhew not only asserted the right of subjects to resist an unjust ruler but leveled an attack against the Anglican clergy, which he claimed still harbored sympathies for the tyrannical Stuarts. He accused Charles I of endeavoring to enslave his subjects through the Anglican clergy which would "set up a monstrous hierarchy like that of Rome."[6] Given this background, it is not surprising that Mayhew came to the fore as the leading opponent of an American episcopacy during the 1760s. He attacked the SPG and the Anglican Church in a series of pamphlets. Only his untimely death at the age of forty-six in 1766 ended Mayhew's crusade against episcopacy.

Mayhew explained in no uncertain terms why New Englanders must oppose an episcopal settlement in the New World. He drew on the traditional history of New England, with which his audience was certainly familiar, to explain the necessity of opposition to the Anglican Church.

When we consider the real constitution of the Church of England; and how alien her mode of worship is from the simplicity of the gospel, and the apostolic times: When we consider her enormous hierarchy, ascending from . . . the dirt to the skies . . . When we reflect on what our Forefathers suffered from the mitred, lordly successors of the fisherman of Galilee for non-conformity to a non-instituted mode of worship; which occasioned their flight into this Western world: when we consider that to be delivered from their unholy zeal and oppressions, countenanced by scepter'd tyrants, they threw themselves, as it were, into the arms of Savages and Barbarians: When we consider that one principal motive to this exchanging . . . Britain . . . for America, was, that they might here enjoy, unmolested, God's holy word and ordinances without such heterogenous and spurious mixtures as were offensive to their well-informed consciences . . . we cannot well think of that Church's gaining ground here to any great degree, and especially of seeing bishops fixed among us.[7]

In this passage Mayhew cleverly employed all the codewords of anti-popery. When he described "an enormous hierarchy ascending from the dirt to the skies," and "mitred, lordly" bishops who pursued "unholy zeal and oppressions," he was using the terms usually employed to describe the Catholic Church. Rhetorically, Mayhew linked the two churches. The association was deliberate, subtle, and very effective. Anti-episcopal forces repeated this association throughout the Episcopal Controversy with telling effect. By 1775 many New Englanders held the Anglican Church to be but one small step away from the idolatry of the Roman Church.

Mayhew could be less subtle in indicting the Anglicans as well. Earlier in the same sermon he indicated that Anglicans were actually crypto-Catholics: "I myself hear some episcopalians amongst us, who were reckoned very good church-men, say, that they should prefer the communion of the Church of Rome to ours; and would sooner go to mass than come to our assemblies."[8] Similarly, Noah Welles wrote a satire, purportedly from the Anglican perspective, to describe an Anglican service: "by these ceremonies . . . which for the most part are borrowed from the romish church, our worship is tolerably agreeable to the more moderate Papists, for whom we have a much greater love and more tender regard than for any protestant dissenters."[9] Congregationalists had long criticized the "popish" ceremonies of the Anglican Church. The revival and repetition of the charge in the 1760s and 1770s by critics such as Mayhew and Welles made it easy for New Englanders to identify the English with popery in the decade before the Revolution.

The debate over episcopacy was not confined to ministers and their pamphlets and sermons. The Episcopal Controversy made for good copy and improved newspaper circulation. The newspapers carried many columns reflecting almost every conceivable opinion on the question of a bishop for America. Colonial newspapers fanned the flames of the debate by printing unsubstantiated rumors. In January 1764 the *New Hampshire Gazette* reported that a bishop of Albany would be created with a "Salary of £1,500 per annum to be paid out of His Majesty's Quit Rents in America."[10] The notion that an ecclesiastical officeholder would live off the quitrents paid by Congregationalist farmers was sure to strike terror in the readers of the *Gazette*. New Englanders well knew that the popish cycle of poverty, corruption, and damnation began when a grasping hierarchy seized the money and blunted the initiative of the people.

Opposition to the establishment of an Anglican episcopate did not die with Jonathan Mayhew in 1766. The issue persisted until the Revolution. The continuing newspaper debate and the publication of Charles Chauncy's 474-page *A Complete View of Episcopacy* in May 1771 are testimony to ongoing interest in the episcopal question.[11] Like a geyser, the episcopal question would periodically bubble to the surface of New England's consciousness and dominate public affairs, as it did in 1763 and 1764. At other times, it receded before more pressing issues such as the Stamp Act or the Townshend Duties. Nonetheless, the issue was a permanent feature in the deteriorating relationship between Britain and its colonies. Not until the controversy over the Quebec Act in 1774 was the distress over the prospect of the appointment of an American bishop finally eclipsed. With the Quebec Act, New Englanders came to fear that the English were determined to establish popery itself in North America rather than simply to give precedence to the popish Anglican Church. The Quebec Act played a critical role in the estrangement between the colonies and Britain which the Episcopal Controversy had helped foster.

III

New Englanders linked the question of an Anglican bishop to their anxiety over the Catholicism of their neighbors, the Quebecois. After the conquest of Canada, secured by the Peace of Paris in 1763, New Englanders found themselves to be fellow subjects of George III with their traditional Catholic enemies to the north. As the joy of their victory faded, New Englanders worried about the corrupting influence that Quebec's Catholicism might have on the British Empire. When London granted Catholics the right to hold government positions in Quebec under the new British administration in 1765, Thomas Hollis warned Jonathan Mayhew, "You . . . Men of New England, have need to look sharp at these backfriends."[12]

The men of New England needed little warning. They kept a wary eye on their neighbors in Quebec. They were greatly concerned when rumors spread that the pope had appointed a Catholic bishop for the vacant see at Quebec.[13] During the summer of 1766, the *New Hampshire Gazette* reported that "the Pope's galleys will be employed this summer in carrying the Bishops of his Church to Canada . . . together with a proper cargo of relicts, indulgences and other popish valuables."[14] New Englanders' fears were realized on July 3, 1766, when Bishop Jean-Olivier Briand arrived at Quebec City, "which gave such a general satisfaction to the Canadians that many of them were seen to weep Tears of Joy. It was really affecting . . . to see them afterwards run in Crowds to the Parish Church to see this Bishop, whom they look upon as the support of their Religion, & as a pledge of the King's paternal Goodness to them."[15] If the king pledged his paternal goodness to the Quebecois, it must have come at the expense of his loyal subjects in New England. The manichean outlook fostered by the anti-papal persuasion meant that the king could not promote the religious interests of his subjects in both Quebec and New England. Against the backdrop of Canadian events, New England fears of an episcopal settlement are more meaningful. After the appointment of a Catholic bishop at Quebec, American Anglicans began to ask why, if even the papists in Canada had their own bishop, should they not have one of their faith?[16] These questions caused opponents of episcopacy to view British actions in a still more sinister light. Reverend Andrew Eliot, pastor of the New North Congregationalist Church in Boston, thought the appointment of Briand was part of a plot by the Anglican hierarchy to secure their own bishop in America. He wrote: "they first, contrary to all law, policy and religion, send a bishop to encourage the inhabitants of this newly conquered country in their fatal superstitions . . . and then argue from thence that the [Anglican] hierarchy must be established in other Colonies. Was not that the main thing they had in view in sending this popish bishop?"[17] Many suspicious New Englanders became convinced that there was a popish plot afoot in 1774 with the adoption of the Quebec Act.

Word that Parliament was discussing a bill to reform the government of Quebec reached the American colonies in August 1773. If adopted, the bill would grant French Canadians the same liberties they had had when France ruled Quebec. Catholics would have their faith recognized and protected by English law, and the French legal system, which had formerly prevailed, would be reinstated.[18] The rights of English-speaking Protestants would also be protected in the province. Viewed after two centuries, the Quebec Act seems to be a just piece of reform-minded legislation. Steeped in the tradition of colonial anti-popery, Americans did not view the proposal in the same light. An anonymous Pennsylvanian described the bill as a "barefaced attempt against the success of the Protestant religion."[19] His New England neighbors agreed.

George III signed the bill into law in June 1774. Not only did it recognize Catholic rights and French law, but it extended the southern border of Quebec from the St. Lawrence River to the Ohio River, thereby almost doubling the area where Catholicism was sanctioned. Because the Quebec Act came on the heels of the "Coercive Acts" adopted by Parliament in the spring of 1774 to punish rebellious Bostonians for their famous Tea Party in December 1773, Americans, especially New Englanders, associated the Quebec Act with these "intolerable acts." New Englanders viewed the simultaneous diminution of their own rights and the extension of Catholic rights in an expanded Quebec as related parts of a deliberate plan to enslave them. The *Boston Gazette* exclaimed, "the object of this bill [the Quebec Act] is too evident to be doubted, in the first place TO CUT OFF ALL THE LIBERTIES OF THE REST OF AMERICA by means of Quebec." The *Massachusetts Spy* asked "whether the manifest, and indeed, avowed intention of the Quebec bill, is not to make use of the Canadians as instruments for the enslavement of the British colonies." Such fear only makes sense when the fear and hatred of Catholicism prevalent in colonial New England is taken into account.[20]

It seemed to New Englanders that the British were deliberately promoting popery in Quebec so they could crush resistance to Parliament in New England. From pulpits, newspapers, committees of correspondence, and in daily conversations, New Englanders heard the dreadful consequences of the act described and decried. Samuel Sherwood, the Congregational pastor at Fairfield, Connecticut, explained: "By this act all the French Laws . . . are restored—Popery is established and provision is made for the legal support of the popish clergy by the collection of tythes—Trials by jury are taken away and the whole legislative power lodged in a council appointed by the king."[21] Essentially, all the elements of popish tyranny were to be reestablished at Quebec, with the approval of the British government. The *Massachusetts Gazette and Boston Post-Boy* hinted ominously that the Quebec Act was the first step toward the establishment of military government in New England. The *Providence Gazette* said of the Quebecois, "there is no doubt but every encouragement that can possibly be afforded to those licensed slaves, these children of Popery, supported by a Protestant court, will be given, in order to subdue those head-strong colonists, who pretend to be governed by English laws."[22] One New Englander attributed the following thoughts to Lord North: "We must raise some regiments of Papists in Canada—we may also recruit our army there—they will be glad to cut the throats of those heretics the Bostonians.—A Popish army is by much the fittest for our purpose—they will obey the commands of the crown without hesitation—they have been trained in the principles of passive obedience."[23]

Revived Catholicism meant that New Englanders had to be wary not only of French-Canadians but of a renewed Catholic-Indian alliance along the frontier, a threat made greater by the extension of the southern border of Quebec to the Ohio River. John Lathrop, pastor of the Second Congregationalist Church in Boston, warned: "Should the vast country which is now taken into the vast province of Quebec, be filled up with roman catholics . . . it may be in their power assisted by the Indians to do unspeakable damage to the other colonies."[24] John Sullivan, a New Hampshire delegate to the First Continental Congress, agreed with Lathrop. Sullivan considered "the Canada Bill . . . the most dangerous to American liberties among the whole train" of Parliamentary Acts because Canadian "Territory is so far extended as to include by far a greater part of North America: that this will be a city of Refuge for Roman Catholics who will ever appear in favor of the Prerogative of the Crown . . . assisted by the . . . Indian Nations."[25] To New Englanders, the Quebec Act represented a dire threat to the New England way of life.

New Englanders could not let such a threat go unchallenged. Their response was immediate. Delegates to the Suffolk County Convention gathered at Dedham on September 6 and drafted the famous Suffolk Resolves, which were submitted to the Continental Congress. According to the tenth resolution, "The late act of Parliament for establishing the Roman Catholic Religion, and the French Laws in the extensive country now termed Canada, is dangerous in an extreme to the protestant religion, and to the civil rights and liberties of all America; and therefore as men and protestant christians, we are indispensably obliged to take all proper measures for our security."[26] On September 13 the freeholders of Rochester gathered and condemned the Quebec Act.[27] On September 20 the freeholders of Goshen, Connecticut, declared the act "directly opposite to the British constitution."[28] On September 22 the Cumberland County Congress in Maine endorsed the Suffolk Resolves and called for the stockpiling of weapons for defense against the French and Indians.[29] On September 27, fifty-one delegates from Plymouth County met at Plimpton and declared the Quebec Act was a threat to their "civil and religious rights."[30] Similar resolutions were adopted in Stamford, Connecticut, on October 7, Greenwich on October 17, and Frances Town, New Hampshire, on October 21.[31] From Connecticut to Maine, the seaports to the frontier, New Englanders were united in their opposition to the Quebec Act.

An aversion to popery and the Quebec Act was not limited to New England. On October 14, 1774, the Continental Congress resolved not to submit to the Quebec Act because of "the great dangers from so total a dissimilarity of Religion, Law, and Government of the neighbouring British Colonies, by the assistance of whose blood and treasure the said country was conquered from France."[32] On March 4, 1775, "friends of freedom" assembled under a banner in New York City which read: "GEORGE III REX. AND THE LIBERTIES OF AMERICA. NO POPERY."[33]

Even in Catholic Quebec there were loyal Protestants. On April 30, 1775, eleven days after the fighting at Lexington and Concord, someone in Montreal vandalized a bust of George III. The bust "had its face blackened, a Crucifix was hung around its neck, and a label was affixed to it with the inscription 'The Pope of Canada, and the Fool of England'."[34] Anti-popery, most pronounced in New England, was prevalent throughout the colonies. It helped unify Americans in their opposition to the Quebec Act and in their opposition to Britain.

IV

The identification of George III as "the Pope of Canada" by the Montreal vandal is an example of something more than anti-authoritarian iconoclasm. It was part of a larger rhetorical and ideological shift. Thomas Paine accused George III of "a low papistical design" in *Common Sense* when he attempted to persuade Americans to overthrow monarchy in favor of republican government.[35] Anti-papal rhetoric facilitated the transition to republicanism for many Americans, especially New Englanders. Since the beginning of the Episcopal Controversy, there had been a gradual shift in the anti-papal persuasion in New England. Popery remained the chief system of ideas and symbols to be resisted. However, New Englanders gradually began to identify the English as "popish." Once they were convinced that their British opponents were "papistical," they could easily be identified with evil. As "papists," the English had to be treated in the same manner that Catholics had always been treated by New Englanders. They must be expelled. If resisted, they must be destroyed. Given this subtle refocusing of the anti-papal persuasion, the spectacle of New Englanders taking up arms against Britons in 1775 is not surprising.

Americans, including New Englanders, did not seek independence from Britain solely because they abhorred incipient popery. Their well-known grievances over taxation and representation inspired the American political conflict with Great Britain and the move for independence. However, the intensity of that conflict, and the war that it wrought, cannot be fully appreciated without taking anti-papal feeling into consideration. The fear of incipient popery cast its shadow over Anglo-American relations during the decade from 1765 to 1775. It is not a coincidence that initial opposition to Britain was most pronounced in New England, where the hatred of Catholicism was strongest. By applying the rhetoric of the anti-papal persuasion to the English, New Englanders easily demonized them. The cultural conflict over popery complicated and undermined political relations between the colonies and Great Britain.

The continuing controversy over the settlement of an Anglican bishop in America and the apparent coddling of papists in Quebec confirmed New Englanders in their anti-popery. Throughout their history, New Englanders had confronted Catholic enemies, be they the Stuarts in the seventeenth century, their Jacobite supporters in the eighteenth, the Spanish at Cartagena, or the French at Louisbourg. Most recently they had fought with the English against the French and their Native American allies in what seemed to them a dreadful alliance of popery and savagery. Once again their enemies were Catholic, but instead of lurking in the Vatican, or Versailles, or the Escorial, they came from Canterbury and London. After more than a decade of debate over episcopacy, the adoption of the Quebec Act seemed proof positive to many New Englanders that popery had indeed gained ascendancy in London. Their history taught New Englanders that it was necessary to oppose Catholicism whenever and wherever it reared its head. When they believed papists had gained control in London and attempted to spread their doctrines to America, they had to be opposed by any means necessary.

Because Anglo-American Protestants equated popery with treason, to accuse the Hanoverian king of England of popery was a serious matter indeed. Such a conclusion was not reached easily. New Englanders first resorted to the accusation that the men around the king were suspect. The accusations began during the debate over the episcopal question. In 1767 Andrew Eliot wrote, "I hope there has been no agreement between the bishops and the Papists—but if I hear of a bishop sent to America, I shall fear there is a concaten[a]tion of causes and effects." By 1770 Eliot's fears apparently were realized. He wrote, "There is certainly, of late years, a secret influence in the British court in favour of the Romish church."[36] New Englanders were certain that influence came from France. "Anti-pope" wrote in the *Boston Gazette*, "I [have] not the least doubt but France is at the bottom of the unhappy measures which have so greatly distressed Great-Britain and her Colonies. . . . It is well known that Lord B[ute] . . . is allied to the house of Stuart; and it is likewise to be supposed that he has not the greatest aversion to the religion of that family." Anti-pope later charged a conspiracy existed between "the French King, the Pretender, and Lord B[ute]" and that they had "laid a plan to dethrone King George, enslave Great-Britain with her colonies and to introduce the Romish religion."[37] Anti-pope skillfully invoked the traditional proponents of popery, notably the king of France and the Stuart Pretender, in his indictment of Lord Bute. Such conspiracies were believable to Americans in the 1760s.[38]

With the king's approval of the Quebec Act, it became impossible to maintain the fiction that the king of France or the Pretender were responsible for the rise of popery in England. After the Quebec Act was adopted, all the anti-papal rhetoric of the previous decade returned with a new intensity and focus. Once again New Englanders accused the Anglican bishops of popish sympathies. Enoch Huntington of Middletown Connecticut likened the Quebec Act to a baby, asking his congregation, "shall a whole bench of protestant bishops . . . peculiarly bound to support and defend the protestant religion, and guard against the encroachments of popery, usher into the world a bantling . . . which so strongly bears the features of the scarlet whore and mother of harlots?"[39] The New Englanders singled out the king's ministers for attack as well. The *Essex Gazette* reported that Lord North had received absolution for his part in securing the passage of the Quebec Act. The *Newport Mercury* reported that Lord North received an invitation to go to Rome and receive an office from the pope commensurate with his "good services done the Catholic faith."[40] The *New Hampshire Gazette* carried a satirical list of offices to be given to the major supporters of the act by the Catholic Church.[41] By 1775 the bishops and the king's ministers were tried and true targets for those who abhorred popery. The accusation that they bore complicity for the rebirth of popery had lost much of its potency in constant repetition. After the Quebec Act, New Englanders had new, more formidable targets for their accusations.

After King George signed the Quebec Act, New Englanders even accused the monarch of harboring popish sympathies. This was unprecedented in the New England tradition of anti-popery. The Hanoverian monarchs had always been celebrated as staunch defenders of Protestantism. Nonetheless, when George went to Parliament to give his approval to the act, according to New England newspapers, he was greeted in the streets by thousands of his subjects who gave "a cordial salute of groans and hisses; the universal cry was 'No Popery! No French Laws! No Protestant Popish King!'"[42] New Englanders quickly picked up the cudgel of anti-popery and used it to assault their "Protestant Popish King." The republicanism implicit in such declarations was the most radical consequence of the passage of the Quebec Act.

As Jonathan Mayhew had explained in 1750, Protestant subjects were not obliged to obey unjust tyrants. Popish monarchs by definition were tyrannical. Few New Englanders were willing to declare themselves independent of George III in 1774, though that was the direction their reasoning took them. The Boston Post-Boy asserted that George III's actions were part of "another Restoration." The newspaper did not need to say that the first Restoration ended when the sitting monarch, James II, was deposed for his popish sympathies in the Glorious Revolution. New England readers, well schooled in history and anti-popery, were left to draw their own conclusions.[43] Several months later, Reverend John Lathrop was more explicit. He reminded George III that "that unfortunate Prince, who was obliged to fly from Great-Britain to make way for the Hanoverian succession, was charged among other things with promoting the Roman catholic Religion." Lathrop was treading a fine line, and he knew it. He followed this statement with the declaration, "May the reign of our present rightful Sovereign be long and happy."[44] By the spring of 1775, war between Britain and the colonies would make such declarations unnecessary.

V

When armed conflict broke out in New England in the spring of 1775, anti-popery facilitated the intellectual transition that war with Britain required. In the early years of the Revolutionary War, anti-popery was an important rallying cry for New England soldiers, just as it had been for their fathers and grandfathers.

When Daniel Barber of Claremont, New Hampshire, enlisted in the company of Elisha Humphrey, he noted that many of his comrades believed that George III was a secret papist. Barber recalled: "the real fear of popery stimulated many people to send their sons to join the ranks. The common word then was: 'No King, no Popery.'"[45] Before the Battle of Bunker Hill in June 1775, the rebel soldiers appealed to their British counterparts not to stain their "Hands in the Blood of your Fellow-Subjects in America" simply because the Americans would "not admit to be Slaves and are alarmed at the Establishment of Popery and Arbitrary Power in One Half of their Country."[46] The British answered by their attack on Breed's Hill and the burning of Charlestown on June 17. Such a bellicose response clearly indicated that the British favored popery.

Traditionally, New England's popish enemies had been Frenchmen and their Native American allies. After more than a decade of anti-papal rhetoric, inspired by the Episcopal Controversy and the Quebec Act, New England's popish enemies were now Englishmen. Britain replaced France in New England minds as the source of papal tyranny and oppression. As a consequence, the same rhetoric that had been previously employed against France could be employed against Britain.

The rhetorical shift in the anti-papal persuasion during the early years of the struggle with Britain was not accidental. Leading Whigs consciously employed anti-papal rhetoric in an effort to win support for their cause in the 1770s, just as Jonathan Mayhew and the opponents of episcopacy had done in the previous decade. Perhaps the best example of this deliberate rhetorical shift is the preaching of Reverend Samuel Cooper.

Samuel Cooper was the pastor of the posh Brattle Street Church in Boston. Gifted with a degree of eloquence that earned him the sobriquet "Silver-tongued Sam," Cooper was among the more influential ministers in New England. He counted among his parishioners the wealthiest and most powerful families in Massachusetts. On a given Sunday, Cooper preached to the leaders of the Whig resistance. A fervent Whig, Cooper was deeply involved in the politics of revolutionary Boston, both through his parishioners and his brother William, who served as Boston town clerk. Because he was both a revolutionary and a cultural leader, Samuel Cooper's sermons provide valuable insight into the critical role played by anti-papal rhetoric in promoting armed resistance to Britain. Cooper deliberately and successfully applied anti-papal rhetoric in describing and decrying British actions.[47]

On December 12, 1776, in the wake of the British army's successful campaign in New York and New Jersey (and before Washington's victories at Trenton and Princeton), Cooper mounted his pulpit and delivered a sermon based on Isaiah 45:7 in which he described what was at stake in the war. Cooper declared: "We are engaged against those who would impose upon all they subdue a gross & cruel superstition: a superstition [that] binds ye Lord in Chains, that is a disgrace to his Name & that demands to be supported & propagated by Violence, Torture and Death."[48] The rhetoric Cooper employed to castigate the British is reminiscent of the anti-papal language previously used against the French. The association was deliberate. Cooper previously delivered the same sermon in July 1758 during the French and Indian War. This is not an isolated case; Cooper consistently recycled his sermons from the French and Indian War during the American Revolution.[49]

The repetition of the sermons was not a product of intellectual laziness on the part of Reverend Cooper. Rather, circumstances in the mid-1770s closely resembled those of the late 1750s. Once again New Englanders were confronted by the "oppressions of an inveterate and merciless Enemy," who sought to force popery and tyranny upon New England.[50] What had changed was the source of the popish threat. No longer was France the chief source of popery but England. That Samuel Cooper used the same sermons to admonish Britain that he had previously directed against France is vivid testimony to the refocusing of the anti-papal persuasion. The threat was the same, only its source had changed.

The refocusing of the anti-papal persuasion found expression on the streets as well as in the pulpits. It had long been a custom in New England to parade with effigies of politically unpopular figures, such as the Pretender, along with the pope and the devil on Pope's Day. During the crisis preceding the outbreak of hostilities in North America, anti-British effigies were burned along with the pope during the celebration of Pope's Day. Effigies of Lords Bute and North frequently appeared between 1765 and 1775. For example, in 1768 the pope wore a label that read "Liberty & Property & No [Customs] Commissioners." In this way, the rhetoric of popular anti-popery, as expressed in the streets, was employed against Britain. Britain was graphically indicted for popery in these demonstrations.[51]

The connection between Britain and popery was not lost on those who celebrated Pope's Day. In 1771 an anonymous writer in the *Providence Gazette* compared the Boston Massacre to the Gunpowder Plot. Just as the perpetrators of the Gunpowder Plot sought the "destruction of religion and liberty," so too did the perpetrators of the massacre. In the former case the villains were Catholics, in the latter they were British soldiers. The author felt so strongly about the matter that he proposed "that the 5th of November be disregarded for the future and the 5th of March [the anniversary of the massacre] be observed in its stead forever."[52] Few New Englanders were then willing to part with Pope's Day, and the celebration continued until the early years of the Revolutionary War.

Anti-popery provided colonial New Englanders with a series of images and symbols which they used to order their world and identify good and evil. It was a discourse, a mode of thought, that helped organize their perceptions of the world and persuade others. In this scheme, popery and its attributes had the most negative connotations. Anti-papal Protestantism had the most positive connotations. In the decade before the Revolution, New Englanders interpreted their relations with Britain from their anti-papal perspective. The long debate over an episcopal settlement, followed by the Quebec Act, led New Englanders through a step-by-step process to conclude that Britain and its government, including the monarch, had become popish while they had remained good English Protestants. From this perspective, resistance was not only justified but was essential. While anti-popery did not cause the American Revolution, it certainly eased the way. As a system of religious ideas, anti-popery must be considered among the ideological origins of the American Revolution.

Almost from the outset of the war, however, New England's anti-papal tradition proved an impediment to the rebel war effort. As a consequence, a rift developed between the Whig elite, which sought to eliminate anti-popery to safeguard the Revolution, and the common people, who were reluctant to part with their aversion to Catholicism. The result was a cultural conflict in New England. Ultimately the elite prevailed, and minimal religious toleration resulted. Ironically, the Revolution destroyed the anti-papal persuasion that had helped foster it.

NOTES

1. John Adams to Jedediah Morse, December 2, 1815 in Charles Francis Adams, ed., *The Works of John Adams*, 10 vols. (Boston, 1850-56), X, 185.

2. Carl Bridenbaugh, in *Mitre and Scepter: Transatlantic Faiths, Ideas, Personalities, and Politics, 1689-1775* (New York, 1962), takes the position that the threat of an Anglican episcopacy was a very real possibility, especially in the 1760s. Arthur Lyon Cross, in *The Anglican Episcopate and the American Colonies* (New York, 1902), takes the position that such an establishment was impossible after the Stamp Act riots. Patricia U. Bonomi agrees with Cross in *Under the Cope of Heaven: Religion, Society and Politics in Colonial America* (New York, 1986), 199-209. Bridenbaugh's is the most complete treatment of the Episcopal Controversy.

3. Bridenbaugh, *Mitre and Scepter*, 28.

4. Thomas Bradbury Chandler, *An Appeal to the Public* (New York, 1767), 78; [Thomas Secker (Archbishop of Canterbury)], *An Answer to Dr. Mayhew's Observations* (Boston, 1764), 7.

5. Bernard Knollenberg, ed., "Thomas Hollis and Jonathan Mayhew, Their Correspondence, 1759-1766," *MHSP*, 69 (1947-50), 102-193; quotation, Hollis to Mayhew, April 22, 1764, 148. For the remarkable career of Thomas Hollis, see Caroline Robbins, "The Strenuous Whig," *WMQ*, 7 (1950), 406-453.

6. Jonathan Mayhew, *A Discourse on Unlimited Submission* (Boston, 1750), 52. For further details on Mayhew, see Charles Akers' excellent biography, *Called unto Liberty: The Life of Jonathan Mayhew, 1720-1766* (Cambridge, Mass., 1964).

7. Jonathan Mayhew, *Observations on the Charter of the Society* (Boston, 1763), 155.

8. Mayhew, *Observations*, 79.

9. [Noah Welles], *The Real Advantages which Ministers and People May Enjoy* (New Haven, 1762), 24.

10. *New Hampshire Gazette*, January 27, 1764.

11. Charles Chauncy, *A Complete View of Episcopacy* (Boston, 1771). A notable contribution to the newspaper debate was a series of essays by John Adams published in the *Boston Gazette* on August 12, August 19, and September 30, 1765. Eventually these essays were collected and published in London under the title *A Dissertation on Feudal and Canon Law*, the title by which the piece is remembered. The newspaper debate was so vigorous that an Anglican printer in New York collected all the pieces on the episcopal question printed in New York papers in 1768 and 1769 and published them together as two volumes totaling 837 pages. See John Holt, *A Collection of Tracts From the Late News Papers . . . On the Subject of the Residence of Protestant Bishops in the American Colonies, and in answer to the Writers who opposed it* (New York, 1770). See also Bridenbaugh, *Mitre and Scepter*, 300.

12. Thomas Hollis to Jonathan Mayhew, June 24, 1765, *MHSP*, 69 (1947-50), 170.

13. See the *Boston News-Letter*, June 30, 1763; and the *New Hampshire Gazette*, June 27, 1764.

14. *New Hampshire Gazette*, July 4, 1766.

15. The *Boston News-Letter*, August 11, 1766. New England suspicions and fears were further aroused in 1770 when the English paid for a Catholic missionary to be sent to the Indians of Nova Scotia. *New Hampshire Gazette*, November 9, 1770.

16. For an example of this argument by Anglicans, see Chandler, *An Appeal to the Public*, 42, 44-45.

17. Letters from Andrew Eliot to Thomas Hollis, *MHSC*, 4th series, 4 (1858), 398-461; quotation from letter of November 13, 1767, 410-411. After the death of Jonathan Mayhew, Andrew Eliot became Thomas Hollis' primary correspondent in New England.

18. For the Quebec Act and American reaction to it, see Charles H. Metzger, *The Quebec Act: A Primary Cause of the American Revolution* (New York, 1936).

19. *Pennsylvania Packet*, August 29, 1773.

20. *Boston Gazette*, August 22, 1774 (emphasis in original). *Massachusetts Spy*, October 20, 1774. The *Providence Gazette*, September 3, 1774, reported: "According to advices from Rome, the Chevalier Stuart (commonly called the Pretender) is preparing to set out on a voyage to New-England; and several assert he will go on board

some Spanish vessels which are ready merely for that purpose."

21. Samuel Sherwood, *A Sermon Containing Scriptural Instructions* (New Haven, 1774), 56.

22. *Providence Gazette*, October 27, 1774.

23. This appeared under the heading "Lord North's Soliloquy" in the *Massachusetts Spy*, December 29, 1774.

24. John Lathrop, *A Discourse Preached December 15, 1774* (Boston, 1774), 32.

25. John Sullivan to John Langdon, September 5, 1774, in Otto G. Hammond, ed., *Letters and Papers of Major General John Sullivan*, 3 vols. (Concord, NH., 1930-39), I, 48.

26. *Essex Gazette*, September 20, 1774; *Massachusetts Gazette and Boston Post-Boy*, September 19, 1774.

27. *Boston Gazette*, October 3, 1774.

28. *Connecticut Courant*, October 17, 1774.

29. Peter Force, ed., *American Archives*, 4th series, 6 vols. (Washington, 1837-46), I, 800.

30. *Boston Gazette*, October 10, 1774.

31. Force, *American Archives*, 4th series, I, 827, 888; S. P. Mead, *Ye Historie of ye Town of Greenwich* (New York, 1911), 115-116.

32. Force, *American Archives*, 4th series, I, 912.

33. *Massachusetts Spy*, March 17, 1775.

34. *Massachusetts Spy*, June 7, 1775. The residents of Chester, Vermont, employed similar rhetoric in their struggle against New York authority. They described their opponents in Albany as "Cut throatly, Jacobitish, High Church, Toretical minions of George the third, the pope of Canada & Tyrant of Britain." As quoted in Michael A. Bellesiles, *Revolutionary Outlaws: Ethan Allen and the Struggle for Independence on the Early American Frontier* (Charlottesville, 1993), 107.

35. Michael Foot and Issac Kramnick, eds., *The Thomas Paine Reader* (Harmondsworth, 1987), 81.

36. Andrew Eliot to Thomas Hollis, November 13, 1767 and February 1, 1770, *MHSC*, 4th series, 4 (1858), 410-411, 448-449.

37. *Boston Gazette*, April 25, 1768. Another writer called for the readers of the *New Hampshire Gazette* "to remove these Gallican Pensioners from the Helm" of the British state. *New Hampshire Gazette*, November 11, 1768. Similar sentiments were expressed in the *Newport Mercury*, August 29, 1774.

38. The *New Hampshire Gazette* (July 15, 1774) reported that "the Pretender and the Duke of Cumberland met at the burial of a Cardinal, and after the most courteous silent Address . . . they retired in the most princely stile." For American fears of conspiracy during the American revolutionary era see Bernard Bailyn, *Ideological Origins of the American Revolution* (Cambridge, Mass., 1967), 144-159; and Gordon S. Wood, "Conspiracy and the Paranoid Style: Causality and Deceit in the Eighteenth Century," *WMQ*, 39 (1982), 410-441.

39. Enoch Huntington, *A Discourse Delivered at Middletown* (Hartford, 1775), 20.

40. *Essex Gazette*, September 13, 1774. The *New Hampshire Gazette*, (September 16, 1774) also reported that Lord North received absolution for his actions. Also see the *Newport Mercury*, November 14, 1774.

41. Among the offices, Lord North would be commissioner of supplies to the College of Jesuits; Charles Fox, archtreasurer of the Holy Roman Empire; Edmund Burke, professor of oratory, University of Padua; the achbishop of Canterbury, sovereign pontiff; and the lord mayor of London, tea man to the pope. *New Hampshire Gazette*, September 30, 1774.

42. *Massachusetts Gazette and Boston Post-Boy*, September 5, 1774.

43. *Boston Post-Boy*, September 12, 1774.

44. Lathrop, *A Discourse December 15, 1774*, 32. Also see Philip Davidson, *Propaganda and the American Revolution, 1763-1783* (Chapel Hill, 1941), 128.

45. Daniel Barber, *The History of My Own Times* (Washington, 1827), 17. Late in life, Barber converted to Catholicism. See also Henry Cumings, *A Sermon Preached at Billerica, on the 23d of November 1775*, 12 n. for a good example of the use of anti-popery as a propaganda tool.

46. Broadside, Salem, July 19, 1775, as quoted in Davidson, *Propaganda and the American Revolution*, 127-128.

47. The most complete study of Cooper is Charles Akers, *The Divine Politician: Samuel Cooper and the American Revolution in Boston* (Boston, 1982); see also Charles Akers, "The Lost Reputation of Samuel Cooper as a Leader of the American Revolution," *NEHGR*, 130 (1976), 23-34. Akers has persuasively argued that Cooper played an important role in the American Revolution in New England, comparable to that of Samuel Adams, but that his contribution has largely been ignored by historians because much of his activity was hidden by his activities as a minister.

48. Sermon on Isaiah 45:7, CP 3:170.

49. For example, Cooper delivered sermons on Jeremiah 17:7, March 26, 1752, March 1755, April 3, 1760, September 1765, April 1769, and March 16, 1775, CP 3:124; Chronicles 20:3-4, July 3, 1755 and August 8, 1777, CP 3:149; Psalm 20:7, July 22, 1756 and August 1, 1776, CP 3:157; Psalm 16:84, March 20, 1757, March 1767, November 1768, January 1774, November 1777, December 10, 1780, and January 1781, CP 3:159; John 14:6, October 2, 1757, October 1758, January 22, 1763, December 1771, February 2, 1777, CP 3:161; Psalm 2:11, November 17, 1757, December 1, 1768, December 18, 1777, November 1778, CP 3:162; Acts 8:5-6, March 1758, January 1762, September 1776, November 1780, CP 3:165; Psalm 23:5, April 2, 1758, December 1759, December 1765, May 1774, August 1777, CP 3:166; Joshua 5:13-14, April 6, 1758, March 7, 1776, September 1777, October 9, 1777, CP 3:167; Isaiah 3:170, July 1758, April 1762, December 12, 1776, June 1780, CP 3:170.

50. Joshua 5:13-14, CP 3:167.

51. Anne Hulton, *Letters of a Loyalist Lady* (Cambridge, Mass., 1927), 8; *Boston Gazette*, November 12, 1770. Peter Shaw has delineated the use of Pope's Day rhetoric and images by anti-British protesters. See Peter Shaw, *American Patriots and the Rituals of Revolution* (Cambridge, Mass., 1978), 12, 179, 197-199.

52. *Providence Gazette*, February 23, 1771.

4

However Erroneous It Might Appear to Me as a Protestant: The Beginning of Religious Toleration for Catholics

I

The anti-papal outlook that facilitated rebellion and revolution in New England proved cumbersome and difficult once the conflict was under way. While anti-popery promoted a unified outlook in the region, the American Revolution embraced the thirteen British colonies along the Atlantic seaboard, including colonies such as Maryland and Pennsylvania that had substantial numbers of Catholics. Participation in a national struggle, rather than a regional contest, required that New Englanders tone down their most strident exclamations of anti-popery so as not to offend their Catholic comrades. Moreover, from the outset, the struggle for American independence relied on outside aid, most of which came from Catholic France. Partially as a consequence of these circumstances, New Englanders gradually jettisoned anti-popery as the cornerstone of their outlook during the American Revolution.

New Englanders moved away from anti-popery for several reasons, and the most obvious was self-interest. It was not in the best interest of New Englanders to give vent to their deepest held notions about the evils of popery while they depended for their survival on French supplies in their battle with Britain. The contradiction between anti-popery and the Revolution would become all the more pronounced in 1778 when French soldiers and sailors joined the cause of

American independence.

Material self-interest, however, is too facile an explanation for a tremendous cultural shift such as the abandonment of anti-popery. Ironically, the Revolution undermined the anti-papal persuasion which had contributed so significantly toward making a break with Britain possible. Once the British preempted the French as the primary "popish" threat to New England, New Englanders fundamentally altered the anti-papal persuasion. Anti-popery had appealed to New Englanders because it allowed them to affirm their identity as good, free, British Protestants. Once New Englanders fought Britons, anti-popery lost its relevance to them. The anti-papal persuasion could not explain a world in which New Englanders allied with French Catholics to fight British tyranny. Simply put, the Revolution rendered anti-popery obsolete.

The decline of anti-popery was uneven and difficult. During the early years of the conflict, most New Englanders did not recognize, nor would they have welcomed, the decline of anti-popery. By the end of the Revolution they codified it into law by extending religious freedom to Catholics. The rejection of anti-popery represents a dramatic cultural shift. New England's Whig elite, especially its religious, political, and military leaders, was primarily responsible for this transformation. Rebel leaders recognized early in the struggle for independence that anti-popery, while valuable as propaganda, was an impediment to their cause. As a consequence, the Whig leaders took steps to reject anti-popery as a cultural formula. Change was not easy. Many in the Whig camp, especially among the population at large, were reluctant to part with their anti-papal ideas. The result was a profound cultural conflict in revolutionary New England. The beginning of the cultural shift over anti-popery began quietly, some six months before the fighting at Lexington, when leading Massachusetts Whigs aided the Continental Congress in its efforts to attract the support of Quebec to the rebel cause.

II

The first New Englanders to confront the contradiction between the region's tradition of anti-popery and the cultural pluralism of the American resistance movement were the delegates to the First Continental Congress which met at Philadelphia from September 5 to October 27, 1774. The city and the body in which the New England delegates found themselves were far more diverse than the region from which they came. John Adams described to his wife, Abigail, the response when fellow Massachusetts delegate Thomas Cushing proposed that the Congress open with a prayer: "It was opposed by Mr. Jay of New York and Mr. Rutledge of South Carolina, because we were so divided in religious sentiments; some Episcopalians, some Quakers, some Anabaptists, some Presbyterians, and some Congregationalists that we could not join in the same act of worship." Eager to display his broadmindedness, Samuel Adams declared "he was no bigot and could hear a prayer from a gentleman of piety and virtue who was a friend of his country." As a consequence, Jacob Duché, an Anglican (and future Loyalist), was summoned, and won high praise from John Adams, "Episcopalian, as he is, Dr. Cooper never prayed with such fervor, such ardor and pathos."[1]

In Philadelphia, the delegates encountered not only Anglican chaplains but Catholic worship. Some observed Catholic rites for the first time, since such practices were illegal in the New England colonies. Among them was a curious John Adams who, on October 9, 1774: "strolled away to the Mother Church, or rather grandmother Church, I mean the Romish Chappell. Heard a good, short, moral Essay upon the Duty of Parents to their Children, founded in Justice and Charity, to take care of their Interests temporal and spiritual." Like a good New Englander, Adams was not taken in by the ceremony. The congressman continued:

The poor Wretches, fingering their Beads, chanting in latin, not a Word of which they understood, their Pater Nosters and Ave Marias. Their holy Water—their Crossing themselves perpetually—their Bowing to the name of Jesus . . . .. The Dress of the Priest was rich with Lace—his Pulpit was Velvet and Gold. The Altar Piece was very rich—little Images and Crucifixes about—Wax Candles lighted up. But how shall I describe the Picture of our Saviour in a Frame of Marble over the Altar at full Length upon the Cross in the Agonies and Blood dripping and streaming from his Wounds. The Musick consisting of an organ, and a choir of singers went all Afternoon, excepting sermon Time, and the Assembly chanted—most sweetly and exquisitely.

Despite his distaste for what he saw as the sensual trappings of idolatry, Adams had to concede the effectiveness of the ceremony: "here is every Thing which can lay hold of the Eye, Ear, and Imagination. Every Thing which can charm and bewitch the simple and ignorant. I wonder how Luther even broke the spell."[2] While attending Mass confirmed most of Adams' prior notions about Catholicism, his willingness to investigate the Roman church indicates a potential to move beyond the crude stereotypes so cherished in New England.

John Adams' willingness to attend Mass while in Philadelphia may well have been the result of his encounters with Catholics who were not only Whigs, but more cultivated and wealthy than himself. While at the First Continental Congress, Adams met Charles Carroll of Carrollton, the Maryland Whig.

Adams described Carroll to James Warren:

He has a Fortune as I am well informed which is computed to be worth Two hundred Thousand Pounds sterling. . . . He had a liberal Education in France and is well acquainted with the French Nation. He speaks their Language as easily as ours; and what is perhaps more important than all the rest, he was educated in the Roman Catholic Religion and still continues to worship his Maker according to the Rites of that Church. In the Cause of American Liberty, his Zeal, Fortitude and Perseverance have been [so] that he is said to marked out for peculiar Vengeance by the Friends of Administration.[3]

That an individual could be a Whig and a Catholic was a revelation indeed. The traditional view in New England had been that Catholics could not be trusted with any civil political power. To New Englanders Catholicism was the religion of absolutism, not liberty. Adams nonetheless recognized that there was no apparent contradiction between Carroll's religion and his politics. He was eager to share this revelation with his politically powerful friend and ally Warren who remained in Massachusetts. Episodes like this and participation in a national political struggle caused the Whig leaders of New England to reassess many of their previously held assumptions about Catholicism and Catholics.

III

The First Continental Congress was not called so that New Englanders could become more broadminded. Its purpose was to air colonial grievances and formulate a coherent strategy to rectify the relationship between the colonies and Britain. The Quebec Act was among the foremost colonial grievances. On October 14, 1774, the Congress declared that the act "damaged the interests of the Protestant religion and these colonies and ought to be repealed."[4] One week later the Congress adopted an *Address to the Inhabitants of Great Britain*, which stated that the British government hoped to use the Quebecois "to reduce the ancient free Protestant Colonies to the same state of slavery with themselves" through the Quebec Act. The Congress further stated, "we [cannot] suppress our astonishment that a British Parliament should ever consent to establish in that country a Religion, that has deluged your island in blood, and dispersed impiety, bigotry, persecution, murder, and rebellion through every part of the world."[5] Congress condemned the Quebec Act and justified its opposition to Britain in the name of a defense against encroaching popery. While such an appeal to anti-popery might encourage sympathy for the

American cause in Britain, such rhetoric clearly would not attract support in Canada.

While it condemned the Quebec Act, Congress also appealed to the people of Quebec to join their cause in resisting Britain. Five days after it adopted the *Address to the Inhabitants of Great Britain*, Congress adopted an *Address to the Inhabitants of Quebec* on October 26, 1774. The second proclamation dealt with the Quebec Act in far different terms than the first. In the *Address to the Inhabitants of Quebec*, Congress argued that the Quebec Act undermined the rights of the Quebecois. According to the proclamation, Parliament had no authority to grant rights that Quebeckers enjoyed naturally. This was especially true in matters of religion. "And what is offered to you by the late Act of Parliament," asked Congress, "Liberty of Conscience in your religion? No. God gave it to you." Indeed, Congress warned the inhabitants of Quebec that when Parliament assumed the right to interfere in religious matters it could misuse its power and establish an inquisition to persecute Catholics. In the name of religious freedom, Congress appealed to the Quebecois to join their southern neighbors in resistance.[6] Congress enlisted the support of Massachusetts leaders in this Janus-like policy.

The resistance leaders in Philadelphia required the aid of their counterparts in Massachusetts to distribute the *Address to the Inhabitants of Quebec*. Philadelphia printers produced two thousand French copies of the address. On November 16, 1774, Congress sent three hundred copies to the Boston Committee of Correspondence for distribution in Quebec.[7] New England Whigs visited Quebec disguised as traders and tried to circulate the document. For example, in February 1775 the Boston Committee of Correspondence sent John Brown of Pittsfield to deliver copies of the address and a letter from the Boston Committee to "some Gentlemen of Montreal and Quebeck," inviting them to join the Whigs and participate in the next session of Congress.[8]

John Brown was ideally suited for his delicate assignment, which required tact and diplomacy. A thirty-one-year-old Yale graduate, who had moved to Pittsfield after unsuccessfully trying to practice law in Providence, Brown was well educated, and a firm adherent to the Whig cause. Moreover, he spoke some French and was not overly offended by the Catholicism of the Quebecois.[9] Brown spent two weeks in March 1775 traveling through Vermont, where he encountered the spring thaw. He reported that the area for twenty miles around Lake Champlain, "especially towards Canada, was under water." After "14 Days having undergone most inconvenient hardships," Brown reported to the Boston Committee that he had, "delivered your Letters . . . and was very Kindly received by the Committee of Correspondence at Montreal." Brown's mission, funded by twenty pounds from the Boston Committee of Correspondence "as directed by the Congress," marked a small but dramatic departure from the New England tradition of anti-popery. Congress, and the Boston Committee of Correspondence, appealed to the people of Quebec in the name of freedom of conscience.[10] The attempt to attract support in Quebec in late 1774 and early 1775 marks the first New England compromise with Catholicism during the Revolution. This early attempt was mostly motivated by self-interest rather than a sincere concern for the rights of conscience in Quebec.

How did the Quebecois respond to the appeals from their new-found New England friends? In December 1774 the *Boston Gazette* optimistically reported that the French in Quebec had refused to arm themselves against the American rebels.[11] Such inactivity was hardly what Congress hoped for when it drafted the *Address to the Inhabitants of Quebec*. Despite his efforts, John Brown detected indifference toward the American cause. He wrote dejectedly from Montreal, "The French People are (as a body) extremely ignorant and Bigoted." Like a good New Englander, Brown attributed their ignorance to the "curat of Priests" which had control of the government "Temporal as well as Spiritual." Brown described his experience in a small village outside Montreal. When he tried to give his landlord a copy of the *Address to the Inhabitants of Quebec*, the landlord immediately took the pamphlet and gave it to the village priests without reading it.[12]

While the Catholic clergy, especially Bishop Briand, were strong supporters of the Quebec Act, and, consequently, opponents of joining the American rebels, clerical interference does not explain the rebel failure to attract Quebec to their cause.[13] Two centuries of American, especially New England, antipathy could not be forgiven with one address which promised religious tolerance. This was especially true because Congress had simultaneously made a contradictory statement in its *Address to the Inhabitants of Great Britain*. An anonymous Anglophone writer from Montreal reported in March 1775 that the *habitants* responded positively to the *Address to the Inhabitants of Quebec*, but when they read the *Address to the Inhabitants of Great Britain*, "they could not contain their resentment, nor express it but in broken curses, 'Oh! the perfidious double-faced Congress; let us bless and obey our benevolent Prince, whose humanity is consistent, and extends to all Religions.'"[14] If Congress had hoped that popish ignorance would keep the Quebecois from reading their *Address to the Inhabitants of Great Britain*, they were mistaken.

Throughout 1775 and 1776 the Congress continued to appeal, unsuccessfully, to the habitants in Quebec. They pursued this policy even while undertaking an expedition in the fall of 1775 to win Quebec from the British by force of arms. In May 1775 Congress adopted a *Letter to the Oppressed Inhabitants of Canada*, which echoed, in more strident tones, the *Address* of the previous October.[15] In October 1775 President John Hancock wrote to General Philip Schuyler, who was undertaking an expedition to Montreal, "You may further declare that we hold sacred, the Rights of Conscience, and shall never molest them in the free Enjoyment of their Religion."[16] In the spring of 1776 Congress sent Benjamin Franklin, Samuel Chase, Charles Carroll, and a Jesuit, John Carroll (Charles Carroll's cousin), on a mission to woo the Canadians. Despite the prominence of the emissaries, further promises of religious freedom from Congress, and the ministrations of Father Carroll, this mission was another failure.[17]

At the same time that Massachusetts leaders assisted Congress in its unsuccessful campaign to attract Canadian support through promises of religious toleration, they also undertook a similar policy with respect to the Indians of Maine. Almost as soon as fighting began between the American rebels and the British, the Catholic Indians of Maine appealed to the government of Massachusetts to allow them a priest. As the rebel position along the eastern frontier deteriorated, Massachusetts agreed to provide a priest for the Indians. By 1778 Massachusetts would support the activities of a priest within its jurisdiction. Unlike the campaign to attract Quebec, this effort was both successful and directed exclusively by Massachusetts, not Congress. In sending the priest to Maine, Massachusetts leaders took an unambiguous step in the direction of religious tolerance. They did so in the face of persistent popular antipathy toward Catholics and the Massachusetts anti-priest law of 1700. As with the failed campaign to attract Quebec, Massachusetts embraced limited toleration for Catholicism along its eastern frontier largely due to self-interest.[18]

The campaigns to woo the Quebecois and the Eastern Indians were clumsy efforts. Americans, especially New Englanders, were not sincerely concerned about the religious liberties of their northern neighbors. Rather, they hoped to neutralize the potential military threat from Canada. Despite their selfish motives, the willingness of New Englanders to recognize the right to religion of their Catholic neighbors was unprecedented. The willingness to recognize religious freedom, however, was geographically limited to Quebec and eastern Maine; New Englanders were still not willing to tolerate Catholicism in their midst. It was also limited to New England's Whig elite; the common people remained unmoved from their traditional anti-popery.

Throughout the campaign to attract the Eastern Indians and the Quebecois to the rebel cause, members of the Whig elite in Massachusetts were supportive of the effort. In Congress, New Englanders gave their approval to the *Address to the Inhabitants of Quebec*. Through the agency of John Brown, the Boston Committee of Correspondence helped distribute the pamphlet in Quebec. While

New Englanders in Congress and the Boston Committee of Correspondence supported Catholicism in Quebec, they did so as covertly as possible. They did not seek to advertise their actions to the population at large.

The correspondence of John and Abigail Adams reveals the reluctance of leading Whigs to make widely known the effort to extend religious toleration. John Adams had written to his wife in February 1776 describing the impending mission to Canada of Franklin, Chase, and the Carrolls. He said of the Jesuit, John Carroll: "[he] is to go with the Committee. The Priests of Canada having refused Baptism and Absolution to our Friends there."[19] Adams, and his fellow Congressmen, hoped Father Carroll's presence would testify to American sincerity in recognizing religious freedom. Several weeks later Abigail Adams answered her husband: "I was very much pleased with your choice of a committee for Canada. *All those to whom I have ventured to shew that part of your Letter* approve the Scheme of the Priest as a master-stroke of policy."[20] While Abigail Adams certainly appreciated the possible contribution of Father Carroll to the rebel cause in Quebec, she also recognized that many of her fellow New Englanders would not share her appreciation. Consequently, she told only a select few about the mission. While Whig leaders in New England—men and women like John and Abigail Adams, John Hancock, James Warren, and John Brown—appreciated that anti-papal feeling would prove an impediment to their cause, they were also aware of its popularity. Rather than foster conflict within Whig ranks, they sought to promote nominal toleration while hiding their actions from all but a few of their peers.

IV

Between 1774 and 1778, the Revolution began to undermine the foundation of anti-popery in New England. Anti-popery proved an obstacle to Whig goals in Quebec and eastern Maine. As a consequence, Whig leaders were willing to acknowledge a grudging toleration for the Catholicism of the Quebecois and the Eastern Indians. In Quebec this policy failed; in Maine it was successful. In both cases self-interest triumphed over the traditional New England distaste for Catholicism.

Geographically and culturally, Quebec and eastern Maine were the fringes of New England. The steps toward religious toleration were limited to a few who represented the cultural and political elite in the region. The majority of New Englanders, however, were still not willing to jettison anti-popery from their culture during the early years of the Revolution. Indeed, in November 1775

General George Washington had to order his New England soldiers not to burn the pope "at this time when we are soliciting and have really obtained the friendship and alliance of the people of Canada."[21]

It was impossible for the Whig leadership to keep secret its actions with respect to Catholicism. Just as the Quebecois learned of the *Address to the Inhabitants of Great Britain*, New Englanders learned about the *Address to the Inhabitants of Quebec*. The text of the *Address* appeared in the *Boston Gazette* without comment in November 1774.[22] If surprised New Englanders registered their disapproval with the newspapers, then editors sympathetic to the Whig cause refused to print such items.

Coming, as it apparently did, out of the blue, the *Address to the Inhabitants of Quebec* required some explication. Reverend William Gordon of Roxbury took it upon himself to explain the evolving Whig position vis-à-vis Canadian Catholicism in December 1774. In a published fast-sermon Gordon enumerated American grievances against Britain. Among American grievances, Gordon called the Quebec Act "a diabolical design" for enslaving Americans. This interpretation was consistent with traditional New England anti-popery. The minister then stated, "I have no objection to the Canadians being fully secured in the enjoyment of their religion, however erroneous and anti-christian it may appear to me as a protestant."[23] Catholicism remained evil, but if recognizing Canadian Catholicism helped secure redress of American grievances, so be it. Gordon essentially echoed the position of Congress. Coming from a New England Congregational minister, Gordon's statement indicated, in a small way, that toleration might follow revolution in New England.

William Gordon's sermon indicated that anti-popery might not be as relevant a guide to present circumstances as it had been to previous generations. The Revolution presented New Englanders with new circumstances, circumstances in which they had to rely on the assistance of Catholics if they hoped to achieve their goals. Crude stereotypes that equated Catholicism with tyranny did not apply in such a situation. Gordon's sermon marked the beginning of a profound debate over the role of anti-popery in revolutionary New England. In that debate Whig leaders, especially ministers like Gordon, reinterpreted the role of anti-popery in New England life. The debate became especially heated and significant in 1778 when news reached America concerning the conclusion of the Franco-American alliance.

NOTES

1. John Adams to Abigail Adams, September 16, 1774, in C. F. Adams, ed., *Works of John Adams*, 10 vols. (Boston, 1850-56), II, 368, n. 4.

2. John Adams to Abigail Adams, October 9, 1774, in L. H. Butterfield, ed., *The Adams Family Correspondence*, 4 vols. (Cambridge, Mass., 1963-73), I, 166-167.

3. John Adams to James Warren, February 18, 1776, *WAL*, I, 207.

4. Worthington C. Ford, ed., *Journals of the Continental Congress*, 34 vols. (Washington, 1904-37), I, 69-70.

5. *Journals of the Continental Congress*, I, 81-90, quotations, pp. 87, 88.

6. *Journals of the Continental Congress*, I, 105-113. For the Canadian situation, see Robert McConnell Hatch, *Thrust for Canada: The American Attempt in Quebec in 1775-1776* (Boston, 1979), especially chap. 1; Justin H. Smith, *Our Struggle for the Fourteenth Colony: Canada and the American Revolution*, 2 vols. (New York, 1907), especially chap. 3; Gustave Lanctot, *Canada and the American Revolution, 1774-1783*, trans. Margaret M. Cameron (Cambridge, Mass., 1967); and George M. Wrong, *Canada and the American Revolution* (Toronto, 1935).

7. *Journals of the Continental Congress*, I, 122.

8. Boston Committee of Correspondence to John Brown of Pittsfield, February 21, 1775, in Henry A. Cushing, ed., *The Writings of Samuel Adams*, 4 vols. (New York, 1907, repr. 1968), III, 182-188.

9. J. E. A. Smith, *History of Pittsfield, 1734-1800*, 2 vols. (Boston, 1869), I, 181, 211-213.

10. John Brown to the Boston Committee of Correspondence, March 29, 1775, MA 193:41-44.

11. *Boston Gazette*, December 19, 1774.

12. John Brown to the Boston Committee of Correspondence, March 29, 1775, MA 193:44.

13. For the role of the clergy, see *Journals of the Continental Congress*, IV, 148-149. In 1776 John Adams described the Catholic clergy in Quebec as "the toryfied Priests in Canada." John Adams to James Warren, February 18, 1776, *WAL*, I, 207.

14. Force, ed., *American Archives*, 4th series, 6 vols. (Washington, 1837-46), II, 231.

15. *Journals of the Continental Congress*, II, 68-70. The letter was also published in the *Pennsylvania Packet*, June 19, 1775.

16. John Hancock to Philip Schuyler, October 11, 1775, in Edmund C. Burnett, ed., *Letters of Members of the Continental Congress*, 10 vols. (Washington, 1921-36), I, 227.

17. "Journal of Charles Carroll of Carrollton, During his Visit to Canada in 1776," published in Kate Mason Rowland, *The Life of Charles Carroll of Carrollton, 1737-1832*, 2 vols. (New York, 1898), I, 363-400; John Adams to Abigail Adams, February 18, 1776, *Adams Family Correspondence*, I, 348-349; John Adams to James Warren, February 18, 1776, *WAL*, I, 207; *Journals of the Continental Congress*, IV, 148-149,

217. Also see Ellen Hart Smith, *Charles Carroll of Carrollton* (Cambridge, Mass., 1942); Annabelle M. Melville, *John Carroll of Baltimore: Founder of the American Catholic Hierarchy* (New York, 1955); and William R. Riddell, "Benjamin Franklin's Mission to Canada," *Pennsylvania Magazine of History and Biography*, 48 (1924), 111-158.

18. For a detailed examination of the issues raised in this paragraph, see Francis D. Cogliano, "To Obey Jesus Christ and General Washington: Massachusetts, Catholicism, and the Eastern Indians during the American Revolution," *Maine Historical Society Quarterly*, 32 (1992), 108-133.

19. John Adams to Abigail Adams, February 18, 1776, *Adams Family Correspondence*, I, 348-349.

20. Abigail Adams to John Adams, March 7, 1776, *Adams Family Correspondence*, I, 354 (my emphasis).

21. George Washington, Orderly Book, November 5, 1775, in Worthington C. Ford, ed., *Writings of George Washington*, 14 vols. (New York, 1889-93), III, 200-201.

22. *Boston Gazette*, November 14, 1774.

23. William Gordon, *A Discourse Preached December 15, 1774* (Boston, 1775), 22-23.

5

The Perfidy of My Countrymen: Whigs, Tories, and the French Alliance

On the morning of April 19, 1778, Samuel Cooper sat in his study putting the finishing touches on a sermon he was to deliver that day. As he completed his work, Simeon Deane of Connecticut interrupted the minister. Deane was the brother of Silas Deane, one of the American Commissioners at Versailles. He had come directly from Paris with a letter from Benjamin Franklin to Cooper. In his letter, Franklin outlined the details of the newly concluded American alliance with France. Cooper quickly revised his sermon, adding the news from France. On the third anniversary of the war, Samuel Cooper made the first public acknowledgment of the alliance.[1]

The French alliance forced New Englanders to confront the issue of anti-popery. No longer could they marginalize and skirt the contradiction between their aversion to Catholicism and their reliance on Catholics. Anti-popery, which had proved a source of unity during the colonial period, had become a source of division during the Revolution. Anti-popery divided New Englanders in complex ways. The Whig-Tory division remained constant. After the conclusion of the French alliance, Loyalists employed anti-papal rhetoric as one of their chief weapons in attacking the supporters of the Revolution. The supporters of the Revolution were divided between those cultural and political leaders who sought to promote toleration and eliminate anti-popery, and the majority of the people who, though they welcomed French support, were not eager to see toleration for Catholicism result from the relationship between France and the United States. Thus supporters of the alliance and of religious toleration found themselves challenged from within and without. Beginning in the spring of 1778 and continuing until the end of the war in 1783, leading New England Whigs were forced to explain and defend their alliance with Catholic France. At the same time, New England Tories embraced anti-popery all the more fervently in an effort to expose the hypocrisy of their foes. This chapter explores the debate over the French alliance engaged in by the leading Whigs and their Tory opponents.

From the outset of the American war with Britain, the rebels relied on the support of France. Beginning in 1775 France covertly supplied the rebels with money, supplies, and arms that were critical to the American war effort. The French did not support the American rebels because they shared a commitment to republican government. Rather, they sought to avenge their defeat in the Seven Years' War and to deal a blow to their age-old rivals, the British.[2]

Many Americans felt that the rebels could not defeat the British without direct French military intervention in the conflict. The French foreign minister, the Comte de Vergennes, favored such intervention, yet he needed a demonstration of the viability of the American rebellion before he committed his nation to war with Britain for the second time in a generation. For the first two years of the war, the Americans were unable to defeat the British in a major battle. Vergennes received an indication of American credibility in October 1777 when General Horatio Gates captured General John Burgoyne's combined force of British regulars, Hessians, Canadians, and Indians, numbering approximately six thousand soldiers, at the battle of Saratoga.

Saratoga was the most significant American victory in the first years of the war. Americans, especially New Englanders, celebrated the triumph. New Englanders interpreted the victory at Saratoga as another in a series of triumphs over the forces of evil by God's chosen people. In a thanksgiving sermon delivered immediately after the victory, Samuel Cooper gave the standard rendition of New England history, telling his listeners how "There is no People whose circumstances . . . more nearly resemble those of the Israelites when they were conducted by the divine hand of Canaan, than these States, & particularly the N. England ones." Cooper went on to explain the recent victory: "What a change to have that whole army that threatened war and devastation &c. surrendered into our hands. It is the Lord's Doing, and it is marvellous in our Eyes. I will sing unto the lord for he has triumphed gloriously. The Lord is our Strength & Song."[3] Cooper's rhetoric was typical of that employed after a New England victory. It differed little from that of his predecessors after such triumphs as those at Louisbourg in 1745 or Quebec in 1759. One key difference was the focus of Cooper's sermon. The British, not the French, were the villains of the tale. For those who attended Cooper's sermons regularly, and had previously noted the shift in his application of anti-papal rhetoric, this was nothing new.

Samuel Cooper ended his sermon on a decidedly different note, which must have shocked even the most indifferent of his listeners. He concluded with the following words: "May Heaven bless the Monarch of France & his Dominions; and still honor him as Defender of the Rights of Mankind. With joy we look forward to the Blessings of Peace upon the Basis of Liberty may God realize this bright Prospect."[4] While New Englanders might have to give grudging thanks for the covert aid the French provided, calling on God's blessing for King Louis XVI was another matter entirely. In the traditional anti-papal scheme of things, the king of France was only slightly less dangerous than his master, the pope, as a source of evil and tyranny. For a New England minister to pray for the king of France must have been a shock. In so doing, Cooper anticipated one of the most radical developments of the conflict wrought by colonial anti-popery—an American alliance with Catholic France.

Cooper not only expected an American alliance with France, he actively promoted it. In a letter written a week after Saratoga, the minister asked his friend Benjamin Franklin, who was negotiating with Vergennes at the time: "What expect you of France and Spain? Can they hesitate a moment about acknowledging our Independence, Entering into an Alliance with us; and protecting their own trade to this Quarter?" The minister continued sarcastically, "are they afraid of war?" Cooper hinted further that France should enter into an alliance with the United States before the British sued for peace. He concluded, "tho we are indebted to France . . . for Secret and important aid, yet their openly keeping aloof from us for so long a time has made such a Plan on the Part of Britain the more practicable."[5] Whether Cooper's arguments influenced the negotiations is unknown. His statements indicate that the leaders of the Revolution in New England, even the author of the 1773 Dudleian lecture, were willing to dispense with anti-popery in order to win American independence.

II

The French alliance was not only a diplomatic and military triumph for the United States, but it was the beginning of a cultural and intellectual revolution in New England. Massachusetts congressman Elbridge Gerry described the situation:

What a miraculous change in the political world! The ministry in England advocates for despotism, and endeavouring to enslave those who might have remained loyal subjects of the King. The government of France an advocate of liberty, expousing the cause of protestants and risking a war to secure their independence. The king of England considered by every whig in the nation a tyrant, and the king of France applauded by every whig in America as the protector of the Rights of man! The king of Great Britain aiding the advancement of popery, and the king of France endeavouring to free his people from ecclesiastical power! Britain at war with America! France in Alliance with her! These, my friends are astonishing changes.

Astonishing changes indeed. Such radical developments had to be accounted for. Gerry posited his own explanation, "Perhaps one principle, self-interest, may account for all."[6] While self-interest may have been a satisfactory explanation for accepting Catholicism in Quebec and among the Eastern Indians, a sea change like the alliance with France required more substantive explanation.

Intellectually, the problem with an alliance based on self-interest was twofold. First, if the Americans were acting out of self-interest, then the French must be as well. What would happen if those interests collided? "The Honest Politician" wrote to the *Massachusetts Spy* in October 1779 and argued "France has made a wise judgement of our situation, and pursued her best interests in connection with us; we are not unmindful at the same time that she entertained a real goodness or predilection for our cause."[7] In other words, though the French acted out of self-interest, their interests did not conflict with American interests. This was a feeble argument for people who had been raised to fear and hate the popish cunning and duplicity of the French.

A second problem with basing the Franco-American alliance on self-interest was that such a relationship would be completely secular. In such a view, the American rebels made their alliance based solely on temporal political concerns. There were precedents for such unions. As Reverend David Rowland of Providence declared: "such an alliance is not unexampled; England has been in alliance with Portugal, the inhabitants of which are almost if not wholly Roman Catholics; and France with Holland, yet the Hollanders are chiefly Presbyterians."[8] While such an explanation was reasonable, it did not satisfy New Englanders, who were acutely aware of their Protestant historical tradition. While alliances with papists might be good enough for the English or the Dutch, New Englanders had to answer to a higher authority. Indeed, English sympathy for popery had helped bring about the conflict in the first place. New

Englanders believed their activities were of providential import. Were they to behave in an ungodly manner, all the military aid in the world would not avail them in their struggle. The French alliance required religious justification. For the remainder of the war, New England leaders, especially ministers, were required to explain, justify, and defend the alliance.

In 1779 Reverend Rowland observed, "It has been a matter of speculation to some, that the Americans should be so fond of forming an alliance with France, on account of her religious sentiments, being in general Roman Catholics."[9] As cultural and social leaders who overwhelmingly supported the Revolution, it fell to New England's ministers to answer this criticism. This was especially so because New England's ministers had done so much to keep the anti-papal tradition alive during the colonial period. It fell to the ministers to formulate a justification for the alliance. How, then, did those ministers, like Rowland, who supported the Revolution explain the American alliance with Catholic France? There are several answers to this question. Most ministers did not endorse one or the other of the explanations but usually a combination of several.[10]

New England ministers sought a religious justification for the alliance with France. The easiest explanation for the alliance came from ministers who claimed that the union was an example of Providence's mysterious working which could not be comprehended by mortal men. Phillips Payson, the pastor at Chelsea, was one of the first to put this view forth when he delivered the Massachusetts election sermon in May 1778. "We must be infidels," Payson told the assembled clerical and secular dignitaries, "the worst of infidels, to disown, or disregard the hand that has raised us up such a benevolent and powerful assistants in time of great distress. How wonderful, that God . . . should dispose his Most Christian Majesty, the King of France, to enter into the most open and generous alliance with these independent states."[11] Four years later Payson argued that French willingness to overcome their innate prejudices and make an alliance with the Americans "discovers the hand of Providence, the kind influence of Heaven."[12] In other words, God works in mysterious ways; to challenge the alliance is to challenge the will of God.

The argument that the alliance should be accepted as God's will did not satisfy most New Englanders. The argument itself smelled of popery. After all, didn't the papal clergy expect their congregations to blindly accept the most foolish and idolatrous doctrines because they claimed they were God's will? If the New England clergy were to put forth a credible theological defense for the alliance, they would have to ground it, like all the tenets of New England Protestantism, in scripture. New England's ministers needed a biblical justification for the alliance. By necessity, they thumbed through their Bibles searching for precedent for their alliance with France.

The clergy found its precedent in the Book of Ezra. Ezra describes the delivery of the Israelites from the Babylonian Captivity. In Ezra, the temple is rebuilt in Jerusalem and the Israelites delivered from Babylon by the pagan Persian king, Cyrus. As a typology, Ezra seemed to fit New England needs perfectly. New Englanders had always identified themselves with the Israelites. Moreover, they frequently identified the Catholic Church as "the scarlet whore of Babylon" from the Book of Revelation. The Babylonian connection between ancient tyranny and modern popery made the analogy attractive, especially in light of the "popish" sympathies of the British. Cyrus' paganism made the typology still more attractive. The emancipator of the Israelites did not share their religion, but nonetheless God chose him as his instrument.

New England ministers found in the Book of Ezra a compelling scriptural justification for the French alliance. On November 4, 1779, John Murray of Newburyport explained how the typology worked:

Sometimes the great Deliverer chooses a pebble from his own brook to prostrate their most gigantic oppressors, and sometimes he moves the heart of an alien to restore them the liberty which their own kings overthrew. Thus CYRUS a pagan prince, unconnected by nation, and by religion an enemy, monarch of the empire that had persecuted their fathers . . . CYRUS stirred up by the Lord alone . . . proclaims the remains of oppressed Israel, free and independent.[13]

If Cyrus, "by religion an enemy," could deliver the Israelites from Babylonian oppression, then Louis XVI could deliver New Englanders from British oppression. To eighteenth-century New Englanders Louis XVI was Cyrus, the pagan deliverer of God's people. For those who chose to cling to their old anti-French prejudices, Murray asked, "Had a Jew refused the benefit [offered by Cyrus] from educational prejudice against the hand that offered it, or superstitious scruple about the lawfulness of accepting the friendship of a power [which] disowned his religion who could have avoided charging him with a [sin]? . . . May God punish by what hand he will? And may he not deliver by an instrument that none but himself would have thought of?"[14] Here was strong scriptural justification for the French alliance.

There was one major flaw in the comparison between Cyrus and Louis. After Cyrus freed the Israelites, he required them to pay him tribute.[15] Critics of the American alliance with France claimed that the union would result in French subjugation of America—essentially, that the Americans would exchange British for French masters. Ezra seemed to bear this accusation out. Jonas Clarke dealt with this problem in the Massachusetts election sermon of 1781. In a lengthy footnote discussing Cyrus' role in freeing the Israelites, Clarke explained:

I only add, that in my reference to Cyrus and the prophecy concerning him, the judicious reader will easily see, that the main point, was not to illustrate the compleatness or degree of that freedom and liberty, to which God's people were raised, by the kind, generous and effectual interposition of Cyrus, for their redemption or restoration; but the hand of God and wisdom and goodness of all his superintending providence, . . . in the support and relief of an afflicted people, and the redemption and salvation of [the] injured and oppressed.[16]

In other words, the Book of Ezra provided scriptural justification for the alliance if the "judicious reader" took it as an example of God's mysterious ways in delivering his people and nothing further. Ezra should not be read too closely.

For those who sought a religious justification for the alliance, but did not have the will or ability to grapple with the Book of Ezra, some New England ministers provided a simpler explanation. They argued that an alliance with Protestant America would have a beneficial effect on Catholic France. In the 1779 Connecticut election sermon, James Dana explained that an alliance with France would not lead to popery in America: "Popery can prevail only under an arbitrary government, implying a general ignorance of civil rights. Hence the preservation of our religion depends on the continuance of free government. Let our allies have their eyes opened on the blessings of such a government, and they will at once renounce their superstition."[17] According to this interpretation, New Englanders should view the alliance not as a popish threat but a Protestant opportunity to make inroads against popery in France.

Specifically, ministers argued that the Franco-American alliance would ameliorate the conditions of the Huguenots. David Rowland explained: "The Protestants in France are not an inconsiderable part of the nation, who have always been kept under and much out of sight, ever since the repeal of the Edict of Nantz. Now this alliance may have a good tendency to cure the nation of their bigotry, root out their sanguinary notions and introduce an universal toleration."[18] In 1783 the rector of Yale College, Ezra Stiles, reported that "The reformed in France, who were formerly oppressed with heavy persecution, at present enjoy a good degree of religious liberty, though by a silent indulgence only."[19] Zabdiel Adams, the pastor at Lunenburgh, Massachusetts, reported optimistically in 1783 that "the king of France has given free toleration to his Protestant subjects, and allows them to build their churches undisturbed in any part of his kingdom! Spain has put an end to the Inquisition!"[20] According to this argument, as distasteful as an alliance with papists might be, New Englanders should bear it for the sake of their persecuted brethren in France. This line of argument cut two ways: if the alliance produced toleration for Protestants in Catholic France, might it not produce toleration for Catholics in

Protestant New England?

Few Whigs were willing to go so far in 1778. France, after all, remained a Catholic country. By definition, popery and Protestantism were antithetical. If New Englanders were to embrace the alliance with France, they had to be convinced of one of two things: French popery was no longer a threat to New England Protestantism, or New Englanders were threatened by something worse than popery. The former was more difficult to demonstrate than the latter. In August 1778 John Adams, then at Versailles as an American envoy, wrote: "the spirit for cruisading Religion is not in France. The Rage for making Proselytes which has existed in former Centuries is no more. There is a Spirit more liberal here in this Respect than I expected to find. . . . this, I had almost said tollerant, Nation can never endanger our Religion."[21] Coming from Adams, whose anti-papal credentials were impeccable, such a claim seemed credible. Adams benefited from his mind-broadening experience in Philadelphia. His less worldly neighbors were unlikely to believe that French popery did not pose a threat to them.

With little chance of convincing New Englanders that French Catholicism posed no threat, the surest way for Whig leaders to win acceptance for the alliance was to convince them that the English threat was even greater. In 1778 the British threat to New England was obviously far more immediate than that of the French. Phillips Payson succinctly explained why New Englanders ought to support the alliance: "A Friend in need, is a friend in deed. At this day we both see our need of this friendly aid and feel the happy effects of it."[22] Essentially, New Englanders did not need to like the French or their religion. They did need to recognize their dire straits and graciously accept aid from whatever source it came. This justification, which required the least from New Englanders intellectually and emotionally, hearkened back to Elbridge Gerry's less than satisfying statement that "self-interest accounts for all."

Proponents of the Franco-American alliance did not make a clear distinction among the various arguments outlined above. Usually they drew on a combination of them as circumstances dictated. They were required to provide an intellectual and theological defense of the alliance to counter the criticism of New England Tories, who revived the rhetoric of anti-popery to assault the Whigs from 1778 until the end of the war. Indeed, after the French entered the war, anti-popery gave the Tories their most credible and attractive intellectual weapon.

III

Prior to the war, New England Loyalists were as firm adherents to the anti-papal persuasion as their Whig neighbors. In the words of Daniel Leonard, a prominent Massachusetts Loyalist, "the political interests of Britain depend upon our protestant connexion, and the King's being a protestant himself is an indispensable condition of his wearing the crown."[23] They despaired when, in their minds, the Whigs appropriated the language of anti-popery for their own political ends. In the wake of the Quebec Act (which he defended), Leonard lamented:

We often see Resolves and seditious letters interspersed with popery here and there in Italics. If any of the clergy have endeavoured, from this circumstance, to alarm their credulous audiences with an apprehension that their religious privileges were in danger, therebye to excite them to take up arms, we must lament the depravity of the best of men; but human nature stands appalled when we reflect upon the aggravated guilt of prostituting our holy religion to the accursed purposes of treason and rebellion.[24]

For Leonard, and other New England Tories, leading Whigs used anti-papal rhetoric as a canard to dupe the common people into supporting an unjust rebellion.

Some Tories even attempted to accuse the Whigs of popery during the early days of the Revolution. Boston Loyalist Harrison Gray described the Massachusetts delegates to the First Continental Congress as "jesuitical gentlemen." Judge Peter Oliver, whose brother was a favorite target of Boston crowds, wrote of "the Mercy of the Mob who like the Inquisition Coach, would call a Man out of his Bed."[25] Just as supporters of the episcopacy had been unsuccessful in charging their foes with popery, so too were the Tories a decade later. As supporters of a government that most New Englanders suspected of popish sympathies, Tories had little credibility when they made such charges against the professed foes of popery.

The experience of Jonathan Stickney of Rowley, Massachusetts, illustrates the vulnerability of Loyalists with regard to charges of popery during the early years of the Revolution. On April 15, 1776, the Rowley Committee of Safety declared Stickney an "enemy to his Country" because, among other things, he had declared "it an act of grace in his Majesty in establishing Popery in Canada; . . . [and] that his Majesty had a just right to sign any act of Parliament whatever." The General Court sent Stickney to the Essex County jail in Ipswich for his popish expression of free speech.[26]

Ironically, at the same time that Stickney went to jail, Congress was again wooing the Canadians, and Massachusetts leaders were cozying up to the idea of a Catholic priest for the Eastern Indians. Peter Oliver furiously wrote of the 1776 mission to Canada (that of Franklin, Chase, and the Carrolls), "The Congress, who have pretended to be such warms Sticklers against Popery, now made it evident, that they thought evil might be committed, if they could squeeze any Advantage from it to answer their own Purposes."[27] New England Tories were more consistent intellectually on the subject of popery than their Whig counterparts. They remained firm anti-papists throughout the Revolution. In the early years of the struggle, however, they were unable to successfully charge their foes with popery. They could only fume futilely as their enemies promised religious freedom to papists while beating the tocsin of anti-popery to encourage the rebellion against Britain. With the conclusion of the French alliance, Tory accusations of Whig popery gained credibility.

The initial Tory reaction to the French alliance was one of frustration and rage. Anglican missionary Jacob Bailey, a New Englander who had sought exile in Nova Scotia, wrote that the alliance "affords a most striking instance of the perverseness of the human heart, and displays beyond example the obstinacy, the madness, the folly, the perfidy of my countrymen."[28] Salem merchant Samuel Curwen, a refugee in London, was dejected when he heard of the union: "The coup de grâce is given to British glory; its Sun is set! . . . The roar of the British lion will no more be heard; the French cock may now crow and strut undisturbed. America . . . allied itself to her natural, professed, and most dangerous enemy." Another frustrated Loyalist concluded that a people who would enter into such an agreement "deserve no better fate than to become the vassals of France and wear wooden shoes."[29] Frustration gave way to opportunity as Tories realized that the alliance allowed them to make charges of popery stick against their Whig opponents.

New England Whig leaders appreciated that an open alliance with France placed them in a delicate intellectual position. Anti-popery, after all, had been one of the intellectual justifications for the rebellion. Now, a mere four years after the Quebec Act, New England Protestants had allied with French Catholics. Loyalists were quick to expose apparent Whig hypocrisy. James Warren observed: "The Tories are very industrious in Instilling prejudices into the minds of the people against our Connections with France. The danger of Popery is held up to them, and every other Art that Wickedness and weakness can devise is practised, but I hope with little Effect."[30] Beginning in the spring of 1778, the Tories pursued a vigorous anti-papal campaign in which they attacked the French alliance in an effort to win popular support for their cause.

The Tory assault on the alliance with France was carried out in the press.[31] Many Tory propagandists were not encumbered by the truth when they made their case to the American people. For example, Admiral D'Estaing reportedly declared the Congress "a pack of rascals" and promised "A good Frenchman loves monarchy, and let matters go how they may will never permit a Republic to be established on the American continent."[32] In a more remarkable story, it was reported that when an unnamed congressman declared the French alliance absurd, "Count Pulaski [a Catholic] was called immediately and the congressman was beheaded."[33] One enterprising correspondent produced a letter, supposedly captured at sea from the French, which detailed French plans to make Americans French subjects and return them to the Catholic fold.[34]

New England Tories did not need to formulate any new arguments for their attack on the alliance. They had merely to revive the traditional popish cycle of ignorance, idolatry, dependence, and tyranny, with which their audience was well versed. The cycle of popish tyranny culminated in a complete loss of political and religious liberty. Rather than forge a new argument, the Tories merely had to demonstrate that the French alliance endangered the liberty of Americans.

Tory writers argued that cunning French papists had a plan to make Americans "the dupes of their ambition [so] that your children might enjoy the mighty boon of being the slaves of the Most Christian King [Louis XVI]."[35] The plan was very simple. Under the guise of extending aid to the American rebels, the French would take over the American colonies, reducing them to popish servitude. The French plan did not require a sudden political takeover. Rather, the French would gradually insinuate themselves, and undermine American independence while professing friendship for the American cause. "An American Freeman" feared that the debts the rebels had contracted with French merchants would result in French seizure of American property. According to this argument, Congress could obtain credit in France only "by a mortgage or sale of America, or part of it, to secure at a future day the sums lent." According to one report, since Benjamin Franklin had "ceded Canada and Florida to the French and Spaniards, it is hoped that he will give New England to the pretender and make the Pope, Archbishop of North America and the whole continent in the end may go to the devil."[36] This argument played on the traditional image of Catholics as grasping, greedy, and lazy. Catholics sought to swindle the ignorant out of their hard-earned property. The French planned to dupe the ignorant American Whigs into ceding all of America.[37]

For the French plot to succeed, Whig collaboration was necessary. According to the Tories, leading Whigs had sold America in exchange for popish titles and bribes. Tories often accused Congress and notable Whigs of such collaboration. According to "Americanus," the pope would name Samuel Cooper and Noah Welles bishops of Boston and Connecticut, respectively, for their support of the alliance. The pontiff shortchanged Cooper and Welles, for he allegedly promised to canonize Benjamin Franklin and Samuel Adams for their contributions to the French cause.[38]

When congressmen sold American liberty for French gold and popish titles, they sacrificed more than secular freedom. The French alliance endangered American Protestantism. "Under Congress," Charles Inglis, the Anglican rector of New York City, ominously warned, "instead of laws to restrain, the door is thrown wide open to receive popery."[39] "Americanus" described an independent America where denominational distinctions such as Presbyterianism, Congregationalism, Baptism, and Quakerism would not exist because all would "be buried in oblivion and we shall reasonably unite in the venerable title of true Roman Catholics."[40] Another correspondent was even more explicit. He described an America independent of Britain where "Religion with tattered garments and mournful eye, would lament the success which exposed her to the shackles of Popish superstition and the lash of unfeeling persecutors: whilst indignant freedom would fly with disgust, from a land devoted to the arbitrary domination of a French tyrant."[41] The French alliance threatened the temporal and spiritual well-being of America. The alliance allowed Tories to cast the American Revolutionary War as a battle for the soul of America.

Tory propagandists made the most of the opportunity afforded them by the French alliance. In a witty satire, published on March 17, 1779, "Florus" described what America would be like in 1789 if the rebels and French triumphed in the war. Florus described a Boston where "the Bible in the vulgar tongue is strictly prohibited on pain of being punished by discretion of the Inquisition" and Samuel Adams was a priest at the "American Sorbonne"—Harvard. According to Florus, the king of France would parcel out the lands of America to French nobles, take firearms from Americans, outlaw the speaking of English, decree that Americans must ship their trade in French vessels, prohibit American fishing in the North Atlantic, and direct "his Viceroy to send 500 sons of the principal inhabitants of America, to be educated in France, where the utmost care will be taken to imbue them with a just regard for the Catholic Faith, and due sense of subordination to government." Florus' vision of post-war America was an inversion of the Protestant society enjoyed by Americans under British rule. It was a nightmarish vision of the future sprung directly from the anti-papal persuasion. According to Florus, only British victory could forestall such horrendous developments.[42]

Florus' prophecy was reminiscent of Jonathan Mayhew's description of New England after a French victory two decades earlier. The similarity is not coincidental. For New England Tories, the papal threat to New England remained the same in 1778 as 1758: cunning French Catholics sought to destroy

Protestantism in New England. Tories asked if popery had changed in twenty years. Was "it purged from error and become less persecuting?"[43] Since it had not, the popish threat remained unchanged. The Tory response was logical and intellectually consistent. Unlike New England Whigs, Tories did not have to explain a radical change in position. Ironically, the French alliance that materially strengthened the rebel cause simultaneously strengthened the moral cause of Tories.

The Tories expressed their moral confidence with respect to the French alliance in several ways. First, they refused to engage their Whig opponents in debate on the issue. The anti-papal persuasion promoted a manichean outlook which meant that anti-papists were not required to enter the lists of intellectual debate with papists and their sympathizers. Rather than refute arguments based on the Book of Ezra, Tories dismissed such arguments out of hand as jesuitical frippery. More importantly, Tories attacked the alliance whenever they sought to make a popular appeal from the moral high ground. The most notable example of such an appeal is that of Benedict Arnold. Benedict Arnold betrayed the rebel cause and joined the English in 1780 after several years of notable service. When he left the rebels, Arnold, a Connecticut native, appealed to the anti-papal persuasion to justify his actions. In several proclamations issued after he changed his allegiance, Arnold employed anti-papal rhetoric. He claimed to have been offended by the rebel alliance with "the enemy to the Protestant Faith, . . . fraudulently avowing an affection for the liberties of mankind while she holds her native sons in vassalage and chains."[44] Two weeks later, Arnold made an appeal to Continental Army soldiers "who are determined to be no longer the dupes of Congress or of France," asking them to follow his lead and join the British.[45]

Historians have accurately portrayed Benedict Arnold as a shrewd opportunist who was motivated by financial pressures to change his allegiance.[46] But Arnold's own explanation derived from his anti-papal heritage as a New Englander. He condemned Congress for attending Mass in Philadelphia, "participating in the rites of a Church, against whose antichristian corruptions your pious ancestors would have witnessed with their blood."[47] Although his justification did not satisfy his peers or his biographers, it is possible that it did satisfy Arnold. New Englanders had traditionally employed the anti-papal persuasion to order their world, and it is not too much to conclude that it helped one New Englander to justify his treason.

IV

Tory appeals to anti-popery were largely unsuccessful. No Continental soldiers laid down their arms to follow Arnold because congressmen attended Mass. Whig leaders' attempts to justify the French alliance had undermined the intellectual foundation of anti-popery. While Tories made the most of the propaganda opportunity afforded by the alliance, they did so at a time when New Englanders were moving away from anti-popery. Essentially, Tories did not successfully apply the label "papists" to their opponents, until the label had begun to lose its potency and had been abandoned by their adversaries. The Whigs had already successfully attached the attributes of popery onto the British king. While the Tories demonstrated intellectual consistency in their response to the French alliance, Whig leaders demonstrated flexibility. While Whig flexibility smacked of hypocrisy to the Tories, Whig leaders were able to craft a justification for the alliance, which, if not completely consistent or satisfying, was adequate to their needs.

Between 1763 and 1778 leading Whigs refashioned the anti-papal persuasion. Once the British supplanted the French as the chief representatives of tyranny, the fear of popery declined among New Englanders. While most New England Whigs were still no lovers of Catholicism, the papal threat had lost its immediacy for them. When faced with the actual threat of British troops, the abstract threat of Jesuit machinations seemed flaccid. The French alliance was not a radical departure for New Englanders but the culmination of a long transition. It was a transition that New England Tories did not understand or acknowledge, as their retention of traditional anti-papal rhetoric indicates. The French ambassador to the United States, the Chevalier de la Luzerne, best summed up this cultural transition when he visited Boston in 1779. Luzerne noted the decline of anti-popery in New England, observing, "If they wish to make a person odious to his fellows, they charge him with Toryism."[48] By 1779 it was worse in New England eyes to be a Tory than a papist.

Just as the Tories had trouble recognizing and accepting the revisions Whig leaders made to anti-popery, so too did many rank-and-file Whigs who, while willing to accept French aid, were unwilling to accept or tolerate French Catholicism. The result was a cultural conflict between the leading Whigs in New England and their followers. Open conflict over popery occurred in the autumn of 1778 when the fleet of the Comte D'Estaing arrived in Boston.

NOTES

1. William Stinchcombe, *The American Revolution and the French Alliance* (Syracuse, 1969), 10; *Massachusetts Spy*, April 23, 1778; *Providence Gazette*, April 25, 1778.

2. For the background to the French alliance, see Jonathan R. Dull, *A Diplomatic History of the American Revolution* (New Haven, 1985), especially pp. 75-103. Also see Jonathan R. Dull, *The French Navy and the American Revolution: A Study of Arms and Diplomacy* (Princeton, 1975); Ronald Hoffman and Peter J. Albert, eds., *Diplomacy and Revolution: The Franco-American Alliance of 1778* (Charlottesville, 1981); James Breck Perkins, *France and the American Revolution* (New York, 1910, repr. 1970); and Stinchcombe, *The American Revolution and the French Alliance*.

3. Samuel Cooper, A Sermon Preached on the Sabbath after Burgoyne's Surrender, CP Box 3:226.

4. Cooper, Sermon Preached on the Sabbath after Burgoyne's Surrender, CP Box 3:226.

5. Samuel Cooper to Benjamin Franklin, October 25, 1777, CP Box 1:17.

6. Elbridge Gerry to —, May 26, 1778, reproduced in James T. Austin, *Life of Elbridge Gerry*, 2 vols. (Boston, 1828), II, 276.

7. *Massachusetts Spy*, October 7, 1779.

8. David S. Rowland, *Historical Remarks* (Providence,1779), 31.

9. Rowland, *Historical Remarks*, 31.

10. See Alice M. Baldwin, *The New England Clergy and the American Revolution* (Durham, NC, 1928), for the contribution of the standing order to the Whig cause.

11. Phillips Payson, *A Sermon Preached Before the Honorable Council* (Boston, 1778), 30-31.

12. Phillips Payson, *A Memorial of the Lexington Battle* (Boston, 1782), 13-14.

13. John Murray, *Nehemiah: A Discourse Delivered at the Presbyterian Church in Newburyport* (Newburyport, 1779), 16.

14. John Murray, *Nehemiah*, 16-17.

15. Ezra 6:8-10, 7:15-19.

16. Jonas Clarke, *A Sermon Preached Before His Excellency* (Boston, 1781), 47-49.

17. James Dana, *A Sermon Preached Before the General Assembly* (Hartford, 1779), 15.

18. Rowland, *Historical Remarks*, 32.

19. Ezra Stiles, *The United States Elevated to Glory and Honor* (New Haven, 1783), 53.

20. Zabdiel Adams, *The Evil Designs of Men* (Boston, 1783), 24-25.

21. John Adams to James Warren, August 4, 1778, *WAL*, II, 39-40.

22. Payson, *Memorial of the Lexington Battle*, 15.

23. Daniel Leonard, *Letters of Massachusettensis* (Boston, 1775), 74. For New England Tories, see Bernard Bailyn, *The Ordeal of Thomas Hutchinson* (Cambridge, Mass., 1974); Wallace Brown, *The Good Americans: The Loyalists and the American Revolution* (New York, 1969); Robert McCluer Calhoon, *The Loyalists in*

Revolutionary America, 1760-1781 (New York, 1973); North Callahan, *Flight from the Republic: The Tories of the American Revolution* (Indianapolis, 1967); Mary Beth Norton, *The British-Americans: The Loyalist Exiles in England, 1774-1789* (Boston, 1972); Lorenzo Sabine, *Biographical Sketches of Loyalists in the American Revolution*, 2 vols. (Boston, 1864); James H. Stark, *The Loyalists of Massachusetts* (Boston, 1907).

24. Leonard, *Massachusettensis*, 74-75.

25. [Harrison Gray], *A Few Remarks Upon Some of the Votes and Resolutions of the Continental Congress* (Boston, 1775), 10; Douglas Adair and John R. Schutz, eds., *Peter Oliver's Origins and Progress of the American Rebellion* (Stanford, 1961), 97. These were not popular opinions. Gray wrote anonymously, and Oliver's manuscript went unpublished until almost two centuries after the Revolution.

26. Peter Force, *American Archives*, 4th series, V, 950-952, 1282. Stickney also called the Continental Congress "a pack of rascals."

27. *Peter Oliver's Origin and Progress of the American Rebellion*, 137.

28. "Jacob Bailey, Journal, July-August, 1778," reproduced in William S. Bartlet, *The Frontier Missionary: A Memoir of the Life of the Reverend Jacob A. Bailey* (Boston, 1853), 357-358.

29. Samuel Curwen to Isaac Smith, February 25, 1778, in Samuel Curwen, *The Journal of Samuel Curwen, Loyalist*, Andrew Oliver, ed., 2 vols. (Cambridge, Mass., 1972), I, 434, n. 3; *Rivington's Royal Gazette*, March 6, 1779.

30. James Warren to Samuel Adams, May 10, 1778, *WAL*, II, 9. Adams responded on June 1: "The Danger of Popery is particularly held up by the Partizans of the King, who would wish to drain Ireland of its Catholicks to carry on his bloody Purposes in America." *WAL*, II, 15. Adams attempted to fend off charges of popery with an accusation of his own. While this tactic might have worked in 1774, by 1778 the credibility of the charge that Britain would crush freedom in America with Irish Catholics was weakened by the Whig alliance with French Catholics.

31. The chief Tory mouthpieces were *Rivington's Royal Gazette* and the *New York Gazette*, both of which were published in British-occupied New York City. By 1778 most active Tories had fled New England (or had learned to keep their criticisms to themselves). With the exception of the *Newport Mercury*, which published Tory views during the British occupation of Newport in 1778-79, we must rely on printed sources from outside New England to reconstruct the attitudes of New England Tories toward the French alliance.

32. *Rivington's Royal Gazette*, August 25, 1780.

33. *Rivington's Royal Gazette*, October 28, 1778.

34. *Rivington's Royal Gazette*, October 24, 1778.

35. *Rivington's Royal Gazette*, January 2, 1779.

36. *Rivington's Royal Gazette*, August 22, 1778 and October 20, 1779.

37. When French troops landed in New England in 1778 and 1780, the Tory press reported that the French had come to seize territory in payment for their aid. See *Rivington's Royal Gazette*, August 22, 1778; September 16, 1778; August 2, 1780; August 23, 1780; August 25, 1780.

38. *Rivington's Royal Gazette*, March 1, 1780.

39. [Charles Inglis], *The Letters of Papinian* (New York, 1779), 114.

40. *Rivington's Royal Gazette*, March 1, 1780.

41. *Rivington's Royal Gazette*, March 17, 1779.

42. *Rivington's Royal Gazette*, March 17, 1779.

43. [Inglis], *Letters of Papinian*, 114.

44. Benedict Arnold, *To the Inhabitants of America . . . October 7, 1780* (New York, 1780).

45. Benedict Arnold, *To the Officers and Soldiers of the Continental Army . . . October 20, 1780* (New York, 1780).

46. See Willard Sterne Randall, *Benedict Arnold: Patriot and Traitor* (New York, 1990); James Thomas Flexner, *The Traitor and the Spy: Benedict Arnold and John André* (New York, 1953); Carl Van Doren, *Secret History of the American Revolution* (New York, 1951).

47. Arnold, *To the Officers and Soldiers of the Continental Army*.

48. La Luzerne to Vergennes, September 3, 1779, in Henri Doniol, *Histoire de la Participation de la France à l'Établissement des États-Unis d'Amérique: Correspondance diplomatique et documents*, 5 vols. (Paris, 1886-92), IV, 326.

6

Our Ancient Prejudices Were Very Far from Being Eradicated: The French in Massachusetts, 1778–82

I

Initially, New Englanders reacted positively to the French alliance. On April 20, one day after Samuel Cooper announced the alliance, "a Number of Gentlemen" gathered at the American Coffee House in Boston and "congratulated each other on so happy an Event." The gentlemen made thirteen toasts, the third of which they dedicated to Louis XVI.[1] Two weeks later, on May 5, 1778, the French man-of-war *La Nymphe*, commanded by the Chevalier de Sainneville, arrived in Boston harbor. *La Nymphe* was the first French warship ever to visit Boston. The city's leaders gave the crew of the vessel a warm welcome. According to James Warren, "public and private Persons are treating the officers of the French Man of War with every mark of Respect and I understand they are highly pleased with [Boston]." On May 9 the Governor's Council hosted a dinner for the captain and his officers at Marston's Tavern.[2]

The warm welcome extended to *La Nymphe* was superficial. Even among leading Whigs, there was skepticism and apprehension about the French presence. Reverend William Gordon of Roxbury noted that the French ship had failed to observe maritime custom and salute the American flag at Castle William when it entered the harbor. For Gordon there was more at stake than protocol. He feared the symbolic subjugation of America by France. "I hope," he wrote, "the American United States will never suffer their forts to salute first."[3] James Warren questioned whether the dinner at Marston's was "not quite Conformable to the rigid rules and economy of a Young Republic." While Warren concluded that the dinner "may under our present circumstances be good policy," he worried about the display of luxury, a sure sign of popish corruption. The presence of Catholic French officers resplendent in their uniforms must have heightened his anxiety.[4] The common people in Boston were even more apprehensive about the French presence in their midst than their political leaders.

A young Bostonian, Samuel Breck, described the arrival of the first French troops in New England: "the whole town, most of whom had never seen a Frenchman, ran to the wharves to catch a peep at the gaunt, half-starved, soup-maigre crews. How much were my good townsmen astonished when they beheld plump, portly officers and strong vigorous sailors!"[5] Anti-papal antipathy toward the French, however, was deeply rooted. According to one report, some New Englanders clung to their traditional conceptions about the physical characteristics of Frenchmen despite the well-fed examples they met, claiming that the soldiers and sailors sent to America "had been picked on purpose, in order to give them a more advantageous idea of the [French] nation."[6] The Abbé Claude Charles Robin, a Catholic priest, noted that he was well received by the "best families" in Boston but that the "people in general retain their old prejudices."[7]

The pattern of ambivalence and skepticism toward the French present among leaders and common people in the spring of 1778 indicates that anti-popery was still a potent factor in New England culture. It is important to remember that eighteenth-century New Englanders equated things French with things Catholic. In their minds the two were inextricably linked. While it would be incorrect to assume that every instance of Franco-American tension was the result of persistent New England anti-popery, it would be equally incorrect to assume that anti-popery played no role in these disturbances.

The following account chronicles instances of conflict between French soldiers and sailors and their American hosts. Wherever the evidence allows, anti-popery is indicated as a cause (by no means the sole cause) of conflict. In cases where no explicit evidence of anti-popish motivation exists, the incident is examined on the assumption that in such cultural conflicts anti-popery played at least an implicit role. Given the vitality of anti-popery during the early years of the Revolution, and the circumstantial evidence indicating the prevalence of anti-popery after the arrival of the French, such an assumption is warranted, provided the reader recognizes that anti-popery was not the only cause of friction between the allies. The presence of the French prompted an anti-papal reaction among many New Englanders. Their presence was the catalyst for a cultural debate over the place of anti-popery in revolutionary New England. Ultimately, limited toleration would supplant anti-popery. Toleration, however, was preceded by several crises in Franco-American relations.

II

The first crisis in Franco-American relations began in August 1778. On July 29 a naval squadron of fifteen vessels under the command of the Comte D'Estaing arrived off the coast of Rhode Island. D'Estaing had orders to assist General John Sullivan of New Hampshire in capturing Newport from the British. Circumstances seemed to favor the rebels and their new allies. The British garrison in the town was undermanned, and enthusiasm for the action was strong. As one of the besieged defenders wrote in May: "the spirits of the people are now high . . . numbers of them will be found willing to engage for a short time in an enterprize of that nature [an attack on Newport]. It is certainly in their interest to attempt [it], and before we receive any reinforcements from Europe."[8] Located at the southern tip of Rhode Island, Newport was ideally situated for a joint naval and land siege.

American expectations were very high before the siege of Newport. Many Americans viewed the siege as a test of French skill and resolve. Rebel hopes were dashed when the siege collapsed in August 1778. The expedition failed for several reasons. General Sullivan had trouble organizing the New England militiamen who were late to join his Continental soldiers. Miscommunication between D'Estaing and Sullivan exacerbated the situation and delayed the proposed attack until mid-August. Before the Franco-American attack could be launched, Admiral Richard Howe of the Royal Navy arrived off Newport with a fleet from New York on August 10. D'Estaing feared that Howe would trap his fleet in Newport harbor, so he pursued the British vessels into the open sea. After a brief engagement (Howe had only intended to distract D'Estaing and disrupt the siege), D'Estaing's ships were battered by a hurricane on August 14-15.[9]

The American soldiers and militiamen, themselves soaked by the hurricane, impatiently awaited the return of their allies. As each day passed, annoyance with the French increased. After ten days of waiting, Colonel Israel Angell observed, "the French fleet not being yet heard of spread great consternation in the Army."[10] D'Estaing finally limped back into Newport harbor on August 20. The storm had severely damaged five of his eleven ships of the line.

Admiral D'Estaing did not intend to resume the siege. He announced that he would immediately sail to Boston to make repairs to his ships. The American soldiers were furious. Colonel Angell tersely wrote on August 23, "the French fleet Left us to day bound to Boston and I think left us in a most Rascally manner and what will be the Event God only knows."[11] The Americans accused the French of deserting them and causing the collapse of the siege. British Lieutenant Frederick Mackenzie reported that American deserters in Newport "abuse the French for not having been more active in their co-operation and blame them for the failure of the Expedition."[12] One of the first historians of the Revolution, Roxbury minister William Gordon, wrote: "upon the fleet's sailing for Boston, it was said—'There never was a prospect so favorable blasted by such a shameful desertion.' A universal clamor prevailed against the French nation."[13] When the French departed, so too did most of the American militiamen. Only the soldiers of the Continental Army remained before Newport. They withdrew under heavy fire on August 29.

Most of the American soldiers at Newport, both militiamen and Continentals, were New Englanders. New Englanders traditionally believed that papists could not be trusted by Protestants. By nature papists were treacherous. D'Estaing confirmed this attitude by his ill-timed withdrawal from Newport. The Marquis de Lafayette, who was among the Continental soldiers at Newport, wrote to D'Estaing:

I expected that your departure would be displeasing. I counted on some angry responses, but I did not expect the total effect that your leaving produced. No honest or generous soul would have anticipated it. Would you believe that the majority of these people here, forgetting both their general obligations to France and the services specifically rendered by the fleet, let smoldering prejudices flare up again?[14]

He complained to George Washington that the New Englanders had treated the French "as a generous one would be ashamed to treat the most inveterate enemys."[15] Lafayette did not appreciate how close to the surface the "smoldering prejudices" of New Englanders were in 1778. Until recently, of course, the French had been the inveterate enemies of New England. New Englanders responded to D'Estaing's departure in a manner consistent with their anti-papal tradition.

Public opinion in Boston was decidedly anti-French after the debacle in Rhode Island. James Warren lamented on September 2, "we have a foolish Spirit prevailing with rancour against the French for leaving Rhode Island."[16] Many of the Massachusetts militiamen at Newport had been Bostonians under the command of John Hancock. They returned to Boston with tales of French treachery just as D'Estaing's fleet arrived there to refit.

It is unlikely that Bostonians would have welcomed an army of New

Englanders, let alone Frenchmen, in their midst during the summer of 1778. By the third year of the war, food shortages were a major problem in Boston. In March 1778 the Boston Town Meeting petitioned the General Court for price controls on food, and resolved that inhabitants should limit the amount of meat they consumed.[17] More than six thousand hungry sailors manned D'Estaing's squadron. Supporting such numbers could only make the situation worse. D'Estaing could not have chosen a less propitious time to arrive in Boston. The combination of residual anti-popery, recent defeat, summer heat, and want of food made for an unstable relationship between the Bostonians and the newly arrived French.[18]

During the evening of September 8, 1778, several American sailors approached a bakery in Boston established by the French fleet and requested bread from the French bakers. The bakers refused the request, and a fierce fight ensued between the American and French sailors. Two French officers, the Chevaliers de St. Sauveur and de Pleville, attempted to stop the affray and were themselves attacked. St. Sauveur came away from the disturbance with a mortal wound over his right eye.[19]

St. Sauveur was a well-connected man. His brother-in-law was the Comte de Breugnon, and the chevalier had served as the first chamberlain to the Comte d'Artois, the brother of Louis XVI, before he became a lieutenant on the *Tonnant*, the ship that brought him to Boston. His death came barely three weeks after the fiasco at Newport, adding a further strain to an already fragile relationship. Many shared the fear of General William Heath, the American commander in Boston, that "our great & good cause will be Injured Irreparably" by the disturbance. Indeed, Heath went so far as to indicate that Tories, "those who wish to make a Schism at this Time," deliberately initiated the disturbance.[20]

Despite General Heath's claim, it is doubtful that Tories were responsible for the St. Sauveur riot. Such a view, while politically expedient, was not realistic. Historian Dirk Hoerder declared that "the real cause [was] the unalleviated scarcity of provisions and the continuing profiteering" in Boston.[21] There is evidence to support such a claim. The fight, after all, began at a bakery. The arrival of the French had had a deleterious effect on the Boston economy. Abigail Adams explained: "The French Fleet now lies in the Harbour of Boston. The daily supplies which we are obliged to afford them enhances the price of every article of life scarce before but now almost incredibly so." According to the account of the disturbance that circulated among the British at Newport, "a scarcity of Wheat bread" caused the riot. Further evidence reveals that Hoerder's interpretation, while valid in part, is too limited.[22]

While the rising price of bread certainly must have influenced the St.

Sauveur rioters, cultural factors motivated them as well. Such disparate commentators as John Adams, who was then in France, and Thomas Hutchinson, who was exiled in England, heard rumors that the riot stemmed from religious antipathy. Adams reported that he had heard that the row began when D'Estaing seized a Protestant church to celebrate Mass. Hutchinson reported, "There have been frays at Boston between the French and English Seamen, and contentions about suffering the host to be carried in procession to the sick." Hutchinson's mention of the host indicates a connection to the French bakery unrelated to the food shortage. Colonel John Laurens of the Continental Army was a more credible commentator than Adams or Hutchinson. The Carolinian visited Boston in September 1778 and observed, "I saw very plainly when I was at Boston, that our a[n]cient prejudices were very far from being eradicated."[23] While one must recognize the elite bias of these observers, the consistency of the anti-papal theme is difficult to dismiss. This is not to say that the price of bread was not a factor. Rather, that the crowd that attacked the bakery may have had mutliple motives. It is probable that economic concerns and anti-popery combined in a potent and deadly fashion in the St. Sauveur riot. As mariners, St. Sauveur's assailants had probably learned on numerous Pope's Days that anti-popery and economic protest merged quite nicely.

General William Heath, as the highest-ranking American military officer in Massachusetts, was the first official to confront the problem in Franco-American relations after the attack on St. Sauveur. On September 9 Heath wrote to the Massachusetts Council to present the official account of what happened the previous evening. Heath described the affray and warned the council that French "Uneasiness is great. Every Step Possible must be taken to Convince them of our Sincerity . . . or the Consequences may be most disagreeable."[24] The Council heeded the general's warning and immediately took two steps to assuage French unease. First, it offered a reward for information leading to the arrest of the rioters. Second, upon Heath's recommendation, the council forbade the privateer *Marlborough* to leave Boston harbor. Heath believed that members of the crew of the *Marlborough*, many of whom were English deserters, were involved in the riot.[25]

General Heath correctly recognized the disastrous consequences the riot might have for the Franco-American alliance. On September 9 he wrote a diplomatic letter to Admiral D'Estaing, who surely had heard of the tumult from his own officers. Heath explained to the admiral that he suspected crewmen from the *Marlborough* and described the actions he had taken to apprehend those responsible for the assault on St. Sauveur.[26] The initiative now passed to Admiral D'Estaing.

In the wake of the ill-fated Newport expedition, D'Estaing's measured response to Heath on September 10 indicates that the admiral might have been better suited for the diplomatic corps than the navy. D'Estaing took his cue from Heath in placing the blame on the crew of the *Marlborough*. Indeed, D'Estaing went a step further, placing the blame for the attack on British provocateurs who sought to undermine the alliance. D'Estaing echoed Heath's original contention that Tories were responsible for the disturbance when he wrote: "Our Common enemies hesitate at nothing; persuaded that our union both national and private, will render us invincible, & that they must fail eventually, there is nothing they will not try and the agents that they keep among you have only too many opportunities to execute their destructive orders." The admiral absolved Bostonians of any responsibility in the incident: "I should be inconsolable were a single inhabitant of the Metropolis of America to be punished for this fatal incident."[27] By their restrained responses, Heath and D'Estaing helped prevent a possible rupture in Franco-American relations.

General Heath and Admiral D'Estaing made use of familiar scapegoats in blaming Tories and British agents for St. Sauveur's death. New Englanders easily made such accusations. Leading Whigs repeated the accusation, and it became the "official" explanation for the disturbance.[28] John Adams told Edmé-Jacques Genet that British prisoners from Burgoyne's army "probably stimulated by secret Ennemies . . . produced the Disorders which every good Man in Boston abhors." Genet published Adams' comments anonymously in *Affaires de l'Angleterre et de l'Amérique*, a journal sponsored by the French government.[29] Since the British had come to represent popish tyranny, New Englanders ascribed all manner of trickery and guile to them. Ironically, New Englanders even blamed the English for their display of old-fashioned anti-popery toward the French.

Leading Whigs continued to invert traditional New England assumptions about the French and the English when they described D'Estaing's sailors. Despite the conflicts in the streets, commentators consistently praised the French. As Samuel Cooper noted anonymously in the *Independent Ledger*:

there is a striking contrast between the behavior of the British military of this town, and that of the French. The former . . . fired upon the inhabitants of Boston, without any just provocation . . . the latter now become by the oppressions and cruelties of Britain, our allies and protectors, when assaulted themselves, by unknown ruffians, have left their protection and satisfaction, entirely in the hands of the civil magistrate.

William Gordon wrote that, "The behaviour of the French officers and sailors, the whole time that their fleet lay in port, was remarkably good far beyond any thing of the kind before."[30] These views contrasted sharply with traditional anti-papal views of the French, and reveal a determined effort by Whig leaders to foster a better opinion of America's new allies.

An interesting cultural battle took shape in New England during the autumn of 1778. On one side were leading Whigs, military and political leaders such as William Heath and John Hancock, as well as ministers such as William Gordon and Samuel Cooper, who supported the Revolution and the French alliance. These men promoted the view that the British had supplanted the French as purveyors of evil and that anti-popery no longer had a place in New England culture. On the other side were the majority of people, no friends of Britain, who nonetheless still retained vestiges of the traditional anti-papal persuasion. D'Estaing's presence complicated matters in New England. Intellectually, the majority of New Englanders accepted the refocusing of the anti-papal persuasion after the Quebec Act. However, when confronted by real Catholics, even as allies, many New Englanders reverted to their traditional anti-papal persuasion. The leading Whigs attempted to awe the anti-papal majority into accepting the new order of things during the fall of 1778. When this failed, they attempted to suppress anti-papal demonstrations.

On September 11 a regiment of the state militia drilled in the streets of Boston before their general, John Hancock. After the review, Hancock entertained the Massachusetts Council at the Bunch of Grapes Tavern. D'Estaing and his officers had been invited to the review, but were unable to attend because of the rumored approach of an English fleet off Massachusetts. This demonstration of might three days after the St. Sauveur riot was not coincidental. Heath had ordered troops to patrol the streets in the days after the riot.[31] Massachusetts authorities were sending a military message to the people of Boston that they had best accept the French in their midst.

While the troops were drilling in the streets of Boston, the Massachusetts Council met. Inexplicably and without comment, the council voted to allow the *Marlborough* to leave Boston harbor.[32] Whether the members of the crew of the privateer were cleared of any wrongdoing is unknown. That the privateer was released while the militia drilled before the people of Boston indicates that the council felt that the blame for the disturbance lay more with the people of Boston than the crew of the *Marlborough*. While the official cause of the disturbance remained the activity of British agents and provocateurs, the council directed its efforts toward awing the people of Boston.

The unfortunate St. Sauveur died on September 15. French authorities concluded that a Catholic funeral procession through the streets would likely antagonize the citizens of Boston. As a consequence, St. Sauveur was given a quiet funeral in the basement of King's Chapel at ten in the evening on September 16. D'Estaing's secretary described the ceremony: "Eight sailors of the *Tonnant* bore the officer on their shoulders. I preceded them with the sexton and grave digger; the Recollect (a Franciscan monk), MM. de Borda, de Peysegur, and Pierveres followed; the body servant of the deceased, and perhaps two or three other Frenchmen closed the procession." The twenty men "deposited the remains without ceremony" in a vault in the basement of the chapel.[33] The French buried their officer so modestly to avoid further conflict with the citizens of Boston. When the members of the Massachusetts Council voted to attend the ceremony, the French politely declined their presence on the grounds that it would arouse too much attention. The council did vote to erect a monument in St. Sauveur's honor.[34]

Despite the surreptitious internment of St. Sauveur, the presence of six thousand French sailors in a community of fifteen thousand could not be ignored. In the weeks after the death of St. Sauveur, the government of Massachusetts made a concerted effort to publicly welcome the French to Boston. On Tuesday, September 22, D'Estaing and his officers "made a public Entry into this Town." The soldiers at Castle William fired their cannon to honor D'Estaing's party as his launch proceeded through the harbor. Upon landing, a committee representing the civil and military authorities received the French officers. They were then conducted to the Council Chamber where they "received the Compliments and Congratulations of the Gentlemen of the Council and the House of Assembly."[35] After their visit to the General Court, the Frenchmen and the council retired to John Hancock's house where they ate breakfast. At noon D'Estaing's entourage "Drank Punch wine at Headquarters" with General Heath before returning to their ships, saluted again by the guns of Castle William.[36] This public display was intended both to welcome the French and to indicate to the perpetrators of the St. Sauveur riot that the French were in Boston to stay.

Three days later General Hancock sponsored a dinner for more than four hundred French officers and local dignitaries at Faneuil Hall. Before the dinner, French and American troops paraded through the streets. The dinner, described as "plenteous and splendid," was accompanied by twenty-three toasts that "expressed in the most lively manner the great and mutual pleasure diffused by the present happy union between France and these States which British tyranny has now rendered so important to the interest of both nations."[37] On October 29 Hancock sponsored a ball at the Concert Hall for more than two hundred French and American guests.[38] These ostentatious public celebrations of the alliance had two purposes. On one level they were intended to provide a warm welcome to the French and shore up the alliance after an awkward beginning. More importantly, the celebrations were intended to send a message of toleration to the common people despite their misgivings about the Catholicism of their new allies. On this level the celebrations can be seen as a demonstration of what

Edward P. Thompson called "theatrical power" which characterized elite-plebeian relations during the eighteenth century.[39] The Whig elite staged lavish, public celebrations with the express purpose of awing the common people into accepting the French.

Was such a public campaign a success? James Warren wrote to Samuel Adams on September 30, "The disquisition that at first appeared to Cast odium on . . . our new allies seems to have entirely subsided & been succeeded by the most perfect good humour [and] respect shown them."[40] Warren probably overestimated the goodwill engendered by such public extravagance in a time of want. An anonymous letter writer may have expressed the view of the majority in Boston. The writer was critical of the extravagance of the celebrations "in this day of general Calamity, When Providence, Cong[re]ss and every prudent person in America call on us to exercise prudence, economy, and humiliation."[41] The real test of whether the common people accepted the alliance and the French in their midst occurred in the streets.

Despite the public declarations of goodwill, relations between the French and Bostonians remained strained. No arrests were ever made in connection with the St. Sauveur riot, which surely irked the French. The day after the banquet at Faneuil Hall, a drunken French marine was arrested for assaulting a constable. Conversely, French officers from the frigate *L'Aimable* detained a sailor from an American privateer after he and two comrades assaulted one of the passengers from *L'Aimable*.[42] In another incident, the Massachusetts Council ordered the commander of the privateer *Hazzard* to move his ship away from the French ship *Dolphin* because "the hands on board the *Hazzard* treat the people on board the *Dolphin* with very opprobrious language."[43] During the evening of October 5, 1778, large numbers of American and French sailors fought in the streets of Boston. Only swift action by General Heath prevented a larger disturbance on October 6.[44] According to the Chevalier de Borda, who commanded the French troops in Boston, "there happens every day some disagreeable affair."[45] Taken as a pattern, these incidents reveal a tense and potentially explosive relationship between the French and Americans in Boston. While these incidents may not have been directly inspired by anti-popery, cultural differences between the sailors contributed to the disputes. Chief among the cultural differences between the Americans and the French was religion.

The French fleet left Boston on November 4, 1778. Upon departing, D'Estaing wrote to his superiors in Paris. He was concerned about the impact the troubles in Boston might have on French opinion. He wrote, "I hope the King will be satisfied by the public and sincere marks of regret of the Americans; they could do no more and I ought to assure you they would like to have done far more."[46] The willingness of D'Estaing and his American counterparts to put the best face on events kept the discord in Boston from escalating into a major impediment to Franco-American relations.

On the same day that D'Estaing left Boston, the Massachusetts Council authorized the Selectmen and Justices of the Peace in Boston to prevent "some People [who] are so destitute of Consideration" from celebrating Pope's Day.[47] Indeed, it may not be a coincidence that D'Estaing left on November 4. The official and unofficial demonstrations in the streets of Boston in 1778 were part of the cultural debate on anti-popery. The Whig elite, people such as John Hancock, William Heath, James Warren, and Abigail Adams, represented those Whigs who felt that anti-popery was a useless, embarrassing appendage, best removed from the body politic. The sailors of Boston who fought with the French represented other New Englanders who were unwilling to dispense with anti-popery.

The cultural debate over anti-popery did not invariably break along class lines. The intellectual division was not between an enlightened, educated elite and the benighted masses. Although Boston's hungry sailors expressed their displeasure toward the French with brickbats and fists, it is likely they enjoyed the support of many of their neighbors. Abigail Adams lamented that the French "have been neglected in the town of Boston. Generals Heath and Hancock have done their part, but very few if any private families have made any acquaintance with them."[48] Rather, the division was between the small minority of Whigs who held positions of leadership and viewed anti-popery as an impediment to the success of the Revolution, and the overwhelming majority who still retained their prejudices. The attitude of the majority is best characterized as ambivalent. The majority of New Englanders were attracted to the French as necessary allies, yet they were still repelled by their Catholicism. The events of 1778 set the precedent for interaction between the two groups. The advocates of toleration took advantage of their superior social and political position to promote toleration. Their campaign, coupled with a steady influx of French sailors and soldiers throughout the war, undermined the strongest elements of anti-popery.

III

Between 1778 and 1782 a steady stream of Frenchmen visited Boston. Despite the rough treatment of D'Estaing, French warships and merchant vessels put in at the port. The traffic was so heavy that the French ambassador in Philadelphia, Conrad Alexandre Gerard, appointed a consul general, the

Chevalier de Valnais, for Boston in 1779. While Bostonians never again encountered the large numbers of Frenchmen they had in 1778, by 1779 Frenchmen were a familiar sight in the streets and lanes of the town. Prolonged contact with the French was a catalyst for religious toleration in New England.

Among the most notable visitors to Boston was Anne César, Chevalier de Luzerne. Luzerne replaced Gerard as French ambassador to the United States in 1779. He visited Boston in late August on his way to Philadelphia. On Tuesday, August 30, 1779, Luzerne "and a number of other gentlemen of distinction, both French and Americans made a visit to Harvard College, at the invitation of the President and the Corporation." Luzerne passed through a file of Harvard students in their academic robes, "their heads uncovered" as he proceeded to Harvard Hall where he was greeted by the "President, Corporation, Professors and Tutors" of the college. At Harvard, one of the centers of Protestant New England learning and culture, and home of the Dudleian lecture, Luzerne heard "the most respectful mention of our most illustrious ally, His Most Christian Majesty," as well as "the warmest wishes for the perpetuation of the alliance." After the speeches, the entire company repaired "into the large and elegant Philosophy room where a very decent entertainment was provided."[49]

Massachusetts leaders welcomed Ambassador Luzerne according to the pattern established when D'Estaing was in Boston in 1778. Prominent social and political leaders entertained the visiting dignitary, and the event received prominent coverage in the press. In this way, New Englanders became accustomed to the French presence in their midst. General Rochambeau received similar treatment when he visited Boston in December 1780.[50] By 1781 the Boston elite and visiting French officers present in the city socialized regularly. The frequency of Franco-American "entertainments" indicates that the Boston elite learned to enjoy the company of French officers and noblemen. On October 4, 1781, a committee of Boston merchants hosted an entertainment for all the French naval officers and the consul general "as a compliment for the protection they have cheerfully given the Trade of this Commonwealth." After meeting at the Bunch of Grapes Tavern, one hundred and fifty French officers and Boston merchants marched in procession to Faneuil Hall where "the Entertainment was Elegant and Splendid." After dinner, the diners made fifteen toasts. In addition to the standard toasts for the alliance and the king of France, the company also toasted "His Most Catholic Majesty, the King of Spain," who was an ally to America's ally, France, but not to the United States.[51]

The merchants' entertainment is notable not only because of the toast for the king of Spain, but because it was hosted by a committee of private citizens instead of by civil or military officials as previous celebrations had been. The willingness of Boston merchants to sponsor the event and toast the king of Spain indicates an increase in toleration among the upper reaches of Boston society. Three years before Boston merchants, with few exceptions, gave Admiral D'Estaing a very cold welcome. Three years after the conclusion of the alliance, the Whig campaign to promote toleration had succeeded among the city's class of merchants.

Every few months in 1781 and 1782 a notable Franco-American social event was held in Boston. Sometimes the French hosted the entertainments, sometimes the Americans. On August 21, 1781, Governor Hancock held a public dinner to welcome the fleet of the Marquis de Vaudreil to Boston.[52] Several months later, on November 19, 1781, the "Captains of the French ships of war" in Boston sponsored a ball to celebrate the Franco-American victory at Yorktown.[53] On June 12, 1782, "the Rulers of the Commonwealth" sponsored a huge celebration of the birth of the Dauphin, complete with fireworks and a ball in the evening.[54] In November 1782 the Marquis de Viomenil and his troops arrived in Boston. Viomenil had come from Yorktown. He commanded a part of Rochambeau's army as it prepared to embark from Boston to go to the West Indies. Viomenil and his troops stayed in Boston for two months in late 1782. According to Ludwig Von Closen, "Many fetes and balls were given during the army's stay in Boston."[55]

The social whirlwind of 1781 and 1782 indicates that, among the social and cultural elite in Boston, tolerance for the French had developed through long-term contact. Implicit in this toleration was an acceptance of French Catholicism. The increased social interaction indicates that some Bostonians, not just civil and military officials, had learned to appreciate and welcome the French. Most of the Franco-American entertainments excluded the common people. How did Boston's common people, those who traditionally burned the pope, and had fought with D'Estaing's sailors, react to long-term contact with the French? Moreover, was the the deliberate and expensive campaign waged by the Whig elite to promote toleration a success?

The comings and goings of various French and American naval and merchant vessels meant that there was a frequent turnover among the people along the Boston waterfront. Bostonians were recurrently introduced to new groups of French sailors. They freely wandered the streets and taverns. As a consequence, several conflicts occurred between French sailors and Bostonians. In two of the conflicts, Frenchmen killed Americans. The popular response to these incidents reveals that a limited level of toleration for the French had developed among the common people.

During the evening of September 20, 1779, Richard Collingwood, a former British prisoner of war who had signed on as a sailor on the American ship

Queen of France, left his rooming house with several friends. Collingwood reportedly declared "that he would be kill'd or kill somebody" that evening. Collingwood and his friends encountered a group of armed men, "supposed to be Frenchmen." The two groups exchanged words. Unfortunately for Collingwood, he and his friends carried clubs and the French had pistols. An unknown Frenchman shot Collingwood in the back. After an hour of suffering, Richard Collingwood achieved one of his stated goals for the evening: he died.[56]

Although the *Massachusetts Spy* reported that "several sailors are now under confinement . . . taken up in consequence of said affair," there are no court records related to the death of Richard Collingwood.[57] Two historians, William Stinchcombe and Lee Kennett, have demonstrated that French and American authorities covered up several embarrassing incidents that might have damaged Franco-American relations.[58] It is possible that such a coverup occurred after the killing of Richard Collingwood. Unlike the prominent St. Sauveur, Collingwood, a British-born sailor, was a marginal member of the community. He probably had no family in Boston to whom the authorities had to answer. According to the only account of the killing, that which appeared in the *Massachusetts Spy*, Collingwood had gone out looking for trouble.[59] Since Collingwood would not be missed, and his killers were likely Frenchmen, Massachusetts authorities may have decided not to pursue the matter and released the suspects they had taken into custody. The most persuasive evidence in favor of such an interpretation is that Massachusetts authorities behaved in just such a fashion in a subsequent case.

During the evening of December 28, 1780, two weeks after Rochambeau's visit to Boston, a fight occurred on Long Wharf between sailors from the American ship *Alliance* and the French frigate *Surveillante*. At least seven French sailors fought five of their American counterparts. The French got the best of the Americans, leaving two severely wounded and one American, James Bass, dead from a six-inch knife wound in the stomach. At an inquest, a jury concluded that the seven French sailors had murdered Bass. Constables immediately took them into custody to await trial. The seven men appeared before the Supreme Judicial Court of Suffolk County on February 20, 1781. Despite the conclusions of the jury at the inquest and eyewitness accounts from the survivors of the melee, all seven were acquitted.[60]

Leading Whigs figured prominently in the trial of the seven French sailors. Benjamin Hitchborn, a leading Boston lawyer, agreed to defend the men. He found a jury sympathetic to the Whig cause, if not to his clients. The jury foreman was Hitchborn's kinsman, Paul Revere. Other leading Whigs, such as Josiah Eliot, Asa Stoddard, and Uriah Oakes, served on the jury.[61] The political jury came back with a clearly political verdict. A guilty verdict would have fanned the flames of anti-French sentiment in Boston, probably leading to more conflicts. It seems likely that the jury acquitted the men in order to protect the Franco-American alliance.

A comparison of the deaths of St. Sauveur, Collingwood, and Bass reveals a diminution of anti-popery among Bostonians between 1778 and 1780. In 1778 anti-popery motivated the men who killed St. Sauveur. While cultural differences, among which popery was one of the chief differences between Frenchmen and New Englanders, may have contributed to the frays in which Collingwood and Bass lost their lives, there is no firm evidence to support such a claim. More important is the way Bostonians reacted to the killings. If Collingwood and Bass had been killed ten years before and Catholics were suspected, a tremendous popular clamor would have resulted. By 1780 neither murder was solved, despite strong indications that Frenchmen were responsible, and yet the public apparently did not react. Catholics may literally have gotten away with murder in the streets of Boston, and the public was indifferent, in large part because they had come to see the French as valued allies rather than as dangerous papists.

IV

In revolutionary Massachusetts, a small elite imposed religious and cultural toleration on the majority. In Boston the leading advocate of Franco-American friendship was Samuel Cooper. As a leading supporter of the Revolution and Boston's most prominent minister, Cooper played a critical role in promoting harmonious relations between the French and the Americans. This role bears consideration for it reveals the process by which the Whig elite promoted toleration for Catholicism.

Samuel Cooper was probably the strongest advocate for the French alliance in New England. Indeed, the minister was so warm in his support for France that the Loyalist printer James Rivington published anti-French excerpts from Cooper's 1759 thanksgiving sermon on the capture of Quebec to expose the minister as a typical Whig hypocrite. The printer warned New Englanders, "If there is as much stability in the Doctor's religion as there is in his politics, and as ardent desire for independence with regard to the former as the latter, we may expect to see him, in less than twenty years, embrace the scarlet whore, and adorn the first Papal chair in America." Despite such charges, the former Dudleian lecturer never wavered in his support for the French alliance.[62]

In the aftermath of the disaster at Newport in 1778, Cooper played an

important role in closing the breach in Franco-American relations. It was
Samuel Cooper who arranged for the nocturnal burial of St. Sauveur at King's
Chapel.[63] During D'Estaing's stay in Boston, the American minister and the
French admiral became close friends. When he left Boston, D'Estaing wrote to
Cooper, "the truest Auspices are those of friendship . . . love me a little My
Dear Doctor because I love you so much."[64] Cooper drafted a pamphlet
defending D'Estaing's actions during the Newport campaign. The minister did
not publish the pamphlet because he correctly concluded that it would only
upset General Sullivan and revive a controversy best forgotten. The minister did
defend the admiral in his private correspondence.[65]

How is Samuel Cooper's intellectual revolution with respect to the French
to be explained? How did the author of the 1773 Dudleian lecture become a
champion for toleration by 1778, even arranging for a secret Catholic funeral?
In the years between his 1759 thanksgiving sermon on the reduction of Quebec
and his 1773 Dudleian Lecture, Samuel Cooper thoroughly embraced the anti-
papal persuasion. For Samuel Cooper the Quebec Act was an intellectual
catalyst, which caused him to reevaluate the world. Cooper concluded that the
British represented the greatest danger to liberty in America. As a consequence,
Cooper directed his old anti-French sermons against the British. Once the
British supplanted the French in his mind, Cooper ceased to fear and hate the
French. By 1777 Cooper aggressively lobbied for the union of America and
France and praised Louis XVI. When Cooper met Admiral D'Estaing and his
officers in 1778, he became a warm friend of France. It is likely that many other
leading Whigs, including many of Cooper's parishioners, underwent a similar
transformation. They led the campaign to promote the French alliance and
toleration for the French in Massachusetts.

Just as many Americans gave their support to the French because they felt
it was in the best interest of the United States, so too did Samuel Cooper.
Cooper was also motivated by his own self-interest. The minister's support for
the French did not go unnoticed. Conrad Alexandre Gerard, the first French
ambassador to the United States, noted Cooper's pro-French contributions
during the row between D'Estaing and Sullivan which led Gerard to "thank him
for them and to make known my desire to see him use his talents and influence
for the same cause." Gerard chose well. He appreciated "the religious influence
that a leading clergyman must have on a people who maintain a strong tinge of
fanaticism and religious enthusiasm." Cooper's support would undermine those
who attacked the French alliance on the grounds of anti-popery. His imprimatur
would help give the alliance religious credibility in New England.[66]

Gerard dispatched a young French officer with whom Cooper was friendly
to negotiate with the Boston minister. In exchange for £200 per annum "as

compensation for what he lost and suffered for the common cause," Cooper agreed to "inspire the American people with the respect and admiration due the King, esteem for the nation, and confidence in the principles and inclinations of His Majesty by using all the appropriate materials to accomplish this important objective." Thus between 1779 and his death in 1783, Samuel Cooper was a paid agent of the king of France. He correctly realized that anti-popery was the key obstacle to Franco-American harmony, especially in New England. According to Gerard, Cooper believed that "by attacking the unbelievable prejudices to which the British cling to keep the Americans turned against us, he hopes to encourage union and personal trust between the two nations and to destroy the individual aversion to us that the American people continue only too often to display." Until the end of the Revolution, Cooper consciously strove to undermine anti-popery because it was in the the best interest of his country and himself to do so.[67]

Samuel Cooper earned his stipend from Louis XVI in a variety of ways. He squired visiting French dignitaries around Boston.[68] As a member of the corporation that governed Harvard College, Cooper may well have arranged Luzerne's visit to Cambridge in 1779. Additionally, Cooper kept Ambassador Luzerne well informed about matters of interest to the French in Boston. He wrote of the comings and goings of French troops and ships and how they were received.[69] While Cooper's roles as informant and tour director were significant, his most important role was as a propagandist.

Cooper acted as a propagandist in two ways. He hinted at them in a letter he wrote to Luzerne in 1780. The minister wrote, "Knowing Sir the Importance of the Affairs of the ensuing Campaign I have given them a particular attention and endeavor'd to prepare the minds of my Friends in Government as well as among ye people for the most Vigorous Exertions."[70] First, Cooper used his influence within the government of Massachusetts to cultivate a positive attitude toward the French. In this he was usually successful. In so doing he encouraged other leaders to promote toleration for the French among the common people. Cooper's second, more complicated and more important task was to cultivate a positive view of the French among the common people of Boston and New England. He did this through the press and his pulpit.

Between 1779 and 1783 Samuel Cooper submitted a steady stream of anonymous, pro-French articles to New England newspapers. Sometimes Cooper acted on his own initiative; in other cases Luzerne prompted the minister. For example, in November 1779 the ambassador suggested to Cooper that he write about the anticipated campaign of Admiral D'Estaing in Georgia and the Carolinas: "it will be necessary to make it known in your various publications that the two nations are in perfect agreement and to avoid giving more praise to one than the other. But above all it will be useful to make clear that the first concern of the French Admiral . . . was to run to the aid of the three United States which were in danger." Cooper's article appeared in the *Connecticut Courant* at the end of November. The minister precisely conveyed the message the ambassador had wanted.[71]

Cooper's most famous propaganda effort was his defense of Boston's celebration for the birth of the Dauphin. On June 12, 1782, Bostonians extravagantly saluted the birth of Louis XVI's heir. In a widely reprinted account of the celebration, Cooper described how "every order of men, in its own way, shouted benediction to the Dauphin." When they did so, they showed the "good sense of the people who realized the importance in an hereditary Kingdom of such an event." The Dauphin's birth meant that a bloody contest for the crown would be avoided which, according to Cooper, was why "even republicans, as far as they are friends to mankind, may rejoice when the heir to a great empire is born."[72] Placed in the context of Cooper's defense, the celebration, complete with fireworks, banquets, and public illuminations, takes on the aspect of yet another elite display of theatrical power in defense of the French alliance. That Samuel Cooper needed to justify the celebration indicates that the intellectual problem posed by an alliance between Protestant republicans and a Catholic monarchy had not been completely resolved even after four years of such demonstrations. It further emphasizes the important role played by the minister as the chief defender of the alliance.

The movement against anti-popery was very much an elite-directed cultural change. The Whig elite concluded that anti-popery had lost its utility and viability. They demonstrated this in their public actions. They beseeched and, at times, cajoled the common people to accept their view. In general, this campaign was successful as the constitutions of the New England states adopted during the revolutionary era reveal.

NOTES

1. *Exeter Journal*, April 28, 1778; *Providence Gazette*, April 25, 1778.

2. Quotation from James Warren to Samuel Adams, May 8, 1778, *WAL*, II, 8. See also Ezekal Rice, "Diary," *NEHGR*, 19 (1865), 332.

3. William Gordon to Elbridge Gerry, May 9, 1778, Elbridge Gerry Papers, MHS, Reel I.

4. James Warren to Samuel Adams, May 10, 1778, *WAL*, II, 9.

5. Samuel Breck, *Recollections of Samuel Breck* (Philadelphia, 1877), 25.

6. Claude Charles Robin, *New Travels Through North America* (Philadelphia, 1783), 20.

7. Robin, *New Travels Through North America*, 20.

8. Frederick Mackenzie, *The Diary of Frederick Mackenzie*, 2 vols. (Cambridge, Mass., 1930), I, 275-276.

9. William Stinchcombe, *The American Revolution and the French Alliance* (Syracuse, 1969), 48-52. For different views on the siege, see Jeremiah Greenman, *Diary of a Common Soldier in the American Revolution*, Robert C. Bray and Paul E. Bushnell, eds. (DeKalb, 1978); Israel Angell, *Diary of Colonel Israel Angell, 1778-1781*, Edward Field, ed. (Providence, 1899); Mackenzie, *Diary*, II; and Richard K. Showman, ed., *The Papers of Nathanael Greene*, 6 vols. (Chapel Hill, 1976-91), II.

10. Angell, *Diary*, 2.

11. Angell, *Diary*, 4.

12. Mackenzie, *Diary*, II, 387.

13. William Gordon, *The History of the Rise, Progress and the Establishment of the United States of America*, 4 vols. (London, 1788), III, 163.

14. Lafayette to D'Estaing, August 24, 1778, in Stanley J. Idzerda, ed., *Lafayette in the Age of the American Revolution: Selected Letters and Papers*, 5 vols. (Ithaca, 1977-83), II, 143.

15. Lafayette to George Washington, August 25, 1778, Idzerda, *Lafayette in the Age of the American Revolution*, II, 151.

16. James Warren to John Adams, September 2, 1778, *WAL*, II, 46.

17. Boston Record Commissioners, *Report of the Record Commissioners*, 38 vols. (Boston, 1876-1908), XXVI, 8-10.

18. D'Estaing's sailors did not improve the situation. Several French sailors disembarked at Hull in search of provisions. Residents of the town accused the French of stealing hay, grain, flax, corn, potatoes, poultry, utensils and "burning and destroying their effects." The people of Hull complained that the failure to furnish the French "with proper Necessarys is a very great Disadvantage to the inhabitants of Said place." The townsmen correctly recognized that feeding D'Estaing's sailors would pose a major problem for Massachusetts and French authorities. See Petition of the Inhabitants of Hull, September 5, 1778, MA 169:143-144.

19. *Independent Ledger*, September 14, 1778. The death of St. Sauveur and its aftermath has attracted little attention from historians. Two accounts by Fitz-Henry Smith, "The Memorial to the Chevalier de Saint-Sauveur," *Bostonian Society Proceedings* (1918), 31-58, and "The French at Boston during the Revolution," *Bostonian Society Publications*, 10 (1913), 9-75, are useful starting points. A committee was convened by the Massachusetts Senate to investigate the incident in 1905. Their report no. 336, which is in the Senate Resolves for 1905, Chapter 72, at the Massachusetts Archives in Boston (hereafter Mass. Senate Report 336) is also useful.

20. William Heath to the Massachusetts Council, September 9, 1778, MA 200:72-73.

21. Dirk Hoerder, *Crowd Action in Revolutionary Massachusetts, 1765-1780* (New York, 1977), 363-364.

22. Abigail Adams to John Adams, September 29, 1778, in Butterfield, ed., *Adams Family Correspondence*, III, 95; Mackenzie, *Diary*, II, 409. William Gordon reported: "The New England cruisers took such a number of provision vessels on their way from Europe to New-York, as not only supplied thewants of the French, but furnished a surplus sufficient to reduce the rates of the markets at Boston." Letter from Roxbury, November 12, 1778, Mass. Senate Report 336, 19-20.

23. John Adams to James Lovell, November 27, 1778, in Charles Francis Adams, ed., *Works of John Adams,* 10 vols. (Boston, 1854), IX, 473-474; Thomas Hutchinson to Lord Hardwicke, October 30, 1778, Gay Transcripts, MHS; John Laurens quoted in William G. Simms, *Memoir and Correspondence of Col. Laurens in the Years 1777-1778* (New York, 1867), 228. The rumor that D'Estaing had seized a meeting house for Catholic worship was reported in *Rivington's Royal Gazette*, September 19, 1778, and in the *New York Gazette and Weekly Mercury*, September 21, 1778.

24. William Heath to the Massachusetts Council, September 9, 1778, MA 200:72-73.

25. Massachusetts Council Records, 22:443-445; MA 169:152-153. The proclamation offering the $300 reward appeared in the *Independent Chronicle*, September 10, 1778. Boston merchant James Swan owned the *Marlborough*, which was captained by George Waithe Babcock. As a privateer the *Marlborough* captured twenty-eight prizes. See Gardner Weld Allen, *Massachusetts Privateers of the Revolution, MHSC*, 77 (1927), 215.

26. William Heath to Admiral D'Estaing, September 9, 1778, Heath Papers, MHS.

27. Comte D'Estaing to William Heath, September 10, 1778, Heath Papers, MHS.

28. For example, see "Extract from the Log Book of the *Languedoc*," Mass. Senate Report 336, 22 (the *Languedoc* was D'Estaing's flagship); and George Washington to Nathanael Greene, in Fitzpatrick, *Writings of George Washington*, XII, 479.

29. John Adams to Edmé-Jacques Genet, December 30, 1778, in Richard Ryerson and Robert Taylor eds., *The Papers of John Adams,* 8 vols. to date (Boston, 1977-), VII, 324, 325 n. 1.

30. *Independent Ledger*, September 14, 1778; Gordon, *History*, III, 200. For other examples, see James Warren to John Adams, October 5, 1778, Ryerson, *Papers of John Adams*, VII, 111; James Warren to John Adams, October 7, 1778, *WAL*, II, 51; Mercy Otis Warren to John Adams, October 15, 1778, *WAL*, II, 55; and Samuel Cooper to Benjamin Franklin, January 4, 1779, in John Bigelow, ed., *The Works of Benjamin Franklin*, 12 vols. (New York, 1904), VII, 416-418.

31. *Exeter Journal*, September 22, 1778. William Heath Diary, September 9 and 11, 1778, Heath Papers, MHS.

32. Massachusetts Council Records, September 11, 1778, MA 22:448.

33. Mass. Senate Report 336, 26-27. St. Sauveur's modest funeral contrasts with that of another French nobleman who died in New England during the Revolution. When the French admiral, Ternay, died at Newport, Rhode Island, in December 1780, his cortege was carried through the streets of the town and nine priests celebrated a funeral

Mass witnessed by hundreds of Newporters. See Henry J. Yeager, "The French Fleet at Newport, 1780-1781," *Rhode Island History*, 30 (1971), 86-93; and Allan Forbes and Paul Cadman, *France and New England*, 3 vols. (Boston, 1925-27), III, 49.

34. Massachusetts Council Records, September 16, 1778, MA 38:619. The monument was not erected until 1917; see Fitz-Henry Smith, "The St. Sauveur Monument."

35. *Independent Chronicle*, September 24, 1778.

36. Heath Diary, September 22, 1778; MA 219:269-270.

37. *Exeter Journal*, October 6, 1778; *Providence Gazette*, October 3, 1778; *Independent Chronicle*, October 1, 1778; *Independent Ledger*, September 28, 1778.

38. Heath Diary, October 29, 1778; *Independent Chronicle*, November 5, 1778. For other incidents of Franco-American social interaction, see Heath Diary, September 26, 1778; John Gray Diary, October 19, 1778, photostat, MHS; Abigail Adams to John Adams, October 21 and 25, 1778, *Adams Family Correspondence*, III, 109-110; and "Reminiscences of Gen. Wm. H. Sumner," *NEHGR*, 8 (1854), 187-191.

39. E. P. Thompson, *Customs in Common* (London, 1993), 43.

40. James Warren to Samuel Adams, September 30, 1778, photostat, MHS.

41. Anonymous, Fragment of a Secret Letter, October 28, 1778, misc. bound, MHS.

42. Petition of the Chevalier de Borda to the Massachusetts Council, September 29, 1778, MA 184:256-258.

43. Massachusetts Council Records, MA 169:217.

44. See Heath Diary, October 5 and 6, 1778; William Heath to the Massachusetts Council, October 6, 1778, MA 200:132; Massachusetts Council Records, October 6, 1778, MA 169:200.

45. Petition of the Chevalier de Borda, September 29, 1778, MA 184:258.

46. Mass. Senate Report 402, Mass. Senate Resolves, Chapter 104.

47. Resolution of the Council of Massachusetts Bay, November 4, 1778, copy, Lord/Sexton Papers, AABo.

48. Abigail Adams to John Adams, October 25, 1778, in Butterfield, ed., *Adams Family Correspondence*, III, 110.

49. *Massachusetts Spy*, September 2, 1779. Also see "Rapport de la Luzerne du 3 septembre 1779," in Henri Doniol, *Histoire de la participation de la France à l'établissment des États-Unis D'Amérique: Correspondance diplomatique et documents*, 5 vols. (Paris, 1886-92), IV, 326 n. 1.

50. *Independent Chronicle*, December 21, 1780; *Boston Gazette*, December 18, 1780.

51. "Selectmen's Minutes, October 1781," *Report of the Record Commissioners*, 25 (1894), 158; *Boston Gazette*, October 8, 1781.

52. *Independent Chronicle*, August 29, 1782. On August 20 a committee of merchants presented Vaudreil with a gushing letter of welcome. See William Phillips, Chairman of the Committee of Merchants, to Le Mar. de Vaudreil, August 20, 1782, in the Letters of William Bollan, Ezekiel Rice Papers, MHS.

53. *Boston Gazette*, November 26, 1781.

54. *Boston Gazette*, June 17, 1782; Stinchcombe, "Americans Celebrate the Birth of the Dauphin," 65-66.

55. "Freeholder Meeting at Faneuil Hall, December 7, 1782," *Report of the Record Commissioners*, 26 (1895), 275-276; Closen, *Journal*, 272-273.

56. *Massachusetts Spy*, September 30, 1779.

57. *Massachusetts Spy*, September 30, 1779.

58. Stinchcombe, "Americans Celebrate the Birth of the Dauphin," 47; Kennett, *French Forces in America*, 80-87, 120.

59. Of course, if a coverup had occurred, it is possible that the story in the *Spy*, an ardently Whig newspaper, was part of the plot. The story did not appear until ten days after the event. Though the *Spy* was published in Worcester, not Boston, the time lag is unusual.

60. *Boston Gazette*, January 1, 1781; Suffolk County Supreme Judicial Court (hereafter SJC), Docket Book, February 20, 1781, Reel 5, MA, Boston; Claude Blanchard, *Journal*, 85. According to the court records, the men arrested for the murder of James Bass were Philip Eliot, Peter Boudin, Mathurin Limmereau, Francis Cortier, Lewis Dessuages, Francis Gallopee, and Colly Dennis.

61. The jurors were Revere, Eliot, Stoddard, Oakes, James Goodridge, Thomas Holland, Thomas Nolen, Nathan Weld, Ebenezer Oliver, Archibald McNeill, Samuel Downes, and Norton Brailsford. Suffolk County, SJC, Docket Book, February 20, 1781. For the relationship between Revere and Hitchborn, see David Hackett Fischer, *Paul Revere's Ride* (New York, 1994), 299. Additional evidence for a political verdict in the Bass murder trial comes from Claude Blanchard. In January 1781, before the trial, the commissary wrote in his journal: "there was a very warm quarrel at Boston between the sailors of an American frigate, the *Alliance*, and those of the *Surveillante*, a French frigate. The Americans were the aggressors; two were killed. The two sailors who were killed were discovered to be Englishmen in the American Service, which aided in appeasing the quarrel." Blanchard incorrectly noted that two Americans were killed in the disturbance. In his version, the Frenchman implies that a settlement was reached in January, before the case came to trial. Blanchard, *Journal*, 85.

62. *Rivington's Royal Gazette*, July 1, 1778. For Cooper and the French alliance, see Charles Akers, *The Divine Politician: Samuel Cooper and the American Revolution in Boston* (Boston, 1982), chaps. 17-18.

63. Akers, *Divine Politician*, 266.

64. Comte D'Estaing to Samuel Cooper, November 3, 1778, CP Box 1:21.

65. Samuel Cooper to the Comte D'Estaing, February 1781, CP Box 2:9. Also see Samuel Cooper to Benjamin Franklin, November 1778, CP Box 1:1.

66. Conrad Alexandre Gerard to the Comte de Vergennes, January 17, 1779, in John J. Meng, ed., *Desptaches and Instructions of Conrad Alexandre Gerard, 1778-1780: Correspondence of the First French Minister to the United States with the Comte de Vergennes* (Baltimore, 1939), 481.

67. Gerard to Vergennes, January 17, 1779, in Meng, ed., *Desptaches and Instructions*, 482. Charles Akers estimates that after 1781 more than half of Cooper's salary came from Versailles. See Akers, *Divine Politician*, 280.

68. See Samuel Cooper to Anne César de la Luzerne, October 6, 1779, CP Box 1:37; Cooper to Luzerne, December 14, 1780, CP Box 2:60.

69. See Cooper's letters to Luzerne on May 1, 1780, CP Box 2:39; July 13, 1780, CP Box 2:5; December 26, 1781, CP Box 2:18; and November 21, 1782, CP Box 2:23 for examples.

70. Cooper to Luzerne, June 15, 1780, CP Box 2:47.

71. Luzerne to Cooper, November 1, 1779, CP Box 1:66; *Connecticut Courant*, November 31, 1779.

72. Cooper to Luzerne, June 13, 1782, CP Box 2:20; the story appeared in the *Boston Evening Post*, June 15, 1782; *Independent Ledger*, June 17, 1782; *Continental Journal*, June 20, 1782; *Salem Gazette*, June 20, 1782; *Providence Gazette*, June 22, 1782; and *Pennsylvania Gazette*, June 26, 1782. See also Stinchcombe, "Americans Celebrate the Birth of the Dauphin," especially p. 65.

7

An Unalienable Right of All Mankind: Religious Freedom For New England Catholics

I

By the end of the revolutionary era, the four New England states extended minimal religious freedom to Catholics. While Catholics did not achieve full legal equality, Protestant New Englanders relaxed the restrictions that bound them. The toleration extended to New England Catholics by Protestants has largely been ignored by religious historians, who have been more concerned with the emergence of sects such as the Shakers and with the struggle of older groups such as the Baptists and Quakers for equality after the Revolutionary War.[1] The legal emancipation of New England Catholics, however, is the most concrete evidence for the decline of anti-popery in New England during the era of the American Revolution. Historians have often dismissed this evidence because Catholics did not achieve full equality.[2] Nonetheless, while Catholics did not achieve full equality with Protestants, they did secure the right to practice their religion, something that was denied them before the Revolution. This constitutes a significant change in status.

After the Revolution, citizens in two states, Rhode Island and Connecticut, adopted laws granting legal toleration to Catholics. Both Massachusetts and New Hampshire adopted new state constitutions during the 1780s which guaranteed freedom of conscience to Catholics. Massachusetts voters adopted a new constitution in June 1780, after a failed attempt in 1778, and New Hampshire adopted its constitution in 1784. For the historian of anti-popery, the Massachusetts Constitution is the more significant. In Massachusetts there was a vigorous debate in the constitutional convention over those clauses in the proposed frame of government that concerned religious freedom. More importantly, 1,800 copies of the proposed constitution were circulated in every city and town of Massachusetts for approval in the spring of 1780. Most of the communities sent back detailed responses. The responses of the towns, taken as a whole, provide a complete survey of opinion with respect to anti-popery. These responses, from Boston to Berkshire County, the commercial towns of Essex County to the farming villages of Maine, constitute an excellent cross section of New England communities. They are an invaluable source for considering the affect of the Revolution on New England opinion with respect to Catholicism.[3]

II

After the collapse of British authority in Massachusetts in 1774 and 1775, an ad hoc Provincial Convention governed the state. This arrangement was eventually superseded by the creation of the Massachusetts Council and a reorganized Great and General Court. During the summer of 1776 the Great and General Court resolved to draft a more formal, permanent frame of government to replace the defunct royal charter. The General Court did not approve a committee to draft the new frame of government, however, until June 1777. Jeremiah Powell of Cumberland County, Maine, chaired the committee of twelve which took six months to return a draft of the proposed constitution to the legislature. On December 11, 1777, the committee submitted the proposed constitution to the legislature. In February 1778 the legislature of 1777 met as a constitutional convention and considered the draft.[4]

From the perspective of anti-popery, the proposed constitution upheld the traditional New England view. According to the proposal, the offices of governor, lieutenant governor, senator, and representative would be open to "No person unless of the Protestant Religion."[5] The original draft of the constitution did have a provision for liberty of conscience, but stated that, "the Free exercise and enjoyment of Religious Profession and Worship shall for ever be allowed to every Denomination of Protestants within this state."[6] The members of the convention debated the clause for two days on February 11 and 12 before accepting the original wording which became Article 34 of the proposed constitution.[7] The proposed constitution of 1778 was an anti-papal document. It excluded Catholics from office and guaranteed the religious freedom of Protestants only. From an anti-papal perspective, the proposed constitution would maintain the status quo ante bellum.

In March 1778 the General Court distributed copies of the draft constitution to the selectmen of each town in Massachusetts. The selectmen were to submit the document to special town meetings open to all males over the age of twenty-one for consideration. By a margin of five to one, Massachusetts voters rejected the proposed constitution.[8] The voters had multiple reasons for rejecting the plan. Greenwich voters disapproved of having a governor and lieutenant governor. Hardwick voters rejected the constitution because it did not abolish slavery. Boston voters, 968 in all, expressed the most common criticisms of the plan. They unanimously noted "the Impropriety of this Matter's Originating with the General Court," and that "all Forms of Government should be prefaced by a Bill of Rights," which the constitution lacked.[9]

Some citizens took exception to Article 34, which guaranteed the rights of Protestants. "Milton" wrote to the *Independent Chronicle*, criticizing the article, "Which is more important than any other" for its broadness. "Milton" felt "Protestants" was too vague a term and religious freedom needed to be limited to Congregationalists. As it stood, the article "will undoubtedly occasion much dispute and difficulty."[10] Reverend William Gordon also criticized the language of the article. He disliked the use of the word "allowed" in the clause because "we are led to think of a favor's being granted instead of a right's being established."[11]

A small number of critics of the proposed constitution did argue that religious freedom in Massachusetts should include Catholics. William Gordon wrote, "I am also for allowing the free exercise and enjoyment of religious profession and worship to mankind in general . . . upon condition that the persons making such religious profession, do not allow a civil power outside of the State having a right to direct them in civil concerns." In an oblique fashion, Gordon stated that as long as they did not take orders from the Vatican in civil affairs, Catholics should enjoy the same freedom as Protestants.[12] The voters of Essex County concurred.

A convention of Essex County towns met at Ipswich in mid-April 1778 to consider the proposed constitution. The Essex Convention's detailed critique of the constitution was published as the "Essex Result." Newburyport's Theophilus Parsons, the author of the Essex Result, directly assaulted Article 34.

What is a religious profession and worship of God, has been disputed for sixteen hundred years, and the various sects of christians have not yet settled the dispute. What is a free exercise and enjoyment of religious worship has been, and still is, a subject of much altercation. And this free exercise and enjoyment is said to be allowed to the protestants of this state by the constitution, when we suppose it to be an unalienable right of all mankind which no human power can wrest from them.[13]

When they endorsed the Essex Result, voters unequivocally endorsed religious freedom for Catholics. Essex County was an exception in 1778. Few of the other critics of the 1778 constitution objected to its anti-popery.[14]

The rejection of the 1778 constitution meant that Massachusetts still had no formal plan of government. On June 15, 1779, the legislature called for a convention "for the purpose of framing a new constitution," to which delegates would be sent from every town in Massachusetts. Voting for the delegates was open to all men over the age of twenty-one. The General Court waived the usual property requirements in order to solicit the broadest possible input. The next constitution   would more accurately reflect the views of the citizens of Massachusetts than that of 1778.[15]

III

The Massachusetts Constitutional Convention convened on September 1, 1779, at the First Church in Cambridge. The convention consisted of nearly three hundred delegates representing virtually all the regions of the state.[16] On September 2 the convention voted that the proposed constitution should have a separate declaration enumerating the rights of Massachusetts citizens. One of the chief criticisms of the 1778 frame of government had been that it lacked such a declaration. On September 4 a committee of thirty, known as the General Committee, was selected to prepare the Declaration of Rights and the remainder of the constitution. The convention adjourned on September 7 to allow the committee time to draft its report.[17]

The General Committee elected a subcommittee of three—James Bowdoin, Samuel Adams, and John Adams—to draft the constitution. According to John Adams, "When we met, Mr. Bowdoin and Mr. S. Adams insisted that I should prepare a Plan in Writing which I did. When I laid it before them, after deliberating upon it they agreed to it, excepting only to one Line of no consequence, which I struck out."[18] The subcommittee presented Adams' work to the General Committee, which made several changes. When the convention reconvened at Cambridge on October 28, the proposed constitution before it was largely the work of John Adams.[19]

The Massachusetts Constitutional Convention devoted all of its second session (October 28 to November 12) to debating the merits of the Declaration of Rights. On Saturday, October 30, 1779, the convention reached Article II of the Declaration of Rights:

It is right and the duty of all men in society, publicly and at stated seasons, to worship the SUPREME BEING, the great Creator and Preserver of the universe. And no subject shall be hurt, molested, or restrained, in his person, liberty, or estate, for worshipping GOD in the manner and season most agreeable to the dictates of his own conscience; or for his religious profession of sentiments; provided he doth not disturb the public peace, or obstruct others in religious worship.[20]

This article unequivocally extended religious liberty to Catholics. The omission of the word "Protestant," which had appeared in the comparable clause in the 1778 constitution, meant that the right of conscience in Massachusetts was not to be limited to Protestants or even Christians. In the wake of the Essex Result, the delegates to the convention surely understood the implications of the article. In the afternoon of October 30, "the 2d article, after debates and amendments, being accepted, the order of the day was called."[21]

The differences between the version of Article II proposed by Adams and the final version adopted by the convention are minor and cosmetic. The changes, and the brevity of the debate, indicate that the convention adopted Article II with relative ease. Why did the convention of 1779 opt for the toleration of Article II? First, the article was the handiwork of John Adams, who, as a national politician, appreciated more than most the importance of toleration to the Whig cause. Beyond the pragmatic, political reasons for promoting toleration, Adams argued that religious toleration would have a positive influence on the development of the state. He explained the potential salutary effect of Article II:

The Liberality on the Subject of Religion does Us infinite Honor and is admired and applauded everywhere. It is considered not only as an honest and pious Attention to the unalienable Rights of Conscience, but as our best and most refined Policy, tending to conciliate the Good Will, of all the World, preparing an Asylum, which will be a sure Remedy against persecution in Europe, and drawing over to our Country Numbers of excellent Citizens.[22]

By late 1779 most Massachusetts leaders had been convinced by the presence of the French in New England and the assiduous campaigning of men like John Hancock and Samuel Cooper that religious toleration was necessary to defeat the British. This sentiment is reflected in the voting on Article II in the convention.

For those who did not share Adams' belief in the benefits of religious diversity, Article II may have been acceptable in principle because in reality the remainder of the proposed constitution placed checks on religious freedom. On October 30, 1779, the Constitutional Convention began debate on Article III of the Declaration of Rights. A committee of seven men drafted Article III which authorized the legislature to require the "several towns, parishes, precincts and other bodies politic, or religious societies, to make suitable provision, at their own expense, for the public worship of GOD, and for the support and maintenance of public, Protestant teachers of piety, religion, and morality, in all cases where such provision shall not be made voluntarily."[23] Article III mandated public support for the dominant Congregational Church in Massachusetts. As such, it circumscribed the religious liberty guaranteed by Article II, not only of Catholics but also of Quakers, Baptists, Unitarians, and other non-Congregationalists. If both articles were adopted, the rights of Catholics to worship would be guaranteed, but they would not be equal to those of Congregationalists.

Unlike Article II, the delegates vigorously debated Article III. For almost two weeks (October 30 to November 10), they argued over every clause of the controversial article. On November 7 the convention suspended its rule limiting members to speaking twice on a question, and "a free and general debate then ensued." Opponents of the article—Baptists, Quakers and more liberal Congregationalists—felt that Article III contradicted Article II, because requiring taxpayers to support religion undermined freedom of conscience. Proponents of the article, led by the Congregational clergy, argued that the government had a duty to promote morality, which was critical to the survival of a republic. On November 10, the convention adopted Article III.[24]

The Constitutional Convention considered the next twenty-eight articles in the Declaration of Rights in two days before adjourning on November 12, 1779. The convention was scheduled to reconvene on January 5, 1780, to consider the second part of the proposed constitution, the frame of government. Severe cold and snow rendered the roads impassable and delayed the reconvening of the convention from January 5 to January 26.[25] When the convention met at the end of January, barely fifty delegates made it to Boston for the third session. During the session (January 26 to March 2) delegates again encountered the question of toleration for Catholicism.

On February 4 one of the delegates to the convention proposed that a test oath, similar to those employed in Britain to limit officeholding to Protestants, should be added to the constitution. A committee was established "to form a declaration, . . . wherein every person before he takes his seat as a

Representative, Senator, or Governor, or enters upon the execution of any important office or trust in the Commonwealth, shall renounce every principle (whether it be Roman Catholic, Mahometan, Deistical, or Infidel) which has any the least tendency to subvert the civil or religious rights established by this constitution."[26] One of the tenets of New England anti-popery had been that Catholics could not be entrusted with civil political power because they would use their power to oppress Protestants. Since one of the rights established by the constitution was that of freedom of conscience, Catholics might seek high office. The committee sought to strike a balance between these contradictory positions.

On February 17 the Committee on Oaths presented its final report to the convention. Among the oaths required of the governor, lieutenant governor, senators, and representatives was the following: "I do declare that I believe the Christian religion and have a firm persuasion of its truth." Officeholders were also required to swear "that no foreign Prince, Person, Prelate, State, or Potentate, hath or ought to have any jurisdiction, superiority, preeminence, authority, dispensing or other power, in any matter, civil, ecclesiastical or spiritual within this Commonwealth."[27] While the language of the latter oath clearly stemmed from the commonplace belief in the Anglo-American world that Catholic officeholders would be controlled by Rome, the oath fell short of the explicit test sought by anti-papists. Catholics were not denied office, nor were they required to renounce their faith. The report of the Committee on Oaths, incorporated as Chapter 6, Article I of the constitution, is further evidence for the decline of anti-popery at the Constitutional Convention.

The battle over religious toleration continued in the Constitutional Convention when the delegates debated the proper qualifications for governor. According to John Adams' "Frame of Government" the requirements for the office of governor included that the candidate should "be of the Christian religion."[28] While Adams intended to limit the highest office in Massachusetts to Christians, he did not intend to limit it to Protestants. Conceivably a Catholic could become governor of the commonwealth (assuming he was a resident of the state for seven years and worth more than £1000, Adams' other requirements). The convention discussed the issue on February 10, 1780. A motion was made that the word "Protestant" be inserted after the word "Christian" in the clause in order to define more clearly the requirements for office. The 1778 constitution had a similar requirement. By a vote of 40 to 26 the motion was defeated.[29]

By comparison with the proposed constitution of 1778, that of 1780 is not an anti-papal document. Catholics were given the right to worship according to their faith by Article II, and high public offices were open to them. Neither of these rights was a possibility during the colonial period or even as late as 1778. The proponents of toleration defeated the anti-papists at every turn in the Constitutional Convention. The proposed constitution of 1780 is clear evidence of a decline of anti-popery during the Revolution.

On March 2, 1780, the convention sent copies of the proposed constitution to the towns of Massachusetts which were to report their opinions of the document by June 7. As in 1778, special town meetings were to be held, open to all males over the age of twenty-one. If two-thirds of the voters approved the document, it would be adopted. During the spring of 1780, in most of the towns of Massachusetts, meetings were held, and the constitution was voted on, clause by clause. According to two of the foremost students of the Massachusetts Constitution, "the process of devising a new constitution for Massachusetts therefore partook of the nature of a dialogue between the representatives in Boston . . . and the citizens in their towns who gave or withheld their consent. The interchange provided the means for expressing shared assumptions about the polity of a free society."[30] The ratification process also provides an invaluable opportunity to measure shared assumptions about Catholicism.

IV

The returns from the town meetings on the 1780 constitution fill two large volumes in the Massachusetts Archives.[31] They vary widely. In some cases the townsmen simply indicated whether the majority approved or disapproved of the proposed constitution. In other cases the town clerk provided a detailed, clause-by-clause vote on the constitution. In still other cases communities proposed amendments to the clauses they found objectionable and submitted them with their reports. Taken as a whole, the returns allow for a statistical and geographic analysis of the decline of anti-popery in Massachusetts.

The decline of anti-popery can be traced by concentrating on two articles in the proposed constitution: Article II of the Declaration of Rights (hereafter Article II), and Chapter 2, Section 1, Article I of the frame of government (hereafter Chapter 2). The former article guaranteed freedom of conscience in Massachusetts, and the latter stipulated that the governor had to be a Christian. It is possible to measure the decline of anti-popery by evaluating how individual communities responded to these two articles. The overwhelming majority of Massachusetts communities endorsed religious freedom as expressed by Article II of the proposed constitution (Table 1). Of the towns that expressed an opinion, 97.7 percent (171 out of 175) approved Article II. In doing so, the

Table 1
County Voting on Article II and Chapter 2

Table 1 shows how the various counties in Massachusetts voted on the two articles. For the purpose of comparison, I have combined Barnstable and Plymouth counties, and the Maine counties of York, Cumberland, and Lincoln. Nantucket and Dukes counties did not participate in the process. I have provided two sets of figures, "Towns" and "Votes." The former is a breakdown of how the communities in the county that expressed an opinion voted on the particular article. The second figure shows how the voters voted at their town meetings. In many cases towns did not provide a breakdown of the voting on the constitution. The voting figures, while reliable for individual communities, are generally unreliable as a basis of comparison. For example, four communities in Essex County voted against Chapter 2, yet only one dissenting vote was recorded. By contrast, four towns in Plymouth/Barnstable voted against Chapter 2, and 217 negative votes were recorded, far more than the 23 affirmative votes recorded in the ten towns in the county that approved the article. The numbers of "Town" votes do not always correlate because communities did not always specifically respond on every article.

County	Article II				Chapter 2/Section 1/Article I			
	YEA TOWNS	NAY TOWNS	YEA VOTES	NAY VOTES	YEA TOWNS	NAY TOWNS	YEA VOTES	NAY VOTES
Berkshire	8	0	201	0	5	4	70	89
Bristol	9	0	1050	22	4	5	339	344
Essex	11	0	336	12	7	4	157	1
Hampshire	25	0	506	2	13	26	222	540
Middlesex	30	1	780	102	22	11	238	369
Plymouth/Barnstable	15	1	622	1	10	4	23	217
Suffolk	20	0	486	3	14	6	112	47
Worcester	40	2	969	54	19	18	121	309
York/Cumberland/Lincoln	13	0	76	4	7	5	0	0
TOTALS	171	4	5027	200	101	83	1282	1916

Sources: Town Returns, 1780, Massachusetts Archives, vols. 276-277. Oscar and Mary Handlin, *Popular Sources of Political Authority* (Cambridge, 1966).

people of Massachusetts unequivocally extended religious toleration to Catholics. Massachusetts voters did so knowingly. On May 30, 1780, the voters of Dunstable in Middlesex County, one of the few communities to vote against the article, did so because "these Sentences are so general as to Engage full Protection to the Idolatrous worshippers of the Church of Rome."[32] The majority of voters in Massachusetts did not find such protection a danger in 1780.

Toleration is not equality. While Massachusetts voters were willing to tolerate Catholicism, they were unwilling to extend equality to Catholics. As the voters of Wareham explained, "Roman Catholicks may not Enjoy equal privileges with Protestant Christians, yet nevertheless enjoy a Toleration." The reason why Catholics were denied full equality was simple. Many New Englanders tenaciously clung to the belief that "Papists are generally known to be something of a Restless Disposition and Their Religious Principles are of a Persecuting nature and Tendency when ever Power is in their hands."[33] Massachusetts voters, apparently united in the idea of religious toleration, were divided as to whether Catholics should be allowed to aspire to the highest office in the state. Catholicism was the major issue in the debate over the qualifications of the governor.

The town returns concerning Chapter 2 are much more evenly divided than those concerning Article II. Statewide, only 54.9 percent (101 out of 184) of the communities that expressed an opinion approved the article. Among the eighty-three towns that disapproved the article, 97.5 percent (81 out of 83) expressed concern that the use of the term "Christian" in the qualifications for governor was not exclusive enough and, as the voters of Greenwich feared, might allow "a Roman Catholic to be the First Magistrate in this state and because we View it Necessary to the preservation of a free Government and the security of the Protestant Cause that no Papist should be admitted."[34]

Despite the growth of toleration in theory, in practice many New Englanders clung to the old belief that Catholics should not be allowed to wield power over Protestants. Catholics could not be permitted to become governor because their faith itself endangered liberty. The voters of Wells, Maine, explained:

We cannot but think that the safety, peace and welfare of a protestant Commonwealth require that its Governor declare himself to be protestant since it has been found by Experience that a protestant People cannot be happy under the government of those who are of the Roman Church. The Authority and Jurisdiction which the Bishop of Rome claims over the whole Christian World and which all who belong to that Church must be presumed to acknowledge and submit to is We apprehend contrary to a fundamental principal of the Constitution. . . . We apprehend that a Papist is at least as unsuitable to be chosen and admitted to the Office of Governor in this Commonwealth, as one that makes no profession of the Christian Religion.[35]

Thus, while the overwhelming majority of Massachusetts voters were willing to concede toleration to Catholics, many would not trust Catholics with any civil political power. As the voters of Norton succinctly stated, "we think it Dangerous Even to leave an opening for a Roman Catholick to fill the first Seat in the Government."[36]

Table 2
Voting on Chapter 2: Eastern Massachusetts

County	Yea Towns	Nay Towns	Approval Rate (%)
Bristol	4	5	44.4
Essex	7	4	63.6
Middlesex	22	11	66.7
Plymouth/Barnstable	10	4	71.4
Suffolk	14	6	70.0
Totals	**57**	**30**	**65.5**

Table 3
Voting on Chapter 2: Western Masschusetts and Maine

County	Yea Towns	Nay Towns	Approval Rate (%)
Berkshire	5	4	55.6
Hampshire	13	26	33.3
Worcester	19	18	51.4
York/Cumberland/Lincoln	7	5	58.3
Totals	**44**	**53**	**45.3**

Not everyone feared the possibility (remote in the extreme) that a Catholic might become governor of Massachusetts. Almost 55 percent of Massachusetts communities approved of Chapter 2. While this is considerably less than the two-thirds majority the Constitutional Convention required for adoption, it indicates an overall decline of anti-popery.[37] A closer examination of the county votes reveals an interesting geographic pattern in the decline of anti-popery.

The voting patterns concerning Chapter 2 reveal this uneven decline. The counties with the highest approval rates for Chapter 2 are the easternmost counties of Plymouth/Barnstable, Suffolk, Middlesex, and Essex (Table 2). Of the 78 communities that expressed an opinion on Chapter 2 in this region, 53 (67.9 percent) approved the article. The exception to this pattern is Bristol County, where only 44.4 percent of communities (4 out of 9) approved Chapter 2. If the Bristol County figures are added to those of the other eastern counties, the approval rate is 65.5 percent (57 yeas out of 87 towns). Since anti-popery was far and away the number one concern of those who voted against the measure, it is safe to conclude that the overwhelming majority of voters, almost two-thirds, in eastern Massachusetts ceased to be concerned about a popish threat by 1780.

The voting pattern in western Massachusetts and Maine is much different (Table 3). The approval rate for Chapter 2 in the western counties of Worcester, Hampshire, and Berkshire, as well as the Maine counties of York, Cumberland, and Lincoln, is 45.3 percent. Of 97 communities in the two regions, only 44 approved of Chapter 2. If we subtract the two Hampshire County towns, Becket and New Marlborough, which disapproved of Chapter 2, not because of fear of Catholicism but because of the property requirement for governor, then the approval rate for Chapter 2 is 47.4 percent.

The town returns for the 1780 constitution clearly demonstrate that the decline of anti-popery was more advanced in eastern Massachusetts than in western Massachusetts and Maine. The approval rate for Chapter 2 in eastern Massachusetts is 18 percent higher than that of western Massachusetts and Maine. Put another way, 52.5 percent of the communities in western Massachusetts and Maine *disapproved* of Chapter 2 because of their anti-popery, compared to a 34.4 percent disapproval rate in eastern Massachusetts. Although both regions were theoretically committed to religious freedom as expressed in Article II, the people of western Massachusetts and Maine were far more concerned about popery in 1780 than their neighbors and relatives in eastern Massachusetts.

What accounts for the regional disparity? The people of eastern Massachusetts had far more contact with Catholics than their counterparts in western Massachusetts and Maine. Although contact with the French sometimes bred conflict, it also bred familiarity and toleration. Contact with the French undermined many of the previously held assumptions many New Englanders had about Catholics in general and Frenchmen in particular. The 70 percent approval for Chapter 2 in Suffolk County, where the French spent most of their time, is evidence for the correlation between contact with the French and the development of toleration.

The experience of Rhode Island supports the notion that prolonged contact with the French encouraged toleration for Catholics. General Rochambeau's army spent eleven months in Newport during 1780 and 1781. The French sojourn in Rhode Island was remarkably tranquil.[38] In February 1783 Rhode Island legislators adopted an act which declared "That all the Rights and Privileges of the Protestant citizens of this State . . . are hereby fully extended to Roman Catholic citizens."[39] While the legislators may have acted under the influence of Rhode Island's famous colonial tradition of religious toleration, they may also have been influenced by the French soldiers and sailors who visited the state during the war.[40] Taken together, events in Rhode Island and constitutional voting in Suffolk County, Massachusetts, suggest that contact with the French encouraged religious toleration.

The presence of French sailors does not completely explain the decline of anti-popery. More than 47 percent of the communities in the western part of the state and Maine also approved Chapter 2. Statewide, the overwhelming majority of Massachusetts voters endorsed limited toleration. While the presence of French Catholic allies encouraged the growth of toleration and the decline of anti-popery, their presence does not adequately explain such a tremendous cultural shift. Rather, the decline of anti-popery was the product of the efforts made by the Whig elite to promote toleration. This is reflected in the pattern of the voting according to region.

The key to the geographic pattern in voting is the system of cultural diffusion in revolutionary Massachusetts. Historian Van Beck Hall has analyzed Massachusetts politics during the 1780s. Hall's frame of analysis is a "commercial-cosmopolitan continuum" on which he places each of the communities in the commonwealth. Hall based the commercial-cosmopolitan continuum on several economic and cultural factors such as commercial activity, the presence of cultural institutions—newspapers, courthouses, and churches—as well as political representation and participation. Based on his analysis, Hall placed the communities in Massachusetts in three categories: "Group A" towns, which dominated the social and cultural life of Massachusetts; "Group B" towns, which participated in the cultural life of the state but did not direct it; and "Group C" towns, which had a weak connection to society at large and contributed little to the cultural life of the commonwealth.

While Hall found all three types of community in every region of the state, he found that "Group A" towns were most numerous in eastern Massachusetts, while "Group C" towns predominated in western Massachusetts and Maine. The voting patterns on Chapter 2 of the 1780 Massachusetts Constitution conform to Hall's typology.[41]

In the case of anti-popery, cultural change began in the cultural centers and radiated out to the hinterland. The predominance of "Group A" towns in eastern Massachusetts explains the overwhelming vote in the region in favor of Chapter 2. The Whig campaign for toleration was most successful in the cultural centers of the state. Looked at another way, consider the votes of "Group A" towns in the counties where Chapter 2 was defeated. In Bristol County, the only eastern Massachusetts county to vote against Chapter 2, Hall has identified three "Group A" towns, Dartmouth, Taunton and New Bedford.[42] New Bedford did not record a vote on the issue, but both Dartmouth and Taunton voted in favor of Chapter 2 of the Constitution.[43] "Group A" towns in western Massachusetts and Maine followed a similar pattern. The decline of anti-popery began in the cultural centers and spread to the smaller communities of New England.

Anti-popery declined first in communities like Boston, Salem, Worcester, and Northampton which were social, political, and economic centers. These communities had the strongest ties to the outside world. They had the most influential ministers and politicians. Massachusetts newspapers came from the presses of those communities. While the residents of "Group B" and "Group C" communities were certainly opinionated, the residents of "Group A" towns were able to dominate the political, economic, and cultural development of the state. During the Revolution, the Whig leadership, centered in the "Group A" towns, became committed to toleration and used their advantages as cultural leaders to win the agreement of the majority of Massachusetts voters.

The citizens of New Hampshire, like those of Massachusetts, endured a long bout of constitution-making, lasting from 1779 until 1784. When they finally adopted their constitution, Granite Staters declared that, "Every individual has a natural and unalienable right to worship God according to the dictates of his own conscience."[44] Like their southern neighbors, New Hampshire lawmakers placed limits on religious freedom by denying political offices to all but Protestants. The similarities between the constitutions of Massachusetts and New Hampshire with respect to religion is not coincidental. The men who drafted the New Hampshire Constitution consciously imitated their Bay State counterparts who preceded them in defining the parameters of religious toleration.[45] While the same detailed responses to the constitution that exist for Massachusetts are not available for New Hampshire, it is likely that attitudes in the Granite State were similar to those in Massachusetts. New Englanders were willing to concede limited religious toleration to Catholics in the aftermath of the Revolution.

V

Between June 8 and June 16, 1780, the Massachusetts Constitutional Convention held its fourth, and final, session. A committee tabulated the local returns. Although a two-thirds majority was not reached on every article, as the vote on Chapter 2 indicates, according to Samuel Eliot Morison, "every article received a bare majority."[46] The convention voted that the new constitution would take effect after the election of the first governor on October 25, 1780.

The extension of religious toleration to Catholics was the result of a long, complicated process. New Englanders undermined the anti-papal persuasion when they began to apply it to the British during the Episcopal Controversy of the 1760s. When they accused the British of popery, they girded themselves for war. At the same time New Englanders had so changed the message and images of anti-popery that they lost their relevance. When New Englanders opposed the British, they entered a conflict that was more immediate, and more important, to them than their inherited conflict with popery. Once the anti-papal persuasion facilitated the identification of the British as tyrannical, it became unnecessary intellectual baggage for New Englanders. Indeed, Whig leaders actively, and successfully, promoted toleration. As a consequence of the Revolutionary War, anti-popery lost its relevance to most New Englanders. The willingness of almost all Massachusetts towns to approve Article II indicates that anti-popery was in steep decline by 1780.

After the Revolution, some New Englanders tried unsuccessfully to whip up the old phantom of popery. For example, at the Massachusetts Ratifying Convention, which voted on the United States Constitution in January 1788, Amos Singletary of Sutton in Worcester County (a community that had voted against Chapter 2) expressed concern that there were no religious qualifications in the proposed federal constitution because "a papist or an infidel were as eligible as" a Protestant for office. Singletary was a throwback to the old anti-papal persuasion. Despite the criticism of Singletary, the convention approved the United States Constitution without mandating that Catholics be excluded from office. General John Brooke of Medford spoke for the new, tolerant majority when he responded to Singletary, "If good men are appointed, government will be administered well."[47]

Was the rise of toleration and the diminution of anti-popery simply a temporary measure prompted by the expediency of war, or did it signal a more substantive cultural shift on behalf of New Englanders? The experience of the first Catholic congregation in New England reveals that, though there existed a residue on anti-popery, the commitment to toleration among the revolutionary generation was largely sincere. Beginning in 1788 Boston Catholics tested the spirit of Protestant toleration when they began to worship publicly.

NOTES

1. Recent works concerned with the rise of sectarianism during and after the Revolution are Nathan O. Hatch, *The Democratization of American Christianity* (New Haven, 1989); and Jon Butler, *Awash in a Sea of Faith: Christianizing the American People* (Cambridge, Mass., 1990). Also see Stephen Marini, *Radical Sects of Revolutionary New England* (Cambridge, Mass., 1982); and William McCloughlin, *Isaac Backus and the American Pietistic Tradition* (Boston, 1967).

2. See Gayle Kathleen Pluta Brown, "A Controversy Not Merely Religious: The Anti-Catholic Tradition in Colonial New England" (Ph.D. dissertation, University of Iowa, 1990). Brown (p. 289) argues that Catholics did not achieve religious freedom anywhere in New England until 1807 in Vermont.

3. See Arthur J. Riley, *Catholicism in New England until 1788* (Baltimore, 1936), chap. 7. For the development of religious freedom in Connecticut, see Maria Louise Greene, *The Development of Religious Liberty in Connecticut* (Boston, 1905). For the New Hampshire Constitution, see Charles B. Kinney, *Church and State: The Struggle for Separation in New Hampshire, 1630-1900* (New York, 1955). For the Massachusetts Constitution, see Willi Paul Adams, *The First American Constitutions: Republican Ideology and the Making of the State Constitutions in the Revolutionary Era* (Chapel Hill, 1980); Samuel Eliot Morison, "The Struggle over the Adoption of the Constitution of Massachusetts, 1780," *MHSP*, 50 (1916-17), 353-411; Samuel Eliot Morison, *A History of the Constitution of Massachusetts* (Boston, 1917); Ronald M. Peters, *The Massachusetts Constitution of 1780: A Social Compact* (Amherst, 1978); and Robert J. Taylor, "Construction of the Massachusetts Constitution," American Antiquarian Society *Proceedings*, 2nd series, 90 (1980), 317-346. Also useful is Jacob C. Meyer, *Church and State in Massachusetts from 1740 to 1833: A Chapter in the History of Religious Freedom* (New York, 1930, repr. 1968). The town returns in the Massachusetts Archives and the Massachusetts Historical Society have been collected and published in an invaluable volume by Oscar and Mary Handlin eds., *The Popular Sources of Political Authority: Documents on the Massachusetts Constitution of 1780* (Cambridge, Mass., 1966).

4. The Draft of the Proposed Constitution is in MA 156:200-235. The Minutes of the Constitutional Convention, February 1778, are in MA 156:236-293.

5. Draft of the Proposed Constitution, MA 156:230.

6. Draft of the Proposed Constitution, MA 156:230.

7. Minutes of the Convention, MA 156:286-87.

8. The town returns for the 1778 constitution are in MA 156:304-432.

9. Return of the Town of Greenwich, May 3, 1778, MA 156:327; Return of the Town of Hardwick, May 11, 1778, MA 156:329; "Boston Town Meeting, June 1, 1778," Boston Record Commissioners, *Report of the Record Commissioners*, 38 vols. (Boston, 1876-1908), XXVI, 22-24.

10. *Independent Chronicle*, April 9, 1778.

11. *Independent Chronicle*, April 30, 1778.

12. *Independent Chronicle*, April 30, 1778.

13. Theophilus Parsons, Jr., *Memoir of Theophilus Parsons* (Boston, 1861), 386.

14. John Sexton argued that the rejection of the constitution was an unmistakable popular verdict. "By an overwhelming ratio of five to one, the people of Massachusetts thus equivalently demanded a constitutional guarantee of freedom of worship for Catholics, as well as for other non-Protestants." Robert H. Lord, John Sexton, and Edward Harrington, *History of the Archdiocese of Boston in Its Various Stages of Development, 1604-1943*, 3 vols. (Boston, 1943), I, 299. The evidence does not support such an optimistic conclusion. The people of Massachusetts did not reject the constitution of 1778 because of its restrictions on Catholics. Their rejection was not an explicit demand for toleration.

15. Handlin and Handlin, *Sources*, 22-24, quotation, p. 23; Taylor, "Construction of the Massachusetts Constitution," 319-321; Morison, "The Struggle over the Adoption of the Massachusetts Constitution," 354-355.

16. *Journal of the Convention for Framing a Constitution for the State of Massachusetts Bay, 1779-1780* (Boston, 1832) lists 293 delegates. According to Samuel Eliot Morison, the largest number of votes on any question was 247. Morison, "Struggle over the Adoption of the Massachusetts Constitution," 356. The only areas that were not represented were Martha's Vineyard and Nantucket, which were isolated and harassed by British vessels from Newport, and the area of Maine east of the Penobscot River, which was occupied by the British. Handlin and Handlin, *Sources*, 24; Morison, "Struggle over the Adoption of the Massachusetts Constitution," 356, n. 2.

17. *Journal of the Convention*, 28-30.

18. John Adams to William D. Williamson, February 25, 1812, Maine Historical Society, photocopy, Adams Papers, MHS.

19. See John Adams, "The Report of a Constitution or Form of Government for the Commonwealth of Massachusetts," in Charles Francis Adams, ed., *Works of John Adams*, 10 vols. (Boston, 1850-56), IV, 213-267.

20. This is the text as it was finally adopted by the convention. It differs from Adams' version very little. For Adams' version, see Adams, "Report of a Constitution," 221.

21. *Journal of the Convention*, 37.

22. John Adams to Isaac Smith, Sr., May 16, 1780, Letterbook, Adams Papers, MHS.

23. The committee that drafted Article III consisted of Samuel Adams, Caleb Strong, Robert Treat Paine, Theophilus Parsons, Timothy Danielson, Rev. David Sanford, and Rev. Noah Alden. *Journal of the Convention*, 39. According to John Adams, Article III "was the only Article which I omitted to draw. I could not Satisfy my own Judgement with any Article that I thought would be accepted." Adams to Williamson, February 25, 1812. For a thorough treatment of Article III, see Meyer, *Church and State in Massachusetts*, chapter 4.

24. *Journal of the Convention*, 38-46, quotation, p. 39; Meyer, *Church and State in Massachusetts*, 106-109.

25. Robert Treat Paine wrote in his diary on January 21, 1780: "Convention adjourned . . . very cold, Paths filled with blown snow, expecting difficulty passing Teams by reasons of the Depth of Snow." Robert Treat Paine, Diary, Robert Treat Paine Papers, MHS.

26. *Journal of the Convention*, 77. The committee consisted of John Pickering of Salem, Samuel Phillips of Andover, Samuel Adams, Stephen Hall of Medford, and Willis Hall of Sutton.

27. *Journal of the Convention*, 88-89, 119.

28. Adams, "Report on the Constitution," 245. The requirements were in Chapter II, Section 1, Article II of the constitution.

29. *Journal of the Convention*, 97.

30. Handlin and Handlin, *Sources*, 19.

31. MA 276, 277. A few of the missing returns are in the Town Records, MHS. All of the returns have been collected and published in Handlin and Handlin, *Sources*.

32. Return of Dunstable, May 30, 1780, MA 277:10; Handlin and Handlin, *Sources*, 640-642.

33. Return of Wareham, May 29, 1780, MA 277:46; Handlin and Handlin, *Sources*, 711-713.

34. Return of Greenwich, June 5, 1780, MA 276:51; Handlin and Handlin, *Sources*, 561-562. The two towns that objected to the governor's qualifications for other reasons were Becket and New Marlborough in Hampshire County. They both objected to the property requirement for the office. See MA 276:11, 15; Handlin and Handlin, *Sources*, 476, 481.

35. Return of York, May 22, 1780, MA 277:56; Handlin and Handlin, *Sources*, 734-740. See also the returns of Belchertown, MA 276:40, Handlin and Handlin, *Sources*, 538-542; Georgetown, Handlin and Handlin, *Sources*, 627-628; Lexington, MA 277:16, Handlin and Handlin, *Sources*, 659-662; Northfield, MA 276:57, Handlin and Handlin, *Sources*, 571-572; Palmer, MA 276:60, Handlin and Handlin, *Sources*, 587-590; Sutton, MA 277:172, Handlin and Handlin, *Sources*, 876-883; Westhampton, MA 276:70, Handlin and Handlin, *Sources*, 615-617; Williamsburg, MA 276:73, Handlin and Handlin, *Sources*, 624-626.

36. Return of Norton, June 5, 1780, MA 276:34; Handlin and Handlin, *Sources*, 523-526.

37. Samuel Eliot Morison has demonstrated that the Constitutional Convention was remarkably flexible about its two-thirds requirement in interpreting the town returns. See Morison, "The Struggle over the Adoption of the Constitution," 396-401.

38. See Howard C. Rice, Jr., and Anne S. K. Brown, eds., *The American Campaigns of Rochambeau's Army, 1780, 1781, 1782, 1783*, 2 vols. (Providence, 1972); Lee Kennett, *French Forces in America, 1780-1783* (Westport, Conn., 1977); and Elaine Crane, *A Dependent People: Newport, Rhode Island in the Revolution* (New York, 1985).

39. "Roman Catholics in Rhode Island," *MHSC*, 3rd series, 5 (1836), 244. Also see Sidney S. Rider, "An Inquiry Concerning the Origin of the Clause in the Laws of Rhode Island Disenfranchising Catholics," *Rhode Island Historical Tracts*, 2nd series, I (Providence, 1889), 7-53. Connecticut adopted a similar act in 1791.

40. Recently Alison G. Olson has challenged Rhode Island's reputation for religious tolerance. See Alison G. Olson, "Rhode Island, Massachusetts, and the Question of Religious Diversity in Colonial New England," *NEQ*, 65 (1992), 93-116. Certainly anti-Catholicism was as vibrant in Rhode Island during the colonial period as in the other New England colonies.

41. Van Beck Hall, *Politics without Parties: Massachusetts, 1780-1791* (London, 1972). For a discussion of Hall's methodology and categorization, see chap. 1.

42. For a map identifying the "Group A" towns, see Hall, *Politics without Parties*, 10-11.

43. Return of Dartmouth, May 22, 1780, MA 276:29, Handlin and Handlin, *Sources*, 509-510; Return of Taunton, May 25, 1780, MA 276:38, Handlin and Handlin, *Sources*, 531-532.

44. Nathaniel Bouton et al. eds., *New Hampshire Provincial and State Papers*, 30 vols. (Concord, NH., 1867-1910), IX, 853. The most complete discussion of freedom of religion in New Hampshire is Kinney, *Church and State*.

45. See Kinney, *Church and State*, 119-125.

46. Morison, "Struggle over the Adoption of the Massachusetts Constitution," 401.

47. *Debates and Proceedings in the Convention of the Commonwealth of Massachusetts, 1788* (Boston, 1856), 143.

8

How Would Our Fathers Have Stared: New England, Popery, and the Reverend John Thayer

I

On September 4, 1788, the *Independent Chronicle* reported the rather startling news that "Mr. John Thayer, late a protestant minister of the puritan sect in Boston . . . is shortly expected to arrive at Boston, in the character of a Popish Bishop." Although the editor of the *Chronicle* guaranteed the source of the information as a "good authority," the report was only half true.[1] John Thayer, a Catholic priest, though no bishop, did plan to return to his native Boston in 1788. Thayer did not arrive, however, until January 1790. Whether Thayer had been "a minister of the puritan sect" or not was a matter of some debate. He was certainly the first New England native to convert to Catholicism, accept holy orders, and return to his native region to minister to his spiritual brethren.

John Thayer was a cultural pioneer who personified the decline of anti-popery in revolutionary New England. By temperament he was singularly ill-qualified for his task. Thayer was more committed to intrigue and tireless self-promotion than to the spiritual needs of his congregation. Nonetheless, his experiences, and those of the fledgling Catholic congregation in Boston, reveal the extent of the freedom of conscience codified in the Massachusetts Constitution of 1780. Father Thayer's turbulent tenure in Boston reveals that New Englanders took religious freedom seriously and respected the rights, if not the dogmas, of the small number of Catholics in their midst. The Catholic congregation suffered more from the problems wrought by its priests than from any residual anti-popery among its Protestant neighbors.

II

Boston Catholics first worshiped publicly on November 2, 1788. The Boston congregation was drawn from the small French community in the city as well as a growing number of Irish immigrants and a scattering of American converts. All told, the congregation did not number more than one hundred persons. The French parishioners were the minority in terms of numbers but the majority as far as wealth and influence. The setting of the first public Mass was most ironic. The Catholics met in what was known as "the Huguenot Chapel" on School Street. Boston's first Catholic church had been a Huguenot meeting house from 1716 to 1748. From its pulpit Reverend Andrew Le Mercier had exhorted New England soldiers to conquer the anti-Christian papists at Louisbourg in 1745. In 1788 the city's small Catholic congregation rechristened the building as the Church of the Holy Cross.[2]

If any aged Bostonians remembered Le Mercier's sermon, it would have been impolitic for them to mention it in November 1788. Protestant New Englanders regarded the public celebration of Mass with curiosity but without overt hostility. A mixed group of Catholics and Protestants attended Boston's first mass. According to the account in the *Independent Chronicle*, "the concourse of people assembled was so great, as to create an apprehension of some unfortunate accident from the falling of the gallery." Since there were less than one hundred practicing Catholics in Boston at the time, curious Protestants must have made up a large part, if not the majority, of the congregation that attended the Mass. Rather than attack the Catholic ceremony on School Street, so many Protestant Bostonians crowded the church "that they were obliged to make temporary props to this building."[3]

Many New England Protestants, from the soldiers at Louisbourg in 1745, to John Adams in Philadelphia in 1774, to the Newporters who attended Admiral Ternay's funeral in 1780, had been fascinated as well as repelled by Catholic ceremony. The opening of the Catholic church on School Street elicited much curiosity and little hostility. The *Herald of Freedom* published a letter, purportedly from a French resident of Boston to a friend, which said, "A Roman Catholick Chapel is at length opened in this metropolis. This will be pleasing to many of our countrymen. The liberal part of the inhabitants (and to their honour there are but few who are not liberal) are highly pleased with it; and many of the Boston people attend on the worship of god according to the mode prescribed by the Roman Church."[4] That New Englanders casually accepted the celebration of Mass in their foremost city is testimony to the steady decline of anti-popery after the American Revolution.

Abbé Claude Florent Bouchard de la Poterie celebrated the first Mass in Boston. Poterie was a former French naval chaplain with a mysterious past. Reverend Jeremy Belknap described the priest as "a clergyman who was dismissed from ye French fleet in disgrace."[5] Born in Craon in 1751, Poterie had been an unsuccessful parish priest when he left France in early 1788 as a naval chaplain bound for the West Indies. Poterie came to Boston with the fleet of the Marquis de Sainneville in August 1788. When Sainneville left in September, Abbé Poterie remained in the city. Apparently, the cleric's superiors knew of his desertion but decided to ignore it, grateful to be rid of the troublesome priest.[6]

Poterie apparently intended to go to Quebec, but the leaders of the congregation of Catholics in Boston convinced him to stay with them. In early November 1788, Poterie took charge of the small congregation. A shameless, dishonest self-promoter, Abbé Poterie was ill-qualified to lead the congregation. Within six months he had run the small parish into debt. He unsuccessfully solicited donations from Boston Protestants. In the spring of 1789, the archbishop of Paris informed the Boston congregation that he had stripped Poterie of his faculties before he left France. As a consequence, Bishop John Carroll, the head of the American church, dismissed Poterie in May 1789. Poterie went to Quebec to try and make his fortune.[7]

The abrupt departure of Poterie meant that Boston Catholics did not have a cleric to minister to their needs during the summer of 1789. In September a French priest named Louis de Rousselet came to Boston to visit a relative. Abbé Rousselet had spent the previous seven years living with relatives in Dutch Guyana. Bishop Carroll appointed Rousselet to fill the vacant pastorship of the Church of the Holy Cross. Boston Catholics seemed satisfied with the new priest. His transition to his new parish was deceptively easy.[8]

Rousselet encountered trouble when the discredited Poterie returned to New England in December 1789. Poterie had tried unsuccessfully to secure a position in Quebec. He returned to Boston determined to take back his position as pastor of the Church of the Holy Cross. He claimed his dismissal was part of a Jesuit plot against him and published his accusations in a pamphlet.[9]

Poterie insisted that Rousselet permit him to participate in the Christmas services. When Father Rousselet refused, Poterie, like a spoiled child, disrupted the services.[10] On Christmas Eve 1789, as Father Rousselet celebrated midnight Mass at the Church of the Holy Cross, a group of "troublesome people" disrupted the service by overturning and destroying the pews in the church. The following day, William Bentley, a Unitarian minister from Salem, attended afternoon services at the church. Bentley noted, "the behaviour of the crowd was rude, but there was not a disposition to countenance such behaviour in the sober people, & it was principally attributed to the uncomfortable situation in the audience [the pews had not been replaced] that any improprieties ensued."[11] Four days later, Father Rousselet apologized for the disturbances and announced that the Christmas Eve ceremonies the following year would take place at five a.m. on Christmas morning to avoid a recurrence.[12]

It seems strange that Rousselet, the victim of the Christmas disruptions, should apologize for the disturbances. However, only if Poterie was the author of the disturbances, would it explain why his victim, Rousselet, thought it was necessary to apologize publicly. Rousselet's apology was directed at the Protestant community which had demonstrated tolerance for the infant Catholic congregation. Rousselet tried to maintain the dignity of his faith before the Protestant community in the wake of the embarrassing spectacle wrought by his disgruntled rival. Poterie did not act alone. Unfortunately the identities of his accomplices are impossible to determine. Whether they were anti-papists who found themselves in a strange alliance with a former Catholic priest, or a faction of Catholics from the congregation who opposed Rousselet is unknown.

Poterie took his controversy with Rousselet before the reading public in January 1790. He addressed two vicious attacks on his successor "To the Impartial Public," which were published by the *Herald of Freedom*. Poterie called Rousselet: "this very poor orator and bad preacher, not able to persuade a single proselyte, but made to scare everyone by his rough speech and insupportable accent, and by his eyes dark and hollow, this discordant and melancholy singer, in a word this *jesuit*."[13] Whether he did so intentionally or not, Poterie obliquely used the rhetoric of anti-popery when he called Rousselet, who was a Capuchin priest, a Jesuit and when he insulted his appearance. Coming from a former Catholic priest in 1790, the attack was weak and ineffective. The matter was settled once and for all on January 19, 1790, when the Catholic congregation in Boston publicly declared that "the whole congregation have dismissed the Abbé de la Poterie, being fully and in every respect dissatisfied with him."[14] Poterie remained in Boston, pathetic and poverty-stricken, for several months before returning to France.[15] Rousselet's conflict with Poterie was a precursor to the troubles he endured at the hands of John Thayer.

III

The details of John Thayer's early life are sketchy. He was born in Boston on May 15, 1758 to Cornelius Thayer and Sarah Plaisted Thayer. According to Thayer, he was born into "a family in easy circumstances."[16] Raised as a Congregationalist, John Thayer entered Yale during the mid-1770s. Thayer claimed, "At the conclusion of my studies, I was made a Minister of the Puritan sect, and exercised my functions for two years, applying myself to the study of Holy Scripture, and to preaching."[17] One of Thayer's Yale classmates, Noah Webster, remembered a different version of events. Webster claimed that Thayer:

obtained some knowledge of the Latin and Greek languages. With this he went to New-Haven, and by some means, or other, he introduced himself (for he possessed unparalleled impudence) to the acquaintance of some gentlemen, who recommended him to the notice of the President and tutors of the college. . . . Being a total stranger and without money, the gentlemen of the town agreed to board and lodge him, each a certain period, and the governors of the college consented to give him his tuition. He thus subsisted on charity, till the last year of his residence at college, when he was guilty of some disorderly conduct, for which he was dismissed with marks of disgrace. He soon fell upon a plan to get a living. He pretended he had been honored with the usual degree of Bachelor of Arts and forged a license to preach.[18]

Circumstantial evidence supports Webster's version of events rather than that of Thayer. Thayer never received a degree from Yale, nor was he ever ordained a Protestant clergyman, nor did he receive a license to preach.[19]

The contradiction between Thayer's account of his education and Webster's reveals a tendency for self-promotion that Thayer exhibited throughout his life. Thayer demonstrated a remarkable ability to bend the truth to enhance his image or advance his interests. For example, from August 1780 until May 1781, Thayer served as chaplain in Captain William Burbeck's Company at Castle William, commanded by Governor John Hancock. He later claimed that he had been Governor Hancock's personal chaplain.[20] John Thayer was an ambitious man who was willing to lie to advance his career.

While serving as a chaplain at Castle William, Thayer became acquainted with many French officers and resolved to go to Europe "to learn the languages which are most in use, and to acquire a knowledge of the constitution of states, of the manners, customs, laws, and government of the principal nations, in order to acquire, by this political knowledge, a greater consequence in my own country."[21] Until his departure, Thayer had failed to satisfy his vast ambition. He desired to become a person of consequence, yet he had failed at Yale, and his tenure at Castle William, long after the war had moved to the south, was inconsequential. Thayer set out for Europe seeking the notoriety that had eluded him in New England.

At the end of 1781 John Thayer arrived in France. It is unclear how he financed his trip, though his Yale experience indicates that Thayer was adept at convincing wealthy gentlemen that he was a young man worthy of financial patronage. Thayer claimed to have arrived in France "strongly prejudiced both against the nation and the religion of that country." When he became seriously ill shortly after his arrival in France, Thayer remembered that his "first concern was to forbid, that any Catholick Priest should be suffered to come near me, such was my attachment to my own sect."[22] Thayer recovered and he spent the next ten months studying French and traveling. At the end of 1782 he spent three months in Britain before returning to France on his way to Italy.

John Thayer spent a year in Italy. He shed his anti-papal prejudices as he spent more time among Catholics. Thayer wrote, "during my stay in France, I had formed a less unfavourable idea of the Catholick Religion, and my intercourse with the Italians contributed also to remove my prejudices against them." Thayer was especially impressed by the generosity and kindness of the Italians to him, "a stranger, . . . an avowed Protestant."[23] As he shed his prejudices, Thayer became open to other aspects of Italian culture, most notably Catholicism.

While visiting Rome, John Thayer conversed with Catholic clergymen about the differences between Protestantism and Catholicism. He did not intend to convert but "to form an exact knowledge of Catholick doctrine." After several days of conversation with an unnamed Jesuit, Thayer "could not but remark a wonderful harmony through the whole system of the Catholic Religion and a wisdom which seemed to have something divine." Thayer was attracted by the intellectual cohesion he saw in Catholicism, which he felt contrasted sharply to the sectarianism and confusion among Protestants.[24]

At the time that Thayer began to investigate the doctrines of Catholicism, a thirty-five-year-old French nobleman, Benoit-Joseph Labré, died in Rome. Labré had lived as a "holy beggar" among Rome's poor. After Labré's death, miracles were said to occur to those who possessed relics made from his clothing.[25] Thayer, who claimed "of all my prejudices against Catholicks, the deepest rooted was a formal disbelief of the miraculous facts which are said to have happened among them," scoffed at reports of the miracles after Labré's death. He set out to investigate the miracles and became "fully convinced of the reality of each one." By the spring of 1783 Thayer was torn between Catholicism and "all the prejudices which I sucked from my infancy." Finally, after reading a book entitled *Manifesto di un cavaliero convertito alla religione catholica*, the story of the conversion of a Protestant knight to Catholicism, Thayer fell to his knees in tears and vowed to convert to Catholicism.[26] Perhaps Thayer saw himself as a Protestant knight who had finally seen the error of his ways.

On May 25, 1783, John Thayer publicly renounced Protestantism and embraced Catholicism in Rome. Thayer's conversion was a noteworthy event. An Englishman wrote from Rome on June 11: "We have just now before us a conversion which has made a great noise amongst our countrymen in this city. The convert was a Presbyterian teacher at Boston in New England."[27] According to the superior of the Sulpician Seminary in Paris, Jacques André Emery, "[Pope] Pius VI honored [Thayer] with many audiences, and together with the spiritual favours he conferred on him, he made him a present of a new medal on which was engraven his likeness. . . . Many of their Eminences the Cardinals gave him the kind reception that his virtues justly claimed."[28] For a poor Protestant, expelled from Yale in disgrace, Thayer's first days as a Catholic must have been heady ones. By his conversion, John Thayer had finally become a man of consequence.

Not everyone was favorably impressed with Thayer's conversion. Benjamin Franklin, who had encountered Thayer in Paris, both before and after his conversion, sarcastically quipped, "It would be pleasant if a Boston man should come to be Pope. Stranger things have happened."[29] Noah Webster wrote of his former classmate: "This conversion of a little impudent fellow, who was often kicked out of good company in America, was despised by all knew him—publicly disgraced, and guilty of every species of meanness, and of some crimes that should have cost him his ears; this conversion is celebrated by the Roman Catholics thro Europe, and affords them a new and singular cause of triumph."[30] Thayer was a controversial figure in New England, and his conversion did little to improve his reputation. Despite, or perhaps because of, the criticism of his fellow New Englanders, Thayer resolved to study for the priesthood.

John Thayer returned to Paris in 1783 and entered the College of Navarre. After a year of preparation, he entered the Seminary of St. Sulpice on October 18, 1784. Thayer was more successful at the seminary than he had been at Yale. His superior wrote of the convert, "During the whole of the time he was in the seminary never was any one more faithful in observing all the exercises and practices, more obedient to the will of the Superiors, or more charitable towards his brethren."[31] A Scot who met Thayer in 1787 commented: "He had nothing gloomy or melancholy about him, but was on the contrary cheerful and communicative. He entered fully and without reserve on the subject of his conversion, and expressed the most unequivocal and firm persuasion of the truth of the Catholic religion."[32] On the eve of Trinity Sunday 1787, John Thayer was ordained as a Catholic priest.

During his seminary years, Thayer prepared his spiritual autobiography, *An Account of the Conversion of the Reverend John Thayer*, which was published in London in 1787. Thayer's pamphlet was an instant international success. The conversion narrative was translated into six languages and went through many editions.[33] In *An Account of the Conversion*, Thayer not only announced his religious transformation but his "desire to return to my own country, in hopes, notwithstanding my unworthiness, to be an instrument of the conversion of my countrymen."[34] This statement was the source of the rumor that Thayer would soon return to New England.

Thayer did not return to America immediately after his ordination. He spent 1788 working among the poor in London's Southwark district, where he claimed that he had converted "thirty-six heretics, besides a great many whose conversion, though not complete was far advanced when he left London."[35] Thayer returned to Paris in June 1789 before he finally set sail for America.

John Thayer arrived in Baltimore on December 16, 1789 and he traveled to Philadelphia with Bishop John Carroll. Carroll was impressed by the convert's zeal but was wary of his ambition.[36] Like the prodigal son, John Thayer returned to his native Boston on January 2, 1790. As the first New England-born Catholic priest, John Thayer personified the decline of anti-popery in his native New England. His behavior before his departure and his widely celebrated conversion made his visit, in the words of a Protestant minister, "a subject of curious nature."[37] John Thayer would test the limits of toleration in post-Revolutionary New England.

IV

John Thayer celebrated his first Mass in Boston on January 10, 1790. The converted priest described the experience to his former superior: "they came in crowds to hear me; they were very curious to know what was our belief. The toleration granted here to all sects procured me a favourable opportunity of instructing in the Roman Catholic Religion." New Englanders were curious about the priest, if not respectful. Thayer lamented, "the Protestants always testified the same eagerness to hear me, but the greatest number went not further." The intriguing prospect of hearing the liturgy in the nasal tones of a native New Englander more likely drew Bostonians to Thayer's services than a desire to learn the mysteries of Catholicism.[38]

Bishop Carroll hoped that the two priests in Boston would cooperate, particularly after the damage done to the congregation by Poterie. In February 1790 he wrote: "In Boston so far our beginnings have not been auspicious because of the imprudence and bad faith of [Poterie]. . . . He has two successors, of whom one is Mr. Thayer, known undoubtedly to the Congregation at least by reputation. I should wish that both of them should stay for I have found that great inconveniences follow when a priest is all alone." As one of the few priests in America when he returned from Europe in 1776, Carroll well understood professional isolation. His hope for cooperation between the priests at Boston was ill founded. "I see however that this cannot be," he wrote, "because the means of livelihood are inadequate for two and other reasons which cannot be mentioned."[39] The principal reason, which Carroll neglected to mention, was the ambition of John Thayer.

Father Thayer schemed against Father Rousselet from the moment he arrived in Boston. On January 6, 1790, Thayer wrote a letter to Bishop Carroll describing the situation in Boston: "the Catholics are exceedingly few, not above fifty or sixty at most, and those very poor for the most part. I am positive that they must have great difficulty to maintain a single priest much less can they maintain two of us." Thayer had a solution for the problem. He advised the bishop "to place Mr. Rousselet in another parish as soon as possible." Thayer explained that Rousselet "will be in some measure useless here on account of his language. . . . Mr. Rousselet is long and tedious in disposing his chapel exercises." Thayer consistently denigrated Rousselet in private and public throughout the time they shared together in Boston. He did so to undermine Rousselet's credibility and to orchestrate the ouster of the French priest.[40]

By late March the presence of the two priests caused a rift in the small, troubled Boston parish. Baury de Bellerive, a merchant, and Mamie Masson, one of the church wardens, led the French portion of Boston's Catholic community. Not surprisingly, the French in the parish supported Father Rousselet in his growing conflict with Father Thayer.[41] The Irish parishioners, generally poorer than the French, constituted a growing numerical majority in the parish. The presence of the English-speaking Thayer encouraged Boston's Irish residents to attend services at the Church of the Holy Cross. During the first six months of 1790, fifteen people were baptized at the church, twelve Irish and three African Americans. Of the twelve Irish, Thayer baptized eleven. The Irish portion of the congregation, which gravitated toward Father Thayer, was led by the second church warden, a blacksmith named Patrick Campbell.[42]

Bishop Carroll was dismayed at the ethnic division in the Boston parish. He beseeched Boston's Catholics, "since it has pleased divine providence to unite all parts of the United States under one Episcopacy, all would lay aside national distinctions & attachments, & strive to form not Irish, or English, or French Congregations & Churches, but Catholic-American Congregations and Churches." Father Thayer responded to Carroll's call for unity with another attack on Father Rousselet's linguistic ability . "How can you form American churches," asked the American priest, "but by priests who speak ye language of America?" Unable to conciliate the rival factions in the Boston church, Bishop Carroll determined to resolve the dispute.[43]

On June 1, 1790, the bishop appointed Father Rousselet as the superior priest in Boston. He did so because Rousselet was older than Thayer and had preceded him at Boston. Most of all, he did so because he was not fooled by Thayer's machinations. Carroll informed Thayer, "I was not edified with yr. 1st letter . . . rediculing his pronounciation. I assure [you] that observation made me perhaps ye more ready to credit his complaint of yr. assuming too much on yourself as soon as you reached Boston." On July 4 the congregation voted to thank Carroll for appointing Rousselet and officially recognized the Frenchman as "their only Pastor, Publick Teacher, Instructor, and Curate of said Church of the Holy Cross in Boston." It is unclear precisely who voted at the meeting, but both wardens, Masson and Campbell, signed the announcement "In behalf of the Congregation." Apparently the Irish faction yielded to the authority of the bishop and abandoned Thayer.[44]

Rebuffed by both his bishop and his congregation, Thayer went to Salem to investigate the possibility of establishing a parish there. Reverend Bentley of Salem noted in his diary on July 27, "Mr. Thayer called upon me, & mentioned his purpose to open a Mass-house in this town, Mr. Rousselet having an appointment from the Bishop and having been publicly received at Boston. He sinks fast in public esteem & has no prospect of success." Despite the setbacks, Thayer remained defiant. He said of Rousselet, "I acknowledged his superiority over me as far as it existed, tho it was acquired unjustly by perjury." He was not ready to surrender control of the Boston congregation. Thayer's father, Cornelius died in Boston in late July. In August, Thayer returned to Boston to oversee his interest in his father's estate and the Church of the Holy Cross.[45]

Father Thayer returned to Boston on August 9, 1790. He immediately reopened the ethnic division that Bishop Carroll had tried to bridge. Thayer claimed that Rousselet had agreed to allow him to preach on Sunday evenings at the church on School Street. When he tried to obtain the keys to the church from Mamie Masson, the French warden, Masson denied Thayer entrance to the church. According to Thayer, "I was then for 13 days obliged to say Mass in my own chamber." Presumably, Thayer celebrated Mass with some of the Irish parishioners. He told them "that if they'd stay in ye chapel after ye French had finished vespers and keep ye church open I would preach at six." Thayer attempted his ecclesiastical coup on August 22. The American priest gave one of the Irishmen, probably a man named John Lloyd, an advertisement to hang up announcing that he would preach that evening. Lloyd hung the advertisement before Father Rousselet sang vespers. When Mamie Masson tore down the advertisement, Lloyd and another Irishman, "fearing some such thing, took him, one round ye body & another by ye hand, & snatched away the paper & replaced it."[46] Father Rousselet, who probably had visions of the destruction of the previous Christmas on his mind, summoned constables from their own afternoon Protestant services to quell the disturbance. Meanwhile Father Thayer appeared and delivered his sermon. According to Thayer, the bewildered constables listened to his sermon "and declared they saw no appearance of riot."[47]

The ethnic rift in Boston's Catholic congregation had evolved into a serious rupture. On Monday, August 23, Thayer and several of his supporters went to the owners of the building and obtained a lease on it in Father Thayer's name. Meanwhile the French faction went before a grand jury on August 30 to press charges against Thayer and John Lloyd for the assault on Mamie Masson. During early September, Rousselet celebrated Mass with the French faction in his home at 23 Union Street, while Thayer and the Irish used the church on School Street.[48]

The church wardens, Mamie Masson and Patrick Campbell, tried to resolve the dispute. Campbell, having pledged his support to Rousselet in June, remained loyal to the French priest despite renewed Irish support for Thayer. On September 1, the wardens held a meeting with the congregation and voted that Thayer should turn over his lease to the building and that Rousselet was the sole pastor of the Boston church. Since the meeting was held at Rousselet's home, the outcome was not surprising. Although the meeting voted in the name of the congregation, it is likely that only the French faction and those Irish loyal to Rousselet were present. According to the meeting, if Thayer did not comply by September 3, the congregation would "remove all our effects from the church we lately occupied in School Street, and for which we are engaged to pay."[49] True to their promise, on September 3 the French parishioners stripped the church of any and all articles of value, including the altar, tabernacle, and ornaments. It must have amused Protestant Bostonians as they watched French Catholics strip their church of its ornaments, transforming it into a simple meeting house that the original Huguenot tenants of the building would have admired.

A bizarre standoff ensued. Thayer and his supporters possessed the church, and Rousselet and his backers had the articles necessary to celebrate Mass. Unfortunately, Bishop Carroll was in Europe when the dispute occurred. His vicar-general ruled that the priests should have separate jurisdictions until Carroll returned to make a final decision. The vicar-general beseeched the two to try and cooperate in the meantime. Thayer, for his part, continued his intrigues. When Rousselet resolved to go to Maine to visit the Penobscot Indians, Thayer complained "he has frequently said that there are good furs to be had among them, so that I should fear that interest would lead him if he went." Despite Thayer's criticism, Rousselet, unable to compete with Thayer, left his unhappy congregation and went to Maine in late October.[50]

Soon after Rousselet left for Maine, one of his parishioners died. Breckvelt Larive, formerly the treasurer of Guadeloupe, had come to Boston with his family because of ill health during the summer of 1790. He and his family were warm supporters of Father Rousselet. On November 4 he died of an unspecified illness. It seemed that Father Thayer would have to perform the funeral Mass, but Larive's widow refused to allow the American priest to say it. The leaders of the French faction appealed to Reverend Samuel Parker, the Anglican rector of Trinity Church, and asked him to perform an Anglican funeral for the deceased Larive. On the afternoon of Monday, November 8, Larive's cortege, attended "by a very respectable number of citizens," proceeded to Trinity Church where Larive was laid to rest by Reverend Parker according to the ceremony of the Episcopal Church.[51]

Breckvelt Larive was buried under Trinity Church. A dozen years before, another Frenchman, the Chevalier de St. Sauveur, was buried in the basement of another Anglican church in Boston. St. Sauveur's internment had been secret so as not to offend the sensibilities of Boston Protestants. Larive's burial was the result of ecumenical cooperation. Catholics, not Protestants, prevented Larive from being buried according to his faith. Were it not for Protestant toleration, Larive might not have had a funeral.

Catholics again tested Protestant toleration several weeks after the burial of Larive. In early December when Father Rousselet returned from Maine, he asked Reverend Parker if he could perform a belated funeral Mass for Larive in Trinity Church. The wardens and vestrymen of Trinity Church voted unanimously to allow the service. On December 2, in the words of one observer, "Trinity Church was decorated with the insignia of popish *idolatry*," and Rousselet, unable to celebrate Mass in Boston's Catholic church, celebrated Mass there for Larive.[52]

V

The small Catholic congregation surely tested the toleration of Boston's Protestants. Since Christmas 1789, Catholics twice attacked the Church of the Holy Cross, Thayer and Rousselet had carried on an absurd, public power struggle, and the year ended with a Catholic funeral in a Protestant church, because a New England-born Catholic priest would not admit French Catholics into his church. As a New Englander, John Thayer's presence was bound to be controversial. His outrageous behavior made him more so. His presence tested the limits of New England toleration. How, then, did New Englanders respond to the return of their long-lost native son and his subsequent behavior?

When Thayer first arrived in New England, people were curious about him but not overtly hostile. Indeed, some New Englanders viewed Thayer's presence as a special mark of their toleration. An anonymous writer from Portsmouth, New Hampshire, advised Bostonians to greet Thayer "as becomes advocates for religious liberty." If New Englanders could tolerate John Thayer's obnoxious presence, then they could truly call themselves "friends to the equal and just rights of mankind."[53] New Englanders were willing to accept Thayer as they had Poterie and Rousselet. They did not publicly castigate Thayer as an apostate, despite his conversion.

New Englanders thought less of Thayer as his controversy with Rousselet became more public. In late August and September 1790, at the height of the schism with the French, negative comments about Thayer appeared in Boston newspapers. The *Herald of Freedom* published a comment by "John Turncoat" "to certify that John Thayer, formerly a puritan preacher, has preached, and moreover, has told several honest persons, that all who go to protestant or other meetings, were on the path to hell and the synagogue of devils." In September 1790 the same newspaper published an annotated critique of Thayer's *An Account of the Conversion of the Reverend John Thayer*. The critique juxtaposed Thayer's writing with biting satirical commentary. Most of the negative comments were not so much anti-Catholic as anti-John Thayer. In attacking Thayer, his critics resorted to ad hominem insults first and anti-popery second.[54]

By late 1790 anti-popery ceased to interest most New Englanders. When a writer submitted a piece entitled "The Roman-Catholick done over—or the Trinity House of God turned into a Puppet-shew room," for publication after Larive's funeral, the *Columbian Centinel* refused to publish it, declaring that "it would ill comport with the spirit of toleration which is our country's boast." Minister and historian Jeremy Belknap wrote after the funeral Mass at Trinity Church, "the more they expose their religion to the public show; the more its absurdities appear and it is become an object [of] ridicule even to our children."[55] When John Thayer was born in 1758, the popish threat was the primary concern of New Englanders. It was a concern worthy of the foremost minds in the region. By 1790 popery, no longer feared, was a joke for children. John Thayer was not very controversial because, apart from his small congregation, he did not matter. Indifference and tolerance had replaced fear and hatred of popery.

VI

When Bishop John Carroll returned from Europe in late December 1790, he was very alarmed by the situation in Boston. Thayer's behavior infuriated the bishop, who declared "nothing can contribute more to vilify us in the eyes of our Protestant Brethren, or give more pleasure to the enemies of our religion. . . . I am so affected that I would withdraw all powers from him and Mr. R[ousselet], & send a successor to the pastoral office if I had a proper Clergyman." Bishop Carroll vowed to go to Boston and personally clear up the difficulties surrounding the parish as soon as the roads were passable in the spring.[56]

By the time Carroll arrived in Boston, he had only one priest to deal with. In March 1791 Carroll received a letter from France concerning Father Rousselet and matters "very prejudicial" to his character. Carroll advised Rousselet to resign immediately, "for the sake of peace & the prevention of farther scandal. This will be the most effectual method of saving your reputation from the discredit into which it will fall, if the acc[oun]ts from France should be divulged."[57] Whatever Rousselet had done in France, it was so bad that the bishop preferred to have John Thayer in sole control of the Church of the Holy Cross. Rousselet followed Carroll's advice. He resigned immediately, and Thayer became pastor of the parish.[58]

In early June 1791 Bishop Carroll visited Boston to restore harmony to the troubled congregation of Boston Catholics. Carroll was very busy during his visit. On June 2 he confirmed thirty candidates at the Church of the Holy Cross. The following Sunday, June 5, he celebrated Mass in the presence of Governor Hancock. He appointed Thayer as pastor on June 16. The congregation in turn accepted Thayer on the same day. The schism in the Boston congregation was officially over after more than ten months.[59]

Carroll's most symbolic and significant act during his visit to Boston occurred on June 6, 1791, when he participated in the annual election of the Ancient and Honourable Artillery Company, the oldest military organization in

New England. The Puritan founders of Massachusetts had founded the company to protect their colony from its popish enemies. The election of officers in the company, which was accompanied by a sermon and a dinner, was an annual affirmation of the Protestant heritage of New England. After a sermon by Samuel Parker, the Artillery Company escorted a procession of honored guests, including Bishop Carroll, to Faneuil Hall for a banquet. Bishop Carroll and Reverend Parker gave the blessings before the meal. Reverend John Eliot of the New North Church in Boston appreciated the significance of the moment. He wrote in his diary, "An elegant entertainment at the hall, where a clergyman of the C. of England & a Romish Bp. acted as Chaplains. How would our fathers have Stared! Tempora Mutantur &c. and much credit to modern times."[60]

By 1791 anti-popery, once at the heart of New England culture, had entirely lost its relevance to most New England Protestants. Bostonians accepted the Church of the Holy Cross and John Thayer with nary a comment. The experience of Thayer, and the treatment accorded to the small community of Boston Catholics after the Revolution, indicate that religious toleration was not only an ideal but a reality in Boston, the capital of New England.[61]

NOTES

1. *Independent Chronicle*, September 4, 1788.

2. *Boston Gazette*, November 3, 1788; *Independent Chronicle*, November 6, 1788; *Massachusetts Centinel*, November 6, 1788. After 1748 the meeting house was home to the Eleventh Congregational Church. The congregation disbanded when its pastor, Andrew Crosswell, died in 1785. Between 1785 and 1788, the meeting house, owned by Mr. and Mrs. James H.Perkins, fell into disrepair until it was leased by the Catholic congregation. See "A Topographical and Historical Description of Boston, 1794," *MHSC*, 1st series, 3 (1794), 241-231, 264.

3. *Independent Chronicle*, November 6, 1788. When he arrived in Boston in January 1790, John Thayer wrote, "The Catholics are exceedingly few, not above fifty or sixty at most." John Thayer to John Carroll, January 6, 1790, Baltimore Archdiocesan Archives (hereafter BAA), copy in the Lord/Sexton Papers, AABo. As late as 1820 there were only 3,500 Catholics in all of New England. See Timothy Walch, *Early American Catholicism, 1634-1820* (New York, 1988), 9.

4. *Herald of Freedom*, December 22, 1788.

5. Jeremy Belknap, "Interleaved Almanac, November 1788," *MHSP*, 1st series, 3 (1855-58), 308.

6. Percival Merritt, "Sketches of the Three Earliest Roman Catholic Priests in Boston," *Colonial Society of Massachusetts Publications*, 25 (1922-24), 173-229, and Robert H. Lord, John Sexton, and Edward Harrington, *History of the Archdiocese of*

Boston in Its Various Stages of Development, 1604-1943, 3 vols. (Boston, 1943), I, part 2, chapts. 1-2.

7. Merritt, "Sketches of the Three Earliest Roman Catholic Priests in Massachusetts," 173-184.

8. Merritt, "Sketches of the Three Earliest Roman Catholic Priests in Massachusetts," 184-210.

9. Claude Florent Bouchard de la Poterie, *The Resurrection of Laurent Ricci* (Philadelphia, 1789).

10. Merritt, "Sketches of the Three Earliest Roman Catholic Priests in Boston," 193, and Lord et al., *History of the Archdiocese of Boston,* I, 418-419.

11. William Bentley, *Diary of William Bentley,* 4 vols. (Salem, 1905-14), I, 133. *Massachusetts Centinel,* December 26, 1789.

12. *Massachusetts Centinel,* December 30, 1789.

13. *Herald of Freedom,* January 8, 1790. See also Poterie's "To the Impartial Public and Especially the Roman Catholics," in the *Herald of Freedom,* January 15, 1790.

14. *Herald of Freedom,* January 19, 1790.

15. Merritt, "Sketches of the Three Earliest Roman Catholic Priests in Massachusetts," 209.

16. John Thayer, *An Account of the Conversion of the Reverend John Thayer* (London, 1787), 2. Also see Merritt, "Sketches of the Three Earliest Roman Catholic Priests in Boston"; T. E. Bridgett, *A New England Convert or the Story of the Reverend John Thayer* (London, 1897); Arthur J. Connolly, "Historical Sketch of the Rev. John Thayer," read before the United States Catholic Historical Society, October 18, 1888," copy, MHS. Also see Lord et al., *History of the Archdiocese of Boston,* I, part 2, chaps. 1-3.

17. Thayer, *Account of the Conversion,* 2-3.

18. *American Magazine,* 1 (September 1788), 738-739.

19. Merritt, "Sketches of the Three Earliest Roman Catholic Priests in Boston," 211-213.

20. John Thayer to Jacques André Emery, July 17, 1790, reproduced in Bridgett, *New England Convert,* 19-32.

21. Thayer, *Account of the Conversion,* 3.

22. Thayer, *Account of the Conversion,* 4.

23. Thayer, *Account of the Conversion,* 5-6.

24. Thayer, *Account of the Conversion,* 19, 11.

25. Labré (1748-83) was canonized in 1873. See Bridgett, *A New England Convert,* 9-10; Merritt, "Sketches of the Three Earliest Roman Catholic Priests in Boston," 214, n. 1.

26. Thayer, *Account of the Conversion,* 21, 24-25.

27. Quoted in James Barnard, *Life of Benedict Joseph* (London, 1785), 207.

28. Letter from M. Jacques André Emery, September 28, 1790," reprinted in Bridgett, *A New England Convert,* 19-32, quotation, p. 21. Emery's letter has an interesting history. Ursuline Nuns in Sligo, Ireland, lost the original, which they had intended to publish in a book on the life of John Thayer. A copy of the letter was first

published by Charles François Nagot in *Relations de la conversion de quelques protestants* (Paris, 1791).

29. Benjamin Franklin to Jane Mecom, September 13, 1783, *MHSC*, 6th series, 4 (1891), 260.

30. *American Magazine*, 1 (September 1788), 739.

31. Letter from M. Jacques André Emery, September 28, 1790, in Bridgett, *A New England Convert*, 23.

32. Quoted in Alexander Dick, *Reasons for Embracing the Catholic Faith* (Edinburgh, 1848), 18.

33. Percival Merritt, "Bibliographic Notes on 'An Account of the Conversion of the Rev. John Thayer'," *Colonial Society of Massachusetts Publications*, 25 (1922-24), 129-140.

34. Thayer, *Account of the Conversion*, 35.

35. Letter from M. Jacques André Emery, September 28, 1790, in Bridgett, *A New England Convert*, 26-27.

36. Lord et al., *History of the Archdiocese of Boston*, I, 420-421.

37. Bentley, *Diary*, I, 135.

38. John Thayer to Superior Emery, July 17, 1790, reproduced in Bridgett, *A New England Convert*, 35-36; also see the *Boston Gazette*, January 11, 1790.

39. John Carroll to Cardinal Leonardo Antonelli, February 6, 1790, in Thomas O'Brien Hanley, ed., *The John Carroll Papers* (hereafter *JCP*) 3 vols. (Notre Dame, 1976), I, 428.

40. John Thayer to John Carroll, January 6, 1790, BAA; photostat, MHS; typescript Lord/Sexton Papers, AABo.

41. In a letter to Bishop Carroll, John Thayer stated, "Ye number of ye Irish for me is about 60 or 70, against about 8 or 10 French." There were probably more French than Thayer admitted, but the Irish certainly outnumbered the French. John Thayer to John Carroll, May 13, 1790, BAA, copy in Lord/Sexton Papers, AABo. Also see Merritt, "Sketches of the Three Earliest Roman Catholic Priests in Boston," 197.

42. Baptism statistics from Lord et al., *History of the Archdiocese of Boston*, I, 423. Also see *JCP*, I, 441, n. 1.

43. John Carroll to the Congregation of Boston, April 30, 1790, *JCP*, I, 440-441; John Thayer to John Carroll, May 13, 1790, original in BAA, typescript in Lord/Sexton Papers, AABo.

44. John Carroll to John Thayer, May 25, 1790, *JCP*, I, 442-443; *Columbian Centinel*, September 15, 1790. Also see Carroll to Thayer, April 30, 1790, *JCP*, I, 441.

45. Bentley, *Diary*, I, 188; John Thayer to John Carroll, July 27, 1790, original in BAA, typescript in the Lord/Sexton Papers, AABo; *Independent Chronicle*, July 29, 1790.

46. John Thayer to Father Fleming, September 8, 1790, BAA, typescript copy Lord/Sexton Papers, AABo.

47. Thayer to Fleming, September 8, 1790.

48. The court records for the case are in Suffolk County Supreme Judicial Court Files, case no. 105721, at the Massachusetts Archives. Thayer and Lloyd were indicted for assault on August 30, 1790. Warrants were issued for their arrest on December 7. Sheriff Joseph Henderson brought them before the Supreme Judicial Court on February 12, 1791. On February 23 witnesses were summoned for Thayer's trial which was scheduled for March 28. Probably because of the subsequent abrupt departure of Father Rousselet from the parish, the charges against Thayer were dropped on March 28, 1791.

49. *Columbian Centinel*, September 15, 1790.

50. John Thayer to Father Fleming, October 14, 1790, original in the BAA, typescript copy Lord/Sexton Papers, AABo.

51. *Columbian Centinel*, November 10, 1790; *Boston Gazette*, November 8, 1790.

52. Jeremy Belknap to Ebenezer Hazard, December 7, 1790, *MHSC*, 5th series, 3 (1878), 240-241; *Columbian Centinel*, December 1, 1790.

53. *Herald of Freedom*, January 22, 1790.

54. *Herald of Freedom*, August 31, September 3, 10, and 21, 1790. Thayer could not even provoke an anti-papal reaction when he tried to be controversial. In late November 1790, he offered to debate the tenets of Catholicism and "to answer the objections any gentleman would wish to make, either publicly or privately to the doctrine he preaches." Thayer even promised to convert back to Protestantism "if any one can convince him of his errour." *Columbian Centinel*, November 24, 1790. Apparently few New England Protestants were concerned enough about the soul of Thayer to undertake his challenge. For more than a month, Thayer's challenge went unanswered. Not until late December did George Leslie, a Congregational minister from tiny Washington, New Hampshire, begin a newspaper debate with Thayer. Their lackluster debate, carried on over two years, aroused little interest. To their credit, Thayer and Leslie stuck to doctrinal issues and did not resort to insult. Thayer collected and published the articles as *A Controversy Between the Rev. John Thayer, Catholic Missionary, of Boston, and the Reverend George Leslie, Pastor of the Church of Washington, New Hampshire* (Philadelphia, 1793).

55. *Columbian Centinel*, December 4, 1790; Jeremy Belknap to Ebenezer Hazard, December 7, 1790, *MHSC*, 5th series, 3 (1878), 240-241.

56. John Carroll to John Thayer, February 22, 1791, *JCP*, I, 494.

57. John Carroll to Louis Rousselet, March 10, 1791, *JCP*, I, 497.

58. John Carroll to John Thayer, March 10, 1791, *JCP*, I, 496. Rousselet's abrupt resignation and departure probably account for the dropping of the charges against Thayer and John Lloyd from the disturbances of the previous year. Thayer was to be tried on March 23.

59. *Herald of Freedom*, June 7, and 16, 1791; *Columbian Centinel*, June 8, 1791; *JCP*, I, 505-508.

60. John Eliot, Interleaved Almanac, June 6, 1791, MHS; *Columbian Centinel*, June 8, 1791; Bentley, *Diary*, I, 263-264.

61. Thayer remained pastor at Boston until the spring of 1792, when Bishop Carroll replaced him with François Matignon. Thayer spent four years as a missionary in Kentucky. He returned to Europe sometime after 1800 and died in Limerick, Ireland in 1815.

Conclusion

On April 27, 1811, the *Boston Patriot* published an anonymous piece under the heading "THE DEVIL!" The author, a supporter of Napoleon, wrote to advise New Englanders not to believe all they read and heard about the French emperor. In his analysis, the writer concisely summarized the role of anti-popery in colonial New England. According to the Bonapartist:

Ever since the English imported from Holland their heavy race of Kings to crawl in and out before the People, they have never been able to perform their Kingly functions without a Devil to scare their subjects into submission. . . . The most potent and terrific Devil they have ever conjured up to frighten their people was the POPE OF ROME. During two centuries, the stupid People of England were brought up with a full belief that Hell never let loose upon the protestant world a Devil so dangerous to their lives, liberties, property and religion as the Pope of Rome; and all their Bishops, and all their Ministers, and all their Officers, and political writers were hired to describe this detestable destroyer of English liberty in the most frightful forms. They succeeded completely in frightening their own people, and infused the same fear into the hearts of their subjects in the colonies.[1]

While the author, like most New Englanders since the French alliance, incorrectly laid the blame for New England anti-popery at the feet of the British, his description of the role of the pope as demon is as accurate for eighteenth-century New Englanders as for Englishmen.

During the colonial period, anti-popery provided New Englanders with a convenient, coherent system that explained good and evil in the world. New Englanders equated all things "popish" with tyranny and oppression. Conversely, they identified themselves and things Protestant as good. This simplistic, manichean outlook was remarkably durable. Ultimately, anti-papal values facilitated the emotional and intellectual transition required by New Englanders for armed resistance to Britain. While anti-popery did not "cause" the American Revolution, it helped make armed conflict possible in New England.

Once the Revolution was under way, anti-popery lost its currency. While no lovers of Catholicism, New Englanders did not find that anti-popery conveniently explained their world as it had that of their mothers and fathers. New Englanders adapted quickly and found a new devil to replace the pope and his minions: the king of England and his ministers. As the author of "THE DEVIL!" explained, "When we renounced allegiance to Great Britain, we at the same time renounced their Pope and their Devil; and set up George the Third and Lord North in their place."[2] Once the English had supplanted papists as evil in the minds of New Englanders, popery ceased to be a source of anxiety or hatred for them as well. New Englanders gradually transferred their fear and hatred of things Catholic to a fear and hatred of things English. This transition enabled them to ally with French Catholics against British Protestants.

The transition from anti-popery was not easy. Loyalists resisted completely, retaining a more "traditional" view of popery, especially when their Whig rivals allied with France. Many New England Whigs also retained vestigial anti-papal sentiment. Nonetheless, the alliance proved to be a catalyst for change, and by 1780 the fear of popery ceased to concern most New Englanders. Under the direction of the Whig leaders of the Revolution, New Englanders gradually came to accept and tolerate Catholicism.

The article by the anonymous Bonapartist that appeared in the *Boston Patriot* implied that anti-popery was but a distant memory in New England by 1811. Such was not the case. While Catholics enjoyed toleration after the Revolution, they did not enjoy full equality. The Irish parishioners who supported John Thayer were the first wave of an influx of Irish immigrants to New England between the American Revolution and the Civil War. Anti-popery contributed to the hostility with which New England Protestants greeted the Catholic newcomers. In 1832 a Protestant mob burned a convent in Charlestown. The widespread support for the anti-Catholic, xenophobic, Know-

Nothing Party in New England during the 1850s is further testimony to the persistence of anti-papal sentiment in the region well after the America Revolution.[3]

After the Revolution, however, anti-popery would never again be at center of New England culture. The decline of anti-popery there was a dramatic cultural transformation wrought by the Revolution, which permanently undermined the foundation of anti-popery in that region. The decline is vivid testimony to the unforeseen secondary and tertiary effects of cultural upheavals like the Revolution. What began as a relatively simple campaign to defend the rights of Englishmen in America ended not only in political independence and republican government, but in the extension of freedom to people whom New Englanders had previously considered their worst enemies. In the midst of war and crisis, New Englanders gave up not only their allegiance to Britain but one of their most dearly held prejudices.

NOTES

1. *Boston Patriot*, April 27, 1811.

2. *Boston Patriot*, April 27, 1811.

3. Oscar Handlin, *Boston's Immigrants* (Cambridge, 1941); Ray Allen Billington, *The Protestant Crusade* (New York, 1938) and David Brion Davis,"Some Themes of Counter-subversion: An Analysis of Anti-Masonic, Anti-Catholic and Anti-Mormon Literature," *Mississippi Valley Historical Review*, 47 (1960), 205-224. Also see Ira Leonard and Robert D. Parmet, *American Nativism, 1830-1860* (New York, 1971).

Select Bibliography

Unpublished Primary Sources

Adams Family Papers, MHS.
Belknap Papers, MHS.
Samuel Cooper Papers, Huntington Library, San Marino, California.
Dudleian Lectures, Harvard University Archives.
James Freeman, The Notebook of James Freeman of Boston, Describing the
      Activities at Boston from 1745 to 1765, MHS.
Elbridge Gerry Papers, MHS.
William Heath Papers, MHS.
Louisbourg Papers, MHS.
Massachusetts Council Records, MA.
Robert Treat Paine Papers, MHS.
Suffolk County Court of General Sessions of the Peace, Docket Books, MA.
Suffolk County Court Files, MA.
Benjamin Walker, Diary, MHS.

Published Primary Sources (Pre-1800)

Hull Abbot, *The Duty of God's People* (Boston, 1746).

Amos Adams, *A Discourse on Religious Liberty* (Boston, 1768).

Zabdiel Adams, *The Evil Designs of Men* (Boston, 1783).

Nathaniel Appleton, *A Sermon Preached October 9* (Boston, 1760).

East Apthorp, *Considerations* (Boston, 1763).

Benedict Arnold, *To the Inhabitants of America . . . October 7, 1780* (New York, 1780).

————, *To the Officers and Soldiers of the Continental Army . . . October 20, 1780* (New York, 1780).

[A. D. Auborn], *The French Convert* (Boston, 1725).

Pierre Berault, *The Church of Rome Evidently Proved Heretick* (Boston, 1685).

Samuel Bird, *The Importance of the Divine Presence* (New Haven, 1759).

Boston Evening Post.

Boston Gazette.

Boston News-Letter.

John Burt, *The Mercy of God to His People* (Newport, 1759).

Thomas Bradbury Chandler, *An Appeal to the Public* (New York, 1767).

François-Jean de Chastellux, *Travels in North America*, 2 vols. (London, 1787).

Charles Chauncy, *A Complete View of Episcopacy* (Boston, 1771).

————, *The Counsel of Two Confederate Kings* (Boston, 1746).

Jonas Clarke, *A Sermon Preached Before His Excellency* (Boston, 1781).

Colombian Centinel.

Sylvanus Conant, *The Art of War* (Boston, 1759).

Connecticut Courant.

Connecticut Journal.

Continental Journal.

Samuel Cooper, *A Discourse on the Man of Sin* (Boston, 1774).

————, *A Sermon Preached Before His Excellency* (Boston, 1759).

————, *A Sermon Preached . . . Before the Society for the Encouragement of Industry* (Boston, 1753).

Henry Cumings, *A Sermon Preached at Billerica* (Boston, 1775).

James Dana, *A Sermon Preached Before the General Assembly* (Hartford, 1779).

Paul Dudley, *An Essay on the Merchandize of Slaves and the Souls of Men* (Boston, 1731).

Andrew Eliot, *A Sermon Preached October 25, 1759* (Boston, 1759).

Essex Gazette.

Exeter Journal.

Eli Forbes, *God the Strength of His People* (Boston, 1761).

Thomas Foxcroft, *Grateful Reflexions* (Boston, 1760).

Antonio Gavin, *A Master-Key to Popery* (Newport, 1773).

William Gordon, *A Discourse Preached December 15, 1774* (Boston, 1775).

———, *A History of the Rise, Progress and Establishment of the United States of America*, 4 vols. (London, 1788).

William Heath, *Memoirs of Major General Heath* (Boston, 1798).

Herald of Freedom.

William Hobby, *The Happiness of a People* (Boston, 1758).

Enoch Huntington, *A Discourse Delivered at Middleton* (Hartford, 1775).

Independent Chronicle.

Independent Ledger.

John Lathrop, *A Discourse Preached December 15, 1774* (Boston, 1774).

Daniel Leonard, *Massachusettensis* (Boston, 1775).

Massachusetts Centinel.

Massachusetts Gazette and Boston Post-Boy.

Massachusetts Spy.

Jonathan Mayhew, *A Discourse on Unlimited Submission* (Boston, 1750).

———, *Election Sermon* (Boston, 1754).

———, *Observations on the Charter of the Society* (Boston, 1763).

———, *Popish Idolatry* (Boston, 1765).

John Murray, *Nehemiah: A Discourse Delivered at the Presbyterian Church in Newburyport* (Newburyport, 1779).

New Hampshire Gazette.

New London Gazette.

Newport Mercury.

New York Journal.

Phillips Payson, *A Memorial of the Lexington Battle* (Boston, 1782).

———, *A Sermon Preached Before the Honorable Council* (Boston, 1778).

Pennsylvania Packet.

Popish Cruelty Displayed (Boston, 1753).

Claude Florent Bouchard de la Poterie, *The Resurrection of Laurent Ricci* (Philadelphia, 1789).

Providence Gazette.

Claude Charles Robin, *New Travels Through North America* (Philadelphia, 1783).

Rivington's Royal Gazette.

David S. Rowland, *Historical Remarks* (Providence, 1779).

Salem Gazette.

Samuel Sherwood, *A Sermon Containing Scriptural Instructions* (New Haven, 1774).

Ezra Stiles, *The United States Elevated to Glory and Honor* (New Haven, 1783).

John Thayer, *An Account of the Conversion of the Reverend John Thayer* (London, 1787).

Votes and Proceedings of the Freeholders of the Town of Boston (Boston, 1772).

Noah Welles, *The Real Advantages which Ministers of the Gospel and People May Enjoy* (New Haven, 1762).

Edward Wigglesworth, *The Authority of Tradition* (Boston, 1778).

Solomon Williams, *The Duty of Christian Soldiers* (New London, 1755).

Published Primary Sources (Post-1800)

Evelyn M. Acomb, trans., ed., *The Revolutionary Journal of Baron Ludwig Von Closen, 1780-1783* (Chapel Hill, 1958).

Acts and Resolves of the Province of Massachusetts Bay, 21 vols. (Boston, 1869-1922).

Douglas Adair and John R. Schutz, *Peter Oliver's Origins and Progress of the American Rebellion* (Stanford, 1961).

Charles Francis Adams, ed., *The Works of John Adams*, 10 vols.(Boston, 1850-56).

Israel Angell, *Diary of Colonel Israel Angell* (Providence, 1899).

James T. Austin, *Life of Elbridge Gerry*, 2 vols. (Boston, 1828).

Daniel Barber, *The History of My Own Times* (Washington, 1827).

William S. Bartlet, *The Frontier Missionary: A Memoir of the Life of the Reverend Jacob Bailey* (Boston, 1853).

Claude Blanchard, *The Journal of Claude Blanchard* (Albany, 1876).

William Bentley, *Diary of William Bentley*, 4 vols. (Salem, 1905-14).

Boston Record Commissioners, *Report of the Record Commissioners*, 38 vols. (Boston, 1876-1908).

Nathaniel Bouton et al., eds., *New Hampshire Provincial and State Papers*, 30 vols. (Concord, 1867-1910).

Samuel Breck, *Recollections of Samuel Breck* (Philadelphia, 1877).

Edmund C. Burnet, ed., *Letters of Members of the Continental Congress*, 10 vols. (Washington, 1921-36).

L. H. Butterfield, ed., *Adams Family Correspondence*, 4 vols. (Cambridge, Mass., 1963-73).

——, *The Diary and Autobiography of John Adams*, 4 vols. (Cambridge, Mass., 1961).

Anne Rowe Cunningham, ed., *The Letters and Diary of John Rowe* (Boston, 1903).

Henry A. Cushing, ed., *The Writings of Samuel Adams*, 4 vols., (New York, 1907, repr. 1968).

Louis Effingham De Forest, ed., *Louisbourg Journals* (New York,1932).

Guillaume Deux-Ponts, *My Campaigns in America* (Boston, 1868).

F. B. Dexter, *The Literary Diary of Ezra Stiles*, 3 vols. (New York, 1901).

Henri Doniol, ed., *Histoire de la participation de la France à l'établissement des États-Unis d'Amérique: Correspondance diplomatique et documents*, 5 vols. (Paris, 1886-92).

Mathieu Dumas, *Memoirs of His Own Time*, 2 vols. (Philadelphia, 1839).

Peter Force, ed., *American Archives*, 6 vols. (Washington, 1837-46).

Worthington C. Ford, ed., *Journals of the Continental Congress*, 34 vols. (Washington, 1904-37).

——, ed., *Writings of George Washington*, 14 vols. (New York, 1889-93).

John C. Fitzpatrick, ed., *Writings of George Washington, 1745-1799*, 39 vols. (Washington, 1931-44).

"Letters of William Gordon," *MHSP,* 63 (1929-30), 303-616.

Jeremiah Greenman, *Diary of a Common Soldier in the American Revolution* (DeKalb, 1978).

Otto G. Hammond, ed., *Letters and Papers of Major-General John Sullivan*, 3 vols. (Concord, NH., 1930-39).

Oscar Handlin and Mary Handlin, eds., *The Popular Sources of Political Authority: Documents on the Massachusetts Constitution of 1780* (Cambridge, Mass., 1966).

Thomas O'Brien Hanley, ed., *The John Carroll Papers, 1755-1815*, 3 vols. (Notre Dame, 1976).

Anne Hulton, *Letters of a Loyalist Lady* (Cambridge, Mass., 1927).

Stanley J. Idzerda, ed., *Lafayette in the Age of the American Revolution: Selected Letters and Papers*, 5 vols. (Ithaca, 1977-83).

Journal of the Convention for Framing A Constitution for the State of Massachusetts Bay, 1779-1780 (Boston, 1832).

Frederick Kidder, *Military Operations in Eastern Maine and Nova Scotia During the Revolution, Chiefly Compiled From the Journals and Letters of Colonel John Allan, With Notes and a Memoir of Colonel John Allan* (Albany, 1867).

Bernard Knollenberg, ed., "Thomas Hollis and Jonathan Mayhew, Their Correspondence, 1759-1766," *MHSP*, 69 (1947-1950), 102-193.

Armand-Louis Lauzun, *Memoirs of the Duke de Lauzun* (New York, 1912).

Letters from Andrew Eliot to Thomas Hollis, *MHSC*, 4th series, 4 (1858), 398-461.

Frederick Mackenzie, *Diary of Frederick Mackenzie*, 2 vols. (Cambridge, Mass., 1930).

John J. Meng, ed., *Despatches and Instructions of Conrad Alexandre Gerard, 1778-1780: Correspondence of the First French Minister to the United States with the Comte de Vergennes* (Baltimore, 1939).

Frank C. Mevers, ed., *The Papers of Josiah Bartlett* (Hanover, NH., 1979).

Andrew Oliver, ed., *The Journal of Samuel Curwen, Loyalist*, 2 vols. (Cambridge, Mass.,1972).

Theophilus Parsons, Jr., *Memoirs of Theophilus Parsons* (Boston, 1861).

Howard C. Rice, Jr., and Anne S. K. Brown, eds., *The American Campaigns of Rochambeau's Army,* 2 vols. (Providence, 1972).

Richard Ryerson and Robert J. Taylor, eds., *The Papers of John Adams*, 8 vols. to date (Boston, 1977-).

Richard K. Showman, ed., *The Papers of Nathanael Green*, 6 vols. (Chapel Hill, 1976-91).

Paul H. Smith, ed., *Letters of Delegates to Congress*, 10 vols. to date (Washington, 1976-).

Isaiah Thomas, *Three Autobiographical Fragments* (Worcester, Mass., 1962).

Warren-Adams Letters, 2 vols. (Boston, 1917-25).

Secondary Sources

Charles W. Akers, *Called unto Liberty: A Life of Jonathan Mayhew, 1720-1764* (Cambridge, Mass., 1964).

————, *The Divine Politician: Samuel Cooper and the American Revolution in Boston* (Boston, 1982).

————, "The Lost Reputation of Samuel Cooper as a Leader of the American Revolution," *NEHGR,* 130 (1976), 23-34.

Catherine L. Albanese, *Sons of the Fathers: The Civil Religion of the American Revolution* (Philadelphia, 1986).

Fred Anderson, *A People's Army: Massachusetts Soldiers and Society in the Seven Years War* (Chapel Hill, 1984).

Bernard Bailyn, "Religion and Revolution: Three Biographical Studies,"

Perspectives in American History, 4 (1970), 85-167.

Alice M. Baldwin, *The New England Clergy and the American Revolution* (Durham, NH., 1928).

Francis F. Beirne, "Mission to Canada: 1776," *Maryland Historical Magazine,* 60 (1965), 404-420.

John F. Berens, *Providence and Patriotism in Early America, 1640-1815* (Charlottesville, 1978).

Jeremy Black, "The Catholic Threat and the British Press in the 1720s and 1730s," *Journal of Religious History,* 12 (1983), 364-381.

Ruth Bloch, *Visionary Republic: Millennial Themes in American Thought, 1740-1800* (New York, 1985).

Timothy W. Bosworth, "Anti-Catholicism as a Political Tool in Mid-Eighteenth-Century Maryland," *Catholic Historical Review,* 61 (1975) 539-563.

Carl Bridenbaugh, *Mitre and Sceptre: Transatlantic Faiths, Ideas, Personalities and Politics, 1689-1775* (New York, 1962).

————, *The Spirit of '76: The Growth of American Patriotism Before Independence* (New York, 1975)

Gayle Kathleen Pluta Brown, "A Controversy Not Merely Religious: The Anti-Catholic Tradition in Colonial New England" (Ph.D. dissertation, University of Iowa, 1990).

Thomas M. Brown, "The Image of the Beast: Anti-Papal Rhetoric in Colonial America," in Richard O. Curry and Thomas M. Brown, eds., *Conspiracy: The Fear of Subversion in American History* (New York, 1972), 1-20.

Steve Bruce, *No Pope of Rome: Anti-Catholicism in Modern Scotland* (Edinburgh, 1985).

Jon Butler, *Awash in a Sea of Faith: Christianizing the American People* (Cambridge, Mass., 1990).

Joseph J. Casino, "Anti-popery in Colonial Pennsylvania," *Pennsylvania Magazine of History and Biography,* 105 (1981), 279-309.

Robin Clifton, "Popular Fear of Catholics during the English Revolution," *Past and Present,* 52 (1971), 23-55.

Francis D. Cogliano, "Nil Desperandum Christo Duce: The New England Crusade against Louisbourg," *Essex Institute Historical Collections,* 128 (1992), 180-207.

————, "To Obey JesusChrist and General Washington: Massachusetts, Catholicism, and the Eastern Indians during the American Revolution," *Maine Historical Society Quarterly,* 32 (1992), 108-33.

Cedric B. Cowing, *The Great Awakening and the American Revolution:*

Colonial Thought in the Eighteenth Century (Chicago, 1971).

David Cressy, *Bonfires and Bells: National Memory and the Protestant Calendar in Elizabethan and Stuart England* (Berkeley, 1989).

———, "The Protestant Calendar and the Vocabulary of Celebration in Early Modern England," *Journal of British Studies,* 29 (1990),31-52.

Robert Darnton, *The Great Cat Massacre and Other Episodes in French Cultural History* (New York, 1984).

Philip Davidson, *Propaganda and the American Revolution, 1763-1783* (Chapel Hill, 1941).

David Brion Davis, "Some Themes of Counter-subversion: An Analysis of Anti-Masonic, Anti-Catholic and Anti-Mormon Literature," *Mississippi Valley Historical Review,* 47 (1960), 205-224.

Natalie Z. Davis, *Society and Culture in Early Modern France* (Berleley, 1975).

Jay Dolan, *The American Catholic Experience: From Colonial Times to the Present* (Garden City, NY., 1985).

Jonathan R. Dull, *The French Navy and the American Revolution: A Study of Arms and Diplomacy* (Princeton, 1975).

Alice Morse Earle, *Customs and Fashions in Old New England* (Williamstown, Mass., 1969).

John Tracy Ellis, *Catholics in Colonial America* (Baltimore, 1965).

Melvin B. Endy, "Just War, Holy War, and Millennialism in Revolutionary America," *WMQ,* 42 (1985) 3-25.

O. W. Furley, "Pope-burning Processions of the Late Seventeenth Century," *History,* 44 (1959), 16-23.

C. C. Goen, *Revivalism and Separatism in New England, 1740-1800* (Boston, 1962).

Martin Griffin, *Catholics in the American Revolution* 3 vols. (Philadelphia, 1909-11).

K. H. D. Haigh, "'No Popery' in the Reign of Charles II," in J. S. Bromley and E. H. Kassman, eds., *Britain and the Netherlands* (The Hague, 1975), 102-119.

David Hall, *Worlds of Wonder, Days of Judgement: Popular Religious Belief in Early New England* (New York, 1989).

Van Beck Hall, *Politics without Parties: Massachusetts, 1780-1791* (London, 1972).

William Haller, *The Elect Nation: The Meaning and Relevance of Foxe's Book of Martyrs* (New York, 1963)

Thomas O'Brien Hanley, *Charles Carroll of Carrollton: The Making of a Revolutionary Gentleman* (Washington, 1970).

Charles Hanson, "From the Quebec act to the French Alliance: The Catholic Question and the American Revolution in New England" (Ph.D. dissertation, University of California at Berkeley, 1993).

Nathan O. Hatch, *The Sacred Cause of Liberty* (New Haven, 1977).

Robert McConnell Hatch, *Thrust for Canada: The American Attempt on Quebec in 1775-1776* (Boston, 1979).

Alan Heimert, *Religion and the American Mind: From the Great Awakening to the Revolution* (New York, 1966).

Caroline M. Hibbard, *Charles I and the Popish Plot* (Chapel Hill, 1983).

Dirk Hoerder, *Crowd Action in Revolutionary Massachusetts, 1765-1780* (New York, 1977).

Ronald Hoffman and Peter J. Albert, eds., *Diplomacy and Revolution: The Franco-American Alliance of 1778* (Charlottesville, 1981).

W. H. J. Kennedy, "Catholics in Massachusetts before 1750," *Catholic Historical Review*, 17 (1931), 10-28.

John Kenyon, *The Popish Plot* (New York, 1972).

Charles B. Kinney, Jr., *Church and State: The Struggle for Separation in New Hampshire, 1630-1900* (New York, 1955).

Peter Lake, "The Significance of the Elizabethan Identification of the Pope as Antichrist," *Journal of Ecclesiastical History*, 31 (1980), 161-178.

Gustave Lanctot, *Canada and the American Revolution, 1774-1783*, trans. Margaret M. Cameron (Cambridge, Mass., 1967).

Mason Lowance, *The Language of Canaan: Metaphore and Symbol in New England from the Puritans to the Transcendentalists* (Cambridge, Mass., 1980).

Pauline Maier, "Coming to Terms with Samuel Adams," *American Historical Review*, 82 (1976), 12-37.

———, *From Resistance to Revolution: Colonial Radicals and the Development of American Opposition to Britain, 1765-1776* (New York, 1974).

Thomas T. McAvoy, "The Catholic Minority in the United States, 1789-1821," United States Catholic Historical Society, *Records and Studies*, 39 (1952), 33-50.

William McLoughlin, *Isaac Backus and the American Pietistic Tradition* (New York, 1967).

———, "The Role of Religion in the Revolution," in Stephen J. Kurtz and James H. Hutson, eds. *Essays on the American Revolution* (Chapel Hill, 1973), 107-203.

———, "The American Revolution as a Religious Revival: The 'Millennium' in One Country," *New England Quarterly*, 40 (1967), 99-110.

William S. Maltby, *The Black Legend in England* (Durham, NC., 1971).

Annabelle M. Melville, *John Carroll of Baltimore: Founder of the American Catholic Hierarchy* (New York, 1955).

Charles H. Metzger, *Catholics and the American Revolution, a Study in Religious Climate* (Chicago, 1962).

———, *The Quebec Act: A Primary Cause of the Revolution* (New York, 1936).

Jacob C. Meyer, *Church and State in Massachusetts from 1740 to 1833* (New York, 1930, repr. 1968).

John Miller, *Popery and Politics in England, 1660-1688* (Cambridge, 1973).

Perry Miller, "From Covenant to Revival," in James Ward Smith and A. Leland Jamison, eds., *The Shaping of American Religion* (Princeton, 1961), 322-368.

Albert Moore, *Introduction to Religious Iconography* (Philadelphia, 1977).

Samuel Eliot Morison, "The Struggle over the Adoption of the Constitution of Massachusetts, 1780," *MHSP*, 50 (1916-17), 353-411.

E. R. Norman, *Anti-Catholicism in Victorian England* (New York, 1968).

Mary Beth Norton, *The British-Americans: The Loyalist Exiles in England, 1774-1789* (Boston, 1972).

Alison G. Olson, "Rhode Island, Massachusetts, and the Question of Religious Diversity in Colonial New England," *New England Quarterly*, 65 (1992), 93-116.

D. G. Paz, "Anti-Catholicism, Anti-Irish Stereotyping and Anti-Celtic Racism in Mid-Victorian Working-Class Periodicals," *Albion*, 18 (1986), 601-617.

———, "Popular Anti-Catholicism in England, 1850-1851," *Albion* 11 (1979), 331-359.

William Pencak, *War, Politics & Revolution in Provincial Massachusetts* (Boston, 1981).

James Breck Perkins, *France and the American Revolution* (New York, 1911, repr. 1970).

Stow Persons, "The Cyclical Theory of History in Eighteenth-Century America," *American Quarterly*, 6 (1954), 147-163.

A. W. Plumpstead, *The Wall in the Garden* (Minneapolis, 1967).

G. A. Rawlyk, *Nova Scotia's Massachusetts: A Study of Massachusetts-Nova Scotia Relations, 1630-1784* (Montreal, 1973).

Mary Augustina Ray, *American Opinion of Roman Catholicism in the Eighteenth Century* (New York, 1936).

Sidney S. Rider, "An Inquiry Concerning the Origin of the Clause in the Laws of Rhode Island Disenfranchising Catholics," *Rhode Island Historical*

Tracts, 2nd series, I (Providence, 1889), 7-53.

Nicholas Rogers, "Popular Protest in Early Hanoverian London," *Past and Present*, 77 (1978), 70-100.

Kate Mason Rowland, *The Life and Correspondence of Charles Carroll of Carrollton, 1737-1832*, 2 vols. (New York, 1898).

Lorenzo Sabine, *Biographical Sketches of Loyalists of the American Revolution* 2 vols. (Boston, 1864).

Peter Shaw, *American Patriots and the Rituals of Revolution* (Cambridge, Mass., 1981).

Robert B. Shoemaker, "The London 'Mob' in the Early Eighteenth Century," *Journal of British Studies*, 26 (1987), 273-304.

S. E. D. Shortt, "Conflict and Identity in Massachusetts: The Louisbourg Expedition of 1745," *Histoire sociale*, 5 (1972), 165-185.

John Shy, *A People Numerous and Armed* (New York, 1976).

Ellen Hart Smith, *Charles Carroll of Carrollton* (Cambridge, 1942).

Justin H. Smith, *Our Struggle for the Fourteenth Colony: Canada and the American Revolution*, 2 vols. (New York, 1907).

Douglas C. Stange, "The Third Lecture: One Hundred and Fifty Years of Anti-Popery at Harvard," *Harvard University Library Bulletin* , 16 (1968), 354-369.

William Stinchcombe, *The American Revolution and the French Alliance* (Syracuse, 1969).

Harry S. Stout, *The New England Soul: Preaching and Religious Culture in Colonial New England* (New York, 1986).

Ian Y. Thackray, "Zion Undermined: The Protesant Belief in a Popish Plot during the English Interregnum," *History Workshop Journal*, 18 (Autumn, 1984), 28-52.

E. P. Thompson, *Customs in Common* (London, 1993).

John W. Thornton, *The Pulpit of the American Revolution* (Boston, 1860).

Kerry Trask, *In Pursuit of Shadows: Massachusetts Millennialism and the Seven Years' War* (New York, 1989).

Melvin Wade, "Shining in a Borrowed Plumage: Affirmation of Community in the Black Coronation Festivals of New England, ca. 1750-1850," in Robert. B. St. George, ed., *Material Life in America* (Boston, 1988).

Carol Z. Wiener, "The Beleaguered Isle. A Study of Elizabethan and Early Jacobean Anti-Catholicism," *Past and Present*, 51 (1971), 27-62.

———, "Popular Anti-Catholicism in England, 1559-1618" (Ph.D. dissertation, Harvard University, 1969).

George M. Wrong, *Canada and the American Revolution* (Toronto, 1935).

Mark Valeri, "The New Divinity and the American Revolution," *WMQ*, 46

(1989), 741-769.

C. H. Van Tyne, "The Clergy and the American Revolution," *American Historical Review*, 19 (1913-14), 44-46.

Judith A. Wilson, "My Country Is My Colony: A Study in Anglo-American Patriotism, 1739-1760," *The Historian*, 30 (1968), 333-349.

Index